"Raj's first book amazes. At 20 years old, she writes a memoir of uncommon grace and wisdom... A deft, intimate portrayal of a young woman's growth through education"
Kirkus Reviews

"Shilpa Anthony Raj is a powerful new voice for human dignity and opportunity…An important and deeply affecting book narrated in a moving and intimate style."
Sir Ken Robinson, author of *The Element: How Finding Your Passion Changes Everything*

"A visceral portrait of poverty…fascinating and essential reading…. Shilpa's story speaks for millions of families in a way that is immediate, intimate and personal."
Vanessa Roth, *Academy Award Winning Director*

"Shilpa is the future voice for the poor and deprived ….
Uncovering the diamond in the rubble. Read her work."
Sri Viswanath, author of *The Secret of Bhagavad Gita*

"The Elephant Chaser's Daughter will prove to be a milestone in Indian literature…. The arrival of Shilpa on the writers' dice with her splendid first-hand- narrative will surely stimulate a new movement among the socially awakened."
Literary News

"Shilpa's searing, penetrating honesty in the account of her life will change perspectives and impact every reader. It gives hope to the under-privileged and sensitizes the privileged."
Madhu Trehan, editor-in-chief, *Newslaundry*

"In a great measure, her personal account has a universal appeal which evokes the emotions of readers. Shilpa's book will prove to be a landmark."
Alok Mishra, Poet & Author

The Elephant Chaser's Daughter

SHILPA RAJ

@Copyright, Shilpa Raj and George Foundation Inc.,
New Jersey, 2017.

The Elephant Chaser's Daughter

Copyright @ Shilpa Raj and George Foundation Inc.,

New Jersey, 2017

ISBN-10 197649673X

ISBN-13 9781976496738

Printed in the United States

Published by Worldview Books

Dedicated to

Kavya and Dad

Table of Contents

Note

The Elephant Chaser's Daughter is a true story of Shilpa Raj's life, and all events presented are factual based on her recollection. Individuals portrayed in the book are real, but pseudonyms are used for most to protect their privacy.

Chapter One

An Unexpected Departure

It was so unlike him to weep. But there he was, the elephant chaser, all by himself, cowering in the shadow of the peepal tree. I called out to him, but he didn't move.

A chorus of grieving mothers and grim-faced neighbors stood next to my family, mourning the loss of the girl. The priest cleared his throat, preparing to read from the Bible; the family mid-wife asked God to bless the soul of the departed; my mother, whom I call Amma, pleaded for forgiveness.

I looked up from lighting a cheap incense stick to watch the shovel gathering earth. The thunder of dirt hitting the rough coffin resounded like a death knell.

Even today, I wake up to the sound of soil sliding down the spade, slapping the wooden box below. I gasp for breath, prepared to do anything to silence the thud.

I watched the coffin disappear into the ground. As it slipped from view, I remembered our last conversation over the phone. '*Akka*, I want to come home. Put me back to school. Let's start over,' she had pleaded.

I want to forget that desperate call.

I am Shilpa, which means sculpture in Sanskrit. Amma says she named me after a popular Hindi movie actress. It had been more than three years since Kavya, my younger sister, had called me Akka, which means 'elder sister' in our mother tongue, Kannada. She stopped addressing me that way the day our mother bought me a gold chain for my birthday with her meager savings from her job as a housemaid. Kavya was furious. She saw it as yet another injustice she had been subjected to in an ever lengthening list, the biggest being that I was at boarding school receiving a life-changing education while she attended a dilapidated village school. Elders, even older siblings, are venerated in our culture so her calling me by my first name was a blatant sign of disrespect. She might as well have spat at my feet.

Now, over the phone, she was so meek I should have guessed something was wrong. I hadn't heard from her in nine months. I was angry. I didn't want to give in. I told her flatly that I was fine and asked, 'What do you want?'

I suspected that calling me *Akka* was a ploy. It wouldn't have been the first time Kavya had tricked me. Once her boyfriend Prashanth, a gang leader from the neighboring village, had called to say she was missing. I panicked, offering to do anything I could to help find her, only to discover later that she was sitting right next to him. My father, whom I call Appa, had warned me not to be deceived by her again. I had sensed sadness, more than anger, in his voice.

'Please, Akka, let us forget everything that has happened,' Kavya begged. 'Please. I am sorry.' Instead of her customary boldness, there was fear.

I remained unmoved; we had so many old wounds. She had often defied everyone and everything. Grandmother always defended her—even when she stole money from Aunt Maria—explaining away her behavior. 'She's just a child!'

Appa had beaten her on several occasions. Nine months earlier, there had been an especially heated argument with my father. It was about her boyfriend, of course. Appa and I disapproved of him, while Amma was on my sister's side. Kavya was swayed by the luxurious gifts Prashanth had showered on her and the exciting things they did together, like going to the movies in a nearby town, all of it scandalous for an unmarried girl. The neighbors ridiculed us. Finally Appa felt his wild daughter had brought enough disgrace on our family and threatened to set Kavya and her boyfriend on fire if they were to stay together. Kavya must have known this was an empty threat, but she used it as an excuse to get Amma to whisk her away to an unknown place where none of us could find her. She and Amma disappeared completely, until that phone call.

'Akka, please, can you ask Appa to put me back in school?' she pleaded.

My sister had often complained about school and frequently skipped classes for one reason or the other. Now she was asking for my help to get back?

This time I would not fall for her tricks. 'I don't believe you've changed, Kavya. Don't call me again.' I slammed the phone down.

Three days later, I was with my classmates at a surprise birthday party for Ms. Jayanthashree, a long-time manager at Shanti Bhavan, the school where I lived and studied. She and Ms. Denny, the school's senior administrator, were two of the people I had grown closest to in my years at the school. While we were eating and enjoying ourselves, Ms. Denny asked me to join her on the terrace. I stuffed the remaining piece of hamburger quickly into my mouth and followed her.

'Ms. Denny, what's wrong?' I said as soon as we got outside.

She stared silently at me, and then looked away. My nerves tightened.

'Shilpa,' she said softly, 'You have to be strong.' She waited for a moment to watch my reaction. 'Your sister passed away.'

In an instant my legs gave way and I slumped onto the floor. 'It's not true. It's not true,' I cried out over and over again. Ms. Denny tried to calm me, but I was inconsolable. She attempted to lift me, but I crawled away from her frantically, kicking my legs to free myself. I didn't want anyone to touch me. She yelled for help, and Ms. Jayanthashree came running. 'Darling, we are with you. We are with you.' Through my shock and grief, I could barely hear them.

Kavya's last words echoed in my ears. I couldn't escape her gentle voice pleading with me.

I don't know how long I cried, but I was at last able to follow Ms. Denny and Ms. Jayanthashree back into the main hallway. By then my classmates, friends with whom I had grown up from the age of four, had heard the news. They hugged me tightly, but there was nothing they could do to console me.

That night, Ms. Jayanthashree and Ms. Denny took me back to my village. They tried to comfort me through the long drive, but I wasn't listening. Choking with sobs, I shut my eyes and tried to summon my sister back to life with every memory I had. Our fights melted away.

When Kavya was small, she demanded to be carried and I piggybacked her around the village wherever she pointed, as long as she wanted, often ignoring Grandmother's rule about being home before the sun went down. Neighbors saw us a troublesome duo who stirred up mischief at every turn. We played for hours in the lake by the woods, trying to catch tiny fish with our bare hands. At night we slept beside each other, sharing stories; hers filled with imaginary characters, mine about life at my faraway school. I often got the feeling she resented me for having got the chance to study in a 'fancy' school where I spoke English. I promised I would one day educate her to become a school teacher and pay for a grand wedding.

Now she was gone.

If there was ever a girl who was truly free in the village, it was Kavya, not because she was given any freedom by our parents, but by her own making. Even as a child she would wander about like a gypsy, and you wouldn't know whether she was with friends or strangers. But she carried herself with an air of utter confidence, keeping any inner fears to herself. I was never at ease about her and couldn't tell what she was up to. Every time I asked she'd let out a laugh like ringing bells that left me feeling foolish. She was a wildflower that swayed in the wind—a girl with uncontrollable energy and unexplainable dreams.

Nearly three hours of driving brought us to my village, Thattaguppe, in the southern part of Karnataka state, surrounded by lush forests where wild elephants roam. Appa had recently taken a job as an elephant chaser, protecting the village and the sugar cane fields. Life is hard there.

A line of dark trees marked the entrance to the village. As we continued down the road I remembered my previous trips back home and the joy I felt then in reuniting with my little sister.

There was a small crowd by our house—men chatting with each other and women seated on mats by my grandmother's side. No one smiled as I got out of the car. Keeping my head down, I gravitated towards Kavya's body on the dull green cot we had shared as children. Even though unexpected deaths were always a part of village life, I was frightened. I had seen my friends in the neighborhood lose family members to murder, suicide, and illness. But in my own family, I had never seen death up close.

I didn't know what to expect. In her stillness, Kavya appeared peaceful, as if resting. But there was a strange, unnatural hue to her complexion.

I stood dazed staring at her face. Her hair was pulled back tightly, revealing a new fullness in her face. I wiped the sweat off my forehead and reached out to stroke her hair, braided into a long plait draped over one shoulder. It had grown long since the last time I had seen her. I thought of the many times I had complained to Amma that Kavya had smoother, shinier hair than I did. The memory made me cry. She looked older somehow, her youth overshadowed by her stillness.

Appa who had been leaning against the lamppost a few yards away, slowly walked up to Amma and whispered something in her ear. She tried to put her arms around me, but I shrugged her off. She and Kavya had run away and lived together for nine months, hiding from Appa. Kavya was barely fourteen years old, and Amma shouldn't have let her spend time with such an undesirable man. She was responsible for her daughter, and should have known the dangers Kavya was getting into. Why didn't Amma protect her?

A few minutes later I took a chair next to Grandmother. She was seated with her small back hunched and her head bent low in deep prayer.

'Grandmother, please tell me what happened,' I asked.

Grandmother refused to look at me. She whispered, 'Your mother says Kavya killed herself.'

I didn't believe her. I reached for Grandmother's trembling hand. 'How?'

Grandmother looked down, her head bent. She struggled not to cry. 'She hanged herself from the rafter with your mother's sari.'

The air was knocked out of me. I never thought she was capable of killing herself. I saw her as a vibrant girl, looking for fun at every opportunity. But probably I didn't know her well enough. She had never begged for my help before. Even as she pleaded on the phone to return home, she was hiding her other life.

Some in my family believed that Kavya had been murdered. She had spent much of the last nine months with her boyfriend and another man as well. According to Grandmother, these men got her to act in 'backyard movies'. I clapped my hands over my ears, refusing to hear any more. Embarrassed, Grandmother looked to see whether anyone else heard her.

I turned towards Appa. All this while he had been standing alone, some distance away from others, in deep contemplation.

He still hadn't said a word to me. Silence was his way of taking responsibility. He had driven her away, calling her a prostitute and beating her. But no one would blame him for being strict with a rebellious daughter. It was totally unacceptable in our village for a girl to be involved with a man before her marriage.

Amma was weeping. No one came to console her. I heard others say how secretive Amma had been, blaming her for not taking better care of my sister, and even now Amma wasn't telling us everything she knew. She had returned home that morning in an auto-rickshaw with Kavya's body in her arms. It was clear from the condition of the corpse that Kavya had died at least a day or two earlier.

The silence ended with a shriek. 'What has she been letting the girl do?' My father's older sister, Aunt Teresa, was screaming and pointing at my mother. 'She has never been a decent mother. She—'

'You shut up!' Amma snapped, furious. I was shocked to see the flood of shame and rage in her eyes.

Uncle Philip, Appa's younger brother, broke in. 'She might have been pregnant.' He turned to others for agreement.

Grandmother would have none of that. She walked over, not bending her head low in shame as I thought she would, and placed a gentle palm upon Kavya's abdomen. Then she turned around, and declared furiously, 'She wasn't pregnant. Stop your lies.'

The dam was broken, and anger was spilling from all sides. 'You killed her! You killed her!' Aunt Rani, Amma's younger sister, yelled, her body shaking with rage. 'She was murdered by the men she was with. And you. You're only pretending not to know what really happened.' She rushed to strike Amma with one of my sandals, which had been lying by the door. Grandmother lunged into the space between them, taking a blow on her shoulder from Aunt Rani.

Uncle Philip shook his finger at my mother. 'Next will be Shilpa. Who knows what those criminals have in mind.' I got scared, not trusting that my family would be able to protect me.

Another matter could no longer be ignored. We needed to get Kavya's body into the ground. It was almost morning, she had been dead for at least two days, and the stench from her body was becoming unbearable.

Many neighbors objected to burying Kavya in the village graveyard because of the disgrace surrounding her death. But the priest reminded them that they were not the ones to judge a young girl. When they persisted, the priest conceded by directing that the burial take place only in a small, secluded section set aside for those with dishonorable endings—suicide or murder. My little sister, harmless and innocent in the ways of the world, was being discarded in death as she had been in life.

Memories of our childhood rushed in. Incidents that had been buried in my mind for years were coming back. When Kavya was happy and playful, we never stopped laughing, screaming, and running around. There was so much sweetness between us, even in our arguments. Nothing, not even death, could take away what was Kavya's and mine to cherish forever.

I went to sit by the gutter along the road, aimlessly gazing at a crumpled sweet wrapper rotating in a dirty puddle. All I saw was Kavya. I wanted my sister to be the little girl she once was, the one who demanded to be carried around. I wanted to carry her one more time. Unlike me, she had never enjoyed the taste of good food, the comfort of sleeping on a mattress, or travelling. I longed for the conversations we never had, the laughter we hadn't shared, the places we hadn't visited together, and all the happy moments I hadn't spent with her. I prayed to God with all the fervor I could muster, wishing to catapult my way into the heavens for a second chance to say goodbye.

How could the lives of two daughters of the same elephant chaser turn out so differently? The only explanation I could come up with was rooted in my family's spiritual beliefs: Kavya had met her karma and, for some unknown reason, I had been spared the misfortune of my sister.

My feet turned numb. I tried to stand up but my legs felt weak. Sitting down again, I stretched my legs but my body was stiff with anxiety.

It felt strange that I had survived this far. The odds were stacked against me and yet my path had been a charmed one until now. There was nothing I had done to deserve it. I couldn't explain fate having taken me in a different direction.

It all began one day when I was four years old and a blue jeep pulled into my village.

Chapter Two

The Blue Jeep

For years, Amma couldn't get over it. Without me in her daily life, everything was very painful to her—the stillness that had settled like dust in our small hut; the steel trunk containing my faded clothes that Grandmother had carefully sewn from her old saris; my two-year-old brother, Francis, looking around everywhere for me, convinced that I was at our usual game of hide and seek; and most of all, the emptiness on the floor where I had slept between my parents. These memories had reduced her to a sullen, bitter woman, empty of what had been her usual energetic spirit. In the middle of a meal, she'd push her plate away saying she wasn't hungry, or sit lost in thought in front of the kitchen fire, allowing the rice to turn into an overcooked fudgy paste.

'Bring Shilpa back or I'll kill myself,' she'd cry late into the night, refusing to let my father console her. Nor would she give in to his threats of beating her until she behaved herself.

Many a time Appa walked over to Grandmother's house asking her to come put some sense into Amma's head. 'She's acting like her daughter has died. I can't handle her anymore,' he'd complain, letting out a helpless sigh.

Grandmother would try to console Amma, though both hated Appa for what he had done to me. They hung on to the hope that somehow I would be brought back home for good. What transpired between those two women in the months following my leaving home and how the entire family took to my absence were narrated to me years later when I was old enough to understand. The arrival of the blue jeep that fateful morning changed everything for my family and me. It stirred up a storm in our lives and, when it all finally settled, nothing was ever the same again.

No one could be blamed for what happened that day. After all, it was hard to go against the family's beliefs. In this part of the world, they believe that *Vidhiy-Amma*, or mother fate, inscribes the destiny of each child upon his or her forehead at birth. In Kannada we say: *haneli barediddu*—'what is written on the forehead.' My future was laid out for me, and I was expected to fulfill my role as a woman.

My thoughts settle and surrender to the day of my birth, entering the tiny room where I was born. I crane my neck to catch a glimpse of the baby. I discover the new-born on the birth-attendant's lap, in my grandmother's poorly lit hut. The path my life has taken since then—the way it has veered and branched—seems devoid of reason.

Looking out through the window, I see a different world. My days are now spent at Shanti Bhavan, a residential school named 'Haven of Peace,' where children from families who cannot afford even one proper meal a day are well cared for and given a good education. Within its walls are orphans who otherwise would have been trafficked, and the children of construction workers and rag-pickers. I, Shilpa Anthony Raj, the daughter of an elephant chaser and a maid, have been one of these privileged few—children of poverty growing up in a world unrecognizable to those from the one we left behind.

To be here in the present seems unreal. There is no convincing explanation for it. If my good fortune in life is the reward for what my parents and grandparents and their parents and grandparents lived through and suffered, why did it take so long? And why me?

It was November 2, 1997—All Soul's Day. The villagers had risen early to fetch water from the lake and to collect firewood for cooking and bathing. Dirty-looking children who would usually be playing marbles on the narrow, muddy streets were not to be found. Men who ordinarily smelled like sweat and liquor, and servant boys who usually reeked of cow dung, had scrubbed themselves clean. Women had tamed their unruly hair with long black braids, adorning them with white jasmine flowers. Even the poorest were wearing their finest and looking their most respectable to honor and pay homage to their ancestors. On this day, a fateful one for me, the monotony of daily life was broken by the festive atmosphere of the church ceremony. It didn't matter whether it was for the dead or the living.

Everyone had gathered at the church graveyard, a long, narrow patch of land bordered by wild shrubs, at the village's entrance. It looked more like an unkempt field than a place to lay the dead to quiet rest. Candles and cheap incense burned at the heads of earthen tombs covered with wild grass and weeds. Fresh flowers had been placed on the muddy mounds as offerings to the dead.

Out of a sense of reverence, landlords from the Gunna community joined everyone else in prayer at the burial ground. They were dressed in new cotton *lungi* —the traditional garment tied around the waist—and striped shirts, along with glimmering gold rings and chains that displayed their elevated status in the social order.

The few landlords in the village belonged to upper castes. They owned most of the cultivable land and employed people from the lower castes as laborers on their farms and servants in their homes. This was seen by all as the natural order of things. But on this day, they and their beautifully dressed wives and children placed themselves at the front of the crowd at a tolerable distance from the excited *coolies*—unskilled laborers hired cheaply only when needed—who worshipped with them. Everyone stood, at least in appearance, as equals before God.

The priest wore a white cloak delicately accented with gold. He led the cowherds, the coolies, and the brewers of illegal liquor in cries of 'Praise the Lord' and 'Hail Mary,' and a hymn for the dead. Everyone but the landlords, who displayed their privileged status through silence, joined in this spirited show of worship.

Suddenly, the noisy hum of a motor vehicle disturbed the reverent atmosphere. Flocks of goats by the muddy road bleated in panic at the sight of the vehicle speeding towards them. Their master frantically raised his stick and swung it in the air, making animal-like sounds that drove the flock to one side. The goats scattered off the stony road just as a blue jeep sped past them and came to a screeching halt by the gate to the graveyard.

The jeep looked exactly like the vehicles the local police would use to conduct raids for illicit liquor. It was common in our village to see rows of police vans advancing on the village like an army of invaders, honking incessantly to drive the cattle away from the narrow, nameless road, and stop by the huts of the poor. Often on drowsy afternoons when women were cleaning rice or singing lullabies to their infants sleeping in sari-cradles hanging from low rafters, the police would appear without warning. No one could predict when they would come sniffing like hounds for liquor. Was this one of those surprise visits?

'Please, *Anna*, think of me as your sister. I swear on my son's life, we won't do it again,' desperate mothers would cry, after cans containing liquor were found hidden under the soft, clay floors of their huts. Shouting insults at them, the policemen would leave with a warning that they would come back for their husbands.

Any man who was taken later by the police would not be seen for a month, and only after he returned would the village learn what had happened to him. He would have only grave cautions to share with his neighbors. 'Continue making *sarayam* and you will spend your nights in a cold cell. You'll stay warm only from the thrashings you get.'

His message might hit home for a moment but it wouldn't last in anyone's mind for long. Making alcohol was the only way to survive. In no time, men would be back in the woods scraping bark from the *chakki* tree and mixing it with jaggery in steel barrels for fermentation—the local way of making sarayam, a country liquor. Contracts were verbally agreed between suppliers and buyers. Life was a business, and risks were a part of living it.

The families who depended on the translucent liquid for their livelihood were especially unnerved by the jeep's arrival that morning. There was considerable anxious fidgeting in the crowd. Prayers were forgotten, the dead receded to their graves, and the concentrated look of worship vanished from the faces of the congregants. Panic took its customary place. Appa was afraid that the police might be looking particularly for him. Like many others, he too distilled sarayam illegally to support the family, and lived in constant fear of getting caught. No doubt, Thattaguppe was a place where moonshine and God sat side by side.

It was also where I began my life.

Over a century ago, Thattaguppe was a barely inhabited patch of forest. Huge rocky hills rose like a wall around it. No road had ever been carved into its earth, and few even knew of the settlement's existence. In time, its scattered residents found a haven there, safe from outsiders. They lived a meager existence, taking refuge in their faith, Hinduism. Faded pictures of Lord Krishna and other gods hung precariously from nails in the mud walls of their homes. In worship of the many gods who reign in their religion, they built a stone temple with carvings made from simple tools.

In 1896, a plague outbreak in India killed hundreds of thousands of people. Thattaguppe wasn't spared. Its people prayed to their gods, but the deaths kept coming. In their grief, they abandoned the jungle for what they hoped would be more merciful land. All that remained were crumbling huts, the decaying carcasses of cattle, and the stone temple, all of which were soon overtaken by weeds and rats. No incense would be lit in the village for many years.

Not long after, three French missionaries descended on this part of the country looking to convert people to Christianity. They went to villages in many pockets of rural South India seeking the souls of the poor—beggars, coolies, servants. One of the priests, Father Philip Sigeon, went to Somnahalli, a small village adjacent to what was then the wild jungle of Thattaguppe. No one could understand his French, and he couldn't decipher their Kannada. He was a complete stranger to the locals, whom he saw as uncivilized humans, as dark as the rich humus soil they gathered from the lake to build the walls of their huts.

Despite the cultural differences, and after many false starts, Father Sigeon learnt to communicate with the villagers. In time, he gained their friendship and, slowly, with their help, he began to clear away the forest of Thattaguppe. Eventually, a small part of the jungle was cut down to make way for civilization and, as the priest's message began to take hold, a stone church was constructed. Huts were built on the previously abandoned land as people from other villages began to arrive on bullock carts, carrying with them a few bundles of clothes—all they possessed. Little by little, the land came back to life.

The villagers who lived at the farthest end of the rolling contour were nearest to the lake. There lay the furrowed land, rich with jamuns and coconuts, none of which belonged to any rightful owner other than God. Farmers cultivating *ragi*, wheat, rice, and sugarcane depended on the lake for water during the dry season. They carried water for their little farms in large mud pots until newly constructed concrete canals made life easier. When the monsoons arrived, the very lake they revered brought them much sorrow as it often flooded the ragi and rice fields, taking away their staple food crops and the income earned from them.

The growing vegetation eventually brought cattle breeders to adopt this no-man's-land as their own. The cattle were content with the fodder and water available. Soon, with its abundance of fish, the lake drew fishermen to establish dwellings near the cattle breeders. Without the lake, no life would have existed in Thattaguppe. Liquor brewers, farmers, cattle breeders, and fishermen all settled down in a natural progression to pursue their livelihoods. Nobody outside the village cared about the residents of Thattaguppe as they went about their isolated lives in a forgotten corner of the world. Poverty had humbled them; they were as raw as the afternoon sun and as wild as the partheniums that grew aimlessly in the fields.

My family's ancestors had played their part in reclaiming the land and consecrating it to a Christian god. But though we are of a Christian family, we were once of low Hindu caste—part of the social order that has existed in India for over one thousand years. I discovered from my mother that my maternal great-grandfather was considered below a *shudra,* the lowliest position in the caste system that still divides Indian society. I am said to have inherited this *dalit,* or *untouchable,* status—far below the priestly, warrior, merchant, and labor castes. Over time, the caste system assumed a religious character through a belief that God assigned humans to the roles they deserved. My great-grandfather earned his living doing menial jobs like skinning animals, making leather shoes, and burying carcasses—tasks despised by higher castes. I first heard about the caste system during my history lessons at school, and learnt that my family is officially among the 'Scheduled Castes and Scheduled Tribes' that comprise over twenty-five percent of the Indian population. Without an education or opportunities to acquire new skills, tens of millions of people like my parents remain where they have always been—in poverty.

The landlords took great pains to avoid any form of bodily contact with the *sub-humans* who worked for them and lived in squalid, crammed huts with roofs made from coconut leaves. My great-grandfather understood that the only escape from this terribly unjust social order was to convert to Christianity, setting aside years of prevailing traditions and beliefs. Though his wisdom saved me from a life of total indignity, I was still doubly undesirable from the start, being not only poor, but female.

From early on in my life, my parents insisted that my siblings and I pray every night. Grandmother would often gather us around the framed pictures of saints and light candles on evenings when my uncles returned early from work. Still, Jesus wasn't the only God to whom many of the villagers prayed. For favors or mercy, they continued to worship the cooking fire, the full moon, and the ghosts of their ancestors. Divine and human ideals of fraternity didn't seem to have much in common in the day-to-day life of the village.

Long after Father Sigeon had settled in his grave, the stone church lived on as a reminder of the new faith, its toll calling on worshipers to cross themselves in the afternoon and recite the rosary in the evening. Yet on this day, when the entire village had gathered to pray for the souls of the departed, attention quickly shifted to the blue vehicle parked outside the small gate of the graveyard.

Memories of that morning remain etched in my mind like ink blots on sparkling white paper. Parts of the day's events that I couldn't actually remember were retold by my parents so many times that they have become as real as the cobwebs that are a part of our household.

No one had forgotten the jeep. Sister Stella, the elderly nun of the Dona Paula Convent, made her way towards the gate to find out who the intruders were. A woman with short hair and dressed in a colorful sari could be seen descending from the jeep to greet the nun. Shielding her face from the blazing sun with her hand, Sister Stella exchanged a few words with the strangers in the jeep and pointed them in the direction of the village. The visitors smiled, looking genuinely pleased.

The jeep erupted with loud grunts and belches of smoke and headed in the direction Sister Stella indicated. The worshippers returned their attention to the priest. In single file, one head after another bowed to receive Holy Communion from the young women of the convent. Families walked about the burial ground, lighting candles and pressing thin sticks of incense into the covers of the graves that held those with whom they had shared a personal connection.

After paying their respects to the dead, many worshippers surrounded Sister Stella, eager to find out who the visitors were. Appa and I were packed in among them, his arms sealed tight around me. Soon, Amma appeared in the chattering crowd with her hand placed protectively upon her pregnant belly, her eyes searching anxiously for us. She caught up with us just as Appa turned away, his dark face now gleaming with a wide smile. She reached for me over his shoulder, but he kept on walking briskly.

'What has made you so happy?' she asked.

'We must take Shilpa to the hospital immediately,' he replied.

Confusion swept across Amma's face. 'Why the hospital? Shilpa isn't sick.'

'Those strangers have come looking for children to admit to a school they just started. It is free for people like us. The hospital is where they are testing the children for admission.' He was referring to the two-room medical clinic run by the nuns of the convent.

Appa halted in his steps and turned to Amma. 'Shilpa will go to this special school. It is called Shanti Bhavan.' The tone of his voice conveyed what he had decided for me. 'Look, Sarophina,' he said, calling her by her full name as he did when he was upset with her, 'already so many are rushing to the hospital with their children. You better hurry.' Having lived with him for years, Amma knew when he wanted something very badly. She sensed the urgency in his voice and knew it was not the time to argue.

Word that the visitors were screening children had spread fast, and by the time Amma and I reached the hospital, a large noisy crowd of women was already seated upon the muddy ground outside. It was a chaotic scene, with children crying and playing or sleeping in their mothers' laps.

The three visitors from the blue jeep had set up their station in a stand-alone room outside the hospital. Amma pulled her sari tight around her narrow legs and sat on the ground, with me positioned in her lap. As she caressed my scraggly, shoulder-length hair, which was pulled back with a tight cloth band, she listened to the many mothers already seated around her. They appeared unconcerned about the education their children could receive, but were happy that they could live and study in a school without having to pay any fees.

Every so often, Sister Stella would come to the door and call out a name, and a woman would emerge from the crowd and rush in with her child. When the nun called out 'Mary Sarophina,' Amma smoothed my hair with her thin fingers and hoisted me onto her hip.

A man named Dr. Venkatesh was seated at a small desk. With a gentle smile, he asked me to fit some plastic blocks together. I later discovered that he was the school psychologist. Having never encountered toys before, it was an exercise I would remember wistfully for a long time. According to Amma, another of the three, Dr. Maya, asked her several questions about my health. I started to grow restless, so Dr. Venkatesh suggested we take a break.

Upon leaving the room, we saw a group of women excitedly questioning each other about the process. 'They will take the children to America and sell them,' one of the women remarked.

Then another said that she'd heard that the strangers were planning to kill the children and harvest their kidneys and eyes. These women explained that they had come simply out of curiosity to find out what the strangers were up to. Their stories horrified Amma. She wasn't prepared to give me away, her most precious possession, to such people.

Amma didn't care to wait any longer at the hospital. After all, she didn't want to part with me in the first place. She picked me up and ran out of the gate, hugging me tightly and not looking back.

By then, Appa was on his way to find out for himself what was happening. Seeing Amma heading his way, he snatched me from her arms, and asked her what had transpired. He rushed back to the hospital, with Amma struggling to keep pace with him and pleading. She wept in desperation, trying to tear me from his grasp. He was too strong for her even to slow him down by pulling at his shirt from the back. When nothing worked, she yelled at him, accusing him of indifference to me in the past. I was her love, her life's greatest pleasure, and she couldn't put me at such great risk if what the other women were saying was true. Appa was in no mood to listen to what he considered merely the usual talk among foolish women.

Hurrying in through the hospital gate, Appa skidded to a stop, not knowing where to go. Amma stood in front of him, blocking his way, her feet firmly rooted to the ground. But she was no match for his strength. With his free hand, he pushed her aside effortlessly. She kept begging him to stop and briefly caught hold of his hand, but he freed himself with ease. Frustrated, she hit him with both her fists, but he didn't seem affected by it one bit. Nor did he pause to calm her.

Sister Stella saw us from inside a nearby room and summoned Appa. She asked where Amma had taken me, as the doctor had been calling for us. Drenching Amma in foul language, Appa sent us inside with strict instructions to let the strangers do whatever they needed to with me.

I don't remember any of this precisely, but a few memories remain as big, blurry impressions. My parents retell this story often, giving it a place of venerable myth in our household.

The doctor, Dr. Maya, short-haired and chubby, seated me on a small wooden chair before her and examined my eyes, ears, and mouth. She had a warm smile, but the instruments she used on me were as cold as ice. She was so thorough in her inspection of me that it seemed as if she were looking for something important that she had lost. She scribbled something in her notebook, and then looked up as Amma stood in front of her. 'Look at your little one's oval face and pointed nose, so like her young mother.' Dr. Maya smiled but Amma did not smile back.

Dr. Venkatesh called us again to the broken wooden table at which he was seated. Placing coins in front of me, he asked me to count them. His voice was soft, his expression kind, and his Kannada fluent. But I didn't answer; I just stared at him perplexed.

Throughout all this, Mrs. Law, a lean woman with neatly styled short hair and square glasses, was observing us with a stern expression. I later learnt that she was the principal of the school, hired just two months earlier. Though she was barely five feet tall, the seriousness of her bearing gave her the appearance of special importance. Unable to converse with us in our own language, she kept asking Dr. Venkatesh to explain what we were saying.

'*Chinna*,' Amma said warmly, referring to me as her *golden girl*, 'tell the doctor how many coins there are.'

I dragged myself closer to the table and touched the coins, which were arranged in a tidy row, with my little fingers. 'One,' I said. 'Two, three...'

Amma exhaled with relief as, in my lilting voice, I correctly counted the coins. She wiped her sweaty palms on her sari and sat with her legs pressed tightly together. Even if the other women had terrified her with their stories of abduction, she wanted me to do well. It was important to her sense of pride.

Afterward, we found Appa squatting on the ground outside, shoulders slouched, digging in the dirt with a twig to distract himself. He rarely did anything without a purpose, and playing with mud wasn't his preferred manner of spending time. He was pensive, possibly dreaming of a life of good fortune for at least one of his children. He couldn't educate me in a good school, and this would be nothing short of a miracle. Sensing our approach, he suddenly looked up, raising his hand to shield his face from the hot sun. There was no smile; his face was all anxiety. I was singing a tune my grandmother often sang to me and clutching a colorful toffee—my reward from the doctor.

Amma walked towards Appa with slow, heavy steps. 'Well?' he asked.

She didn't answer. But soon her fears took over again. 'Just listen to what everyone is saying. If you let our daughter go with them, she'll never return alive.'

Appa recalled the details vividly, especially because her outbursts were to take place again and again throughout the day. 'Foolish woman, you ran away with Shilpa!' he screamed, worried her panic had cost me a chance at admission to the school.

'I am afraid,' she said, sobbing. 'I will not give my daughter to them.'

'Nonsense. Give her to me, you stupid woman. These people don't look like they would kidnap children. Those who do don't publicize themselves in broad daylight!'

This must have gotten through to Amma in some way because she calmed down enough to explain what had happened inside the testing room. 'They gave two coins to her and asked which was heavier. Instead of saying that the five-rupee coin was heavier than the fifty-paisa coin, she said the other way round.'

Appa's face fell.

'But other than that, she answered all the questions correctly,' Amma continued, her tone a bit lighter. She surely wanted to assure herself and Appa that I was a smart girl. 'They said they will tell us very soon whether or not they will take her.'

Not waiting to see Appa's reaction, she prepared to carry me herself and walk out through the hospital gate. Finding me heavy, she changed her mind, leading me by one hand while flattening the other upon her bulging belly.

Appa appeared satisfied. Finally he had turned calm, his face relaxed. He wanted so badly to remain hopeful. Snatching me up, he walked out onto the muddy road.

'When Shilpa said our names,' Amma said, 'the doctor started laughing. He said our little girl is very smart.'

A big smile spread across Appa's dark face, a sharp contrast to Amma's tense and worried expression. For reasons unknown to me, he seemed sure that I would impress the visitors. But years later, he confessed that all through that day, he was fearful that they would reject me. He wasn't one bit concerned about what Amma had heard from some rumor-mongering women.

Any observant passers-by would have noticed that no cooking smoke rose from our hut that night. All thoughts of dinner had been forgotten as Appa and Amma entangled themselves in a heated argument. At one point, perhaps feeling she had screamed enough, Amma fell silent and proceeded to bang her head against the wall.

'What's wrong with you, woman?' Appa demanded, not wanting her to hurt herself, especially since she was pregnant.

Amma didn't bother to reply.

'Why is it you can't think? Can't you see what this means to us? Don't you want her to study?'

Amma sat still, facing the wall that had just met her head and ignoring his bruising words.

Appa then looked at me—his little girl. I'd heard he was disappointed at my birth because I was a girl, but he always seemed to like me more than my younger brother, Francis, who was then two years old. He had remained weak and thin since his premature birth at seven months. That evening, Appa appeared more caring towards me than ever before. He tickled me, and I let out a peal of laughter. But soon he was lost in thought. I wonder whether he was imagining a better future for me.

'You will not take her away from me,' Amma threatened, turning to face him with sudden boldness.

'You think only *you* care for her?' Appa shot back.

The fight continued into the night until finally Amma, hugging me closely, resorted to desperate pleading. 'Please don't send her away.'

Appa stroked my hair, releasing a sigh. 'Sarophina, we don't know whether she will be selected or not. But I really want her to be chosen. *We* can't educate her. You know that, don't you?'

Amma didn't answer. Instead she cradled me in her arms and sang to me like she did every night. On this night, she hugged me tighter than ever, as though I were all that she had.

A few days later, a knock came on the door of our hut. Amma opened the door and found a young girl from the convent standing in the doorway. Sister Stella had sent her to deliver a message.

I had been chosen to attend the school.

Appa's voice filled the hut as he thanked God—something he rarely did—but Amma burst into furious sobs, her distress running deeper than her husband's happiness. Appa didn't care to hear anything more from the girl, he told me, even though she looked like she had more to say. A new hope was born in him, and there was nothing further to be said. He kept repeating to himself that God had finally heard his prayers, and he ignored Amma completely.

Amma didn't forgive Appa for many years after that. When I was older, she told me a part of her died when she heard of my selection. Having not finished primary school or seen anyone else in the family benefit from an education, she couldn't grasp what good it could do for me. Now, looking back at her early life experiences, I can fully understand why she felt that way. For a woman like her, living was all about serving her husband and bearing his children. In turn, her daughters would look after her in her old age.

Amma wasn't one to surrender without putting up an earnest fight. As they lay on the floor together that night, Appa tried again to reassure her that everything would be fine. On the mat with her back facing him, she kept her arm draped over me protectively. Appa tried to sweep Amma up in his enthusiasm, but when that didn't work, he tried to strike fear in her heart. 'Do you want her to grow up like us, without enough food to eat, no proper clothes to wear, and no money to go to school?'

Amma tensed at his words, but didn't reply, ignoring him as though she hadn't heard him. When he pressed, she retorted, 'We are already sending her to the village school. That is enough.' The plan had been for me to study at Anganwadi, a courtyard shelter run by the local government.

Appa bit his lip to contain his anger. 'You are like a stubborn ox. That school is worthless.' Raising his arms in agitation, he continued. 'Half the time, the teachers don't even show up. Look at me, Sarophina. I can't read or write. I can't even sign my name. Neither of us studied. Do you want our daughter to be like us?'

'Maybe one day she will return to us as a great person,' he continued, once again reversing course, to offer encouragement. 'Maybe she will become a doctor or a lawyer,' he said, pausing to listen to the echo of his own words. But there was no one he could point to as an example of having succeeded from the families he knew. History was against him.

This was the first time Appa had ever spoken with confidence about anything so distant, and Amma was surprised to see what hope could do to a man as wretched as he. But nothing he could say would convince her. In her turn she called him by his formal name, a sign of outright defiance. 'Anthony. I will work. I will even beg on the street if I have to. But I want my daughter to be with me. I won't give her away like an orphan.' She didn't have any dreams for me, or even for herself, and all that was real to her was having me with her.

That was it. Appa gave up trying to convince her. She would fight him to the bitter end, even if that meant getting beaten. She was determined to win, no matter what.

While I could sense the tension in our household, my excitement about travelling to a distant place in the blue jeep was simply overwhelming. I was prepared to leave Amma and Appa for that reason alone. But I can now understand how my mother felt about having to hand over her first child to the care of perfect strangers. I can't blame her for her reluctance. A woman in her situation lives for her children, and we are the only lasting joy my father ever brought her.

Their vicious disagreement over my schooling marked the beginning of a permanent emotional separation between my parents. Appa probably sees what happened that day as simply a twist in the family's fortune. As for me, I have been living a far more comfortable life ever since. Now I do not have to queue patiently for a bucket of water from the village well, as my mother had to. I don't have to huff and puff through a pipe into lit charcoal to start the cooking fire at obscenely early hours of the morning, as all the women in my family have had to do.

I think of my new destiny as pre-planned by Mother Fate, and inscribed on my forehead in the indiscernible ink of the gods. But there is no way to read it without the help of a magic mirror or a fortune teller. It holds a mystery that has haunted me all this while. If we cannot know what our destiny is, how are we to fulfill or escape it? It seems awfully convenient for the Gods and equally maddening for humans. This is *Vidhiy-Amma*'s cunning.

Chapter Three

A Permanent Parting

It had been drizzling all night. Despite the rain, the sun occasionally broke through, offering the promise of a bright morning. In village folklore, that is when the jackals get married—an auspicious time for everyone else.

It wasn't unusual to be woken by chicks walking all over me, pecking at my head. 'Amma, please chase them away,' I cried, raising myself from the floor and pushing the excited birds away. Hens and their chicks were part of our family, spending the night with us in the single room we shared. If Appa bought a goat, a rare occurrence, it would also join us. I didn't think much then about animals and humans living together in such close harmony, all under the same roof.

Over the years, Appa often recounted with great excitement what it was like taking me to school the first time. Amma would listen in while cooking dinner, interrupting to add to Appa's version, which she said didn't explain everything. I never got tired of listening to my story, repeated many times with the same fascination that might attend an unsolved mystery.

Although she was terribly upset and crying, Amma set to work very early on the day of my leaving. She washed my face, combed my hair, and drowned me in a loose skirt that fell all the way to my ankles. She dressed me with great care, tied my hair with a barrette, and pinned onto my blouse a handkerchief she had cut out from one of her old saris. All the while she ignored Appa whenever he attempted to speak with her. He would have liked her to enjoy the moment, but there was nothing he could do. She was still furious and wanted him to know that without me at home they would have no happiness together.

Appa took me to his mother's hut right next to ours, adjoining a cowshed. I wasn't looking forward to this visit as Arpuda Ajji, my paternal grandmother, was not someone I was too fond of. Each time I met her, she would give me a kiss, and I'd try to push her away as she reeked of tobacco and alcohol. Her long, densely matted dreadlocks were a chestnut color, similar to that of a horse I had once seen at the village fair.

Arpuda Ajji had been sick for a while now, buckled over with severe stomach pain that kept her awake most nights. Appa explained that it was for this reason that she had taken up drinking like his father. Each night before lying down to sleep, she'd gulp down three to four glasses of liquor from a cylinder-shaped steel vessel kept behind a stack of firewood in the room.

No one knew that Arpuda Ajji was suffering from some sort of intestinal tumor. The family discovered it years later when Appa and Uncle Philip took her to the city to visit a proper doctor after all the home remedies and treatment by village medicine men had failed. But by then it was too late.

Appa carried me in his arms to his mother as though he were making an offering to God. Ajji was lying on a mat on the floor in a dark room, one hand placed over her abdomen. Her eyes were sunken and lifeless. She forced herself to wrench up a weak smile for Appa's sake.

Arpuda Ajji would die four years later when I turned eight years old, leaving me with many unanswered questions about her life and family history. Every time I went into the room where my paternal grandfather, Joseph Thatha, slept alone, I would see her picture staring coldly down at me from within the broken wooden frame that hung on the mud wall. I would stand in front of that photo and search her hardened face, trying to understand the mystery of her past.

One tale I heard from Amma still troubles me. It was about the unexplained death of Aunt Sagaya, Ajji's youngest daughter, at the age of fourteen. I never knew her, as she died before I was born. Appa explained that her death was an accident, but Amma found the account too convenient to accept.

Allegedly, in the blush of dawn one summer day, a shepherd found Sagaya's bloated body afloat in the stone well at the farthest end of the village. Within an hour of the discovery the sharp tongues of village women had devised many stories to explain her death.

By nightfall, Sagaya was settled at the farthest end of the graveyard. No candles were lit and no flowers placed on the grave; those were the privileges of the wealthy. All that was offered were the few sticks of incense my grandfather, Joseph Thatha, had bought for a rupee. Arpuda Ajji was crying loudly, 'Why did she have to fall into the well? Were we going to kill her? I only beat her because she stole money.'

Her questions didn't remain unanswered for long. Villagers generously offered their own accounts, all rooted in the shared belief that a girl of fourteen years, barely four feet in height, couldn't have jumped over the half-wall around the well. 'Maybe somebody pushed her in,' was the grim conclusion.

Some said that Grandfather Joseph might have beaten his daughter to death in one of his drunken rages and, fearing that others would find out, had thrown the body into the well to make it look like suicide. Others argued that Sagaya had unexpectedly encountered her mother in a close embrace with the shepherd who lived across the street. Afraid that Thatha would kill her if Sagaya revealed to him what she had seen, Arpuda Ajji had her equally frightened lover push Sagaya into the well.

Appa dismissed these stories as ugly tales and putrid gossip, but the memory of his sister was deeply within him. Once he caught sight of me struggling to balance a plastic water vessel on the faint curve of my hip. He burst out laughing and remarked that I was walking just like Aunt Sagaya did when she was my age. 'I used to tell her that even a cow could walk better on two legs,' he said chuckling, his eyes sharp with remembrance. I could see that her death still haunted him, even after all those years. Each time I think about my aunt, I am frightened by my family's past.

'Say good-bye to Ajji,' Appa whispered in my ear as he put me down and gave me a gentle push towards her. I walked forward gingerly, and knelt before her. Ajji wanted to know how often I would return home from school; Appa didn't have an answer for her.

After my short visit with Ajji, Appa instructed Amma to take me to nearby elderly neighbors and relatives to seek their blessings. Whenever we talked about the day I left for school, Amma would tell me that the blessings I received from the elders had helped me on my journey and would follow me for the rest of my life.

My departure was almost as elaborate as a wedding ritual, with just as many onlookers. Curious neighbors gathered outside our hut to ask questions or warn my parents about taking such a dangerous path. Before long, they joined our family in a solemn procession to the convent where the blue jeep was parked. My mother's parents and siblings stayed beside me every step. Uncle Naresh, Amma's youngest brother, then only eleven, sulked along quietly. For Grandmother, this parting was only temporary. She was hoping I would marry Uncle Naresh after some years in school and return to live with the family for the rest of my life. Aunt Maria, Amma's eldest sister, was particularly upset that I was leaving home. She'd grown very much attached to me ever since she fed me her breast-milk when my mother found she did not have enough of her own.

My grandparents would tell me years later that they walked with their heads bent to avoid the sneering voices and mocking eyes of neighbors who were certain that the first granddaughter in our family was being sent to her death. They couldn't understand why I had to go to a distant place in the care of people unknown to anyone in the village. There was no rejoicing at my joining a good school, and there was no talk of what an education would mean for me.

'Who knows what that man wants?' one suspicious neighbor said, referring to the foreigner who had started the school. 'Why should he do anything for us for free?' No one could give an explanation. Poor villagers were not used to being offered life-changing opportunities for their children at no cost to them. In a land where bonded labor is the norm for those who fail to repay loans on time, it was hard to trust generosity and kindness from anyone.

'Anthony doesn't love Shilpa,' Amma moaned to Grandmother. 'Remember, he ordered me to throw her into the *thipai* when she was born.'

The thipai was the landfill next to our house where people went to defecate and discard garbage. This was also where Amma and Grandmother buried the sarayam in a jar to be stored until it was sold. And this was where Appa had wanted to dump me soon after I was born, disappointed that his firstborn wasn't a son.

The sight of the jeep parked outside the convent brought a fresh smile to Appa's face. Upon seeing Mrs. Law, he instantly joined his hands in the traditional greeting of *Namaste*. Appa couldn't understand what Mrs. Law was saying to Sister Stella, but the pleasant look on her face reassured him that everything was all right.

The crowd that had followed us flocked around the vehicle. Appa stepped into the jeep first, and then Amma handed me over to him. She lifted her sari slightly and entered too. It was exciting for the villagers to see the jeep up close and watch my family seated inside. I noticed that my parents weren't looking at each other.

After we got in, Mrs. Law helped a tall, fair-skinned, five-year-old girl with curly hair into the vehicle. 'This is Shoba,' Mrs. Law said. Shoba was gentle and docile, but frightened to be alone without any familiar adult to accompany her. No one was concerned about her, but I was happy that she was going to travel with me.

Appa, like everyone else in the village, immediately recognized the little girl. Her mother had been pregnant with her at a young age but the father denied his role in it. Unable to face the disgrace of bearing a child before marriage, Shoba's mother left the newborn girl with her older brother and fled to Mumbai, leaving Shoba to bear the brunt of her mother's mistake. But neither Shoba's uncle nor his family showed Shoba much affection, and so she retreated into loneliness. In the years to come, Shoba's life would be transformed in ways none of us could fathom then. But on that day, in the blue jeep, the five-year-old looked lost.

The jeep rolled slowly out of the village, its gears whining loudly. I was travelling for the first time through remote villages, thickly populated slums, lush ragi fields, and barren stretches of land. It was a world I never knew existed. The sight of women balancing bundles of dry twigs upon their heads, men digging trenches alongside roads, schoolchildren dressed in uniforms, monkeys sneering at worshippers from temple gates, and many other grand visions excited me beyond words. Cows grazed along the roadside and goats were shepherded by old men over rocky terrain. Occasionally, I stuck my head out the window, pointing to unusual sights along the way: decorated shops, multi-storey buildings, cars, bright yellow buses, and more.

Finally, after long hours navigating muddy roads and around giant potholes, the jeep rolled to a stop. The driver got out and opened the rear door. Appa stepped out first, then Amma who reached for me. Shoba quietly followed. We stood in silence, staring at our new world.

The place looked more like a construction site than a school for children. Piles of concrete blocks and heaps of mud punctuated the barren land around us. The rich red color of the soil showed that it was clay, best suited for making bricks and tiles. We stood upon a gentle hill that I would learn later was part of the Deccan Plateau. The new surroundings appeared stranger than any I could ever have imagined.

A young man appeared from nowhere and asked us to pose for a photograph. The four of us stood in front of the jeep, everyone holding hands, even Shoba. The jeep looked like a paddy wagon, and we probably gave the appearance of fresh prisoners, newly transported to jail. Or did we look instead like immigrants coming to a new world? In my early days at school, I spent innumerable hours staring at that photo of this memorable point in time. I can clearly make out Amma's bulging belly, protruding from beneath the faded blue sari draped untidily around her waist. Appa was dressed in an oversized red shirt, towering over me with his intimidating presence. I realize that I appear frightened. And certainly I must have been, in spite of my excitement. Every time I missed Amma, I would stare at that photograph and cry, holding onto the bittersweet memories of the day that changed my life forever.

We were directed to a table for breakfast. It was the first time any of us had eaten at a table; at home, we ate sitting on the floor. Appa looked uncomfortable at the height. I sat on Amma's lap as she plucked at pieces of *dosa*, a South Indian pancake. No words were exchanged between them, and no signs of surprise were displayed. Both my parents appeared lost in thought.

A tall, elderly woman with a warm smile entered the dining hall. Her black hair streaked with grey was bundled neatly at the nape of her neck. Appa raised himself from his chair.

'No, please sit down; don't get up,' the woman said politely in clear Kannada.

Appa seemed relieved that somebody spoke his language at last. Amma greeted the stranger with a smile and a respectful Namaste. The woman returned the greeting and introduced herself as Ms. Ruth, the dormitory caretaker.

Ms. Ruth led the four of us outside. The grinding sound of a cement mixer followed us wherever we went. Shoba and I were not wearing sandals, and the gravel bit into our bare feet. After a while, Amma picked me up and carried me.

Ms. Ruth escorted us to a nearby building that she explained was a newly constructed dorm for the children who were being admitted to the school. Appa removed his slippers at the doorstep and stepped into the unfinished space, staring curiously at everything around him. The two sections of the dorm were separated by an open courtyard where grass and a few flowering plants were sprouting. Beyond a red-tiled veranda were two large rooms with smooth white and maroon tiles.

Ms. Ruth excused herself for a moment. Alone at last, Amma turned to Appa and whispered, 'Anthu, there is nothing here.'

'This is a new school, Sarophi. It will take time to complete the buildings. What are you grumbling about?' He had made up his mind to let me go, and there was no turning back.

Amma looked away, trying her best to hold back tears. She ran her hand through my hair and held me close. Meanwhile, Shoba stood with her back pressed against the wall, looking frightened and silent save for the sound of her breathing. I was busy looking at everything around me—the colorful curtains, the slippery floor, the empty shoe rack, and the neatly arranged beds. I thought I was in a fairyland, and for a moment I forgot that my parents were even there.

'Amma, come here,' I called out happily.

Wiping her tears with her pallu, Amma rose from the chair and walked towards the large room. She peeped inside the dorm to see two rows of cots lined up neatly. At the end of the dorm was another door that led to a bathroom. Amma stood looking around as though she, too, had discovered something new and exciting. She confessed years later that she was amazed at everything, especially the high ceiling with strong beams—so unlike the low, thatched roof of our hut. Likewise, the smooth tiled floors and colorfully painted walls of the dorm were in sharp contrast to our cow-dung-coated, two-room hut.

Appa eventually joined us. 'This is where my daughter is going to sleep. She will no longer be on the cold floor,' he said, turning towards Amma, hoping for her approval. Instead, her eyes welled with tears as she took in what would become her daughter's second home far away from her.

Appa later related that he had felt left out as I improvised a tour for Amma. However, it only seemed natural to me to share my excitement with my mother who cared for me every day, and not my father who left for the woods before I woke up and returned at night only after I was fast asleep.

Shoba and I were busy investigating the dolls when my parents slipped away. Amma later told me that Ms. Ruth came up to them and said, 'It is time for you to go. We don't let the children know their parents are leaving because it makes it more difficult for them. Don't worry. Shilpa will be happy here.' By then, Amma was somewhat reassured by Ms. Ruth's concern for the children.

My parents were asked to put their signatures in a book that was placed before them. Unable to read or write, Appa pressed his finger into an inkpad and stamped his thumbprint. Neither of them could read what was written in the book as it was in English, but Ms. Ruth explained that they had just acknowledged that they were my parents and were willingly letting their daughter live and study at the school.

Appa joined his hands in Namaste and left the room. Ms. Ruth reciprocated the gesture. Amma couldn't control her tears any longer. She didn't want to even look at Appa's face; she couldn't have hated him more. As they stepped outside, they could hear the excited chattering of children lost in play.

'Please, I want to see Shilpa one last time,' Amma begged, but Appa was resolute.

'Didn't madam tell us that it would be easier for her if we leave like this?' he said, barely controlling his temper.

Ms. Ruth followed my parents as they made their way back to the jeep. They heard a child's loud cry from the dorm, and Amma was certain it was me. For a moment Appa felt unsure whether he had made the right decision. He tried to deafen the sound of his daughter's cries ringing in his head.

Amma composed herself and thanked Ms. Ruth before stepping into the jeep behind her husband. Despite her apprehensions, Amma didn't want to displease Ms. Ruth. She knew this was the person who would care for her daughter in the days to come. Once inside the vehicle, Appa avoided the accusing eyes of his wife.

The jeep made its way out of the gates, bouncing along the bumpy road. Appa distracted himself by staring at the lake near the entrance to the school that reminded him of the one in his village he would pass on the way to sell liquor.

'This is so far away,' Appa said to himself, knowing he would remember this journey for a long time. For my heart-broken mother, it was the beginning of a realization that all that happened that day might have been for the good, as fate would have it.

I don't even know when my parents left me. It might have been while I was busy examining the colorful stuffed toys and sweet dolls I had found in the girls' dorm. Everything was so different and new to me in Shanti Bhavan.

Later that day a young woman dressed in a *churidar* struggled to get me to sit still as she cut my unkempt hair down to a neat bob. I looked strange in the mirror, strange enough to be upset by my new appearance. The woman then took me for a bath into a clean, white bathroom with smooth tiles. It was delightful to feel the gushing water from a tap falling on me, unlike the infrequent baths I had at home with one tiny bucket of water. The woman rubbed me with soap, covered my face with its delightful bubbles, and put shampoo into my hair. It was shampoo from America, I was told, which meant nothing to me since I didn't know what America was. After the bath, I stepped into fresh clothes with beautiful floral patterns. For the first time in my life, I felt clean and pretty.

Until I came to Shanti Bhavan, I had never thought about looking pretty. Most of the time I was dirty and wore simple clothes sewed from my grandmother's worn-out saris. Occasionally Amma cut my hair, crookedly, with blunt scissors when she thought it was too long for me to manage. No one talked about hairstyles. I had never washed my hair with shampoo, worn shoes, or put on face lotion. But the absence of those luxuries didn't matter then as I didn't know they existed.

My new surroundings held many unfamiliar things. In my old world, I cleaned my teeth with a line of charcoal spread on my tiny finger. Now I had a toothbrush and some sort of flavorful paste to brush with. I owned four kinds of footwear: sneakers for play, slippers for the dorm, soft black shoes for daily school, and leather shoes with laces for special occasions. In the beginning, they were a drag on my feet, but soon I began to like their feel. Given that I had arrived barefoot, these were riches beyond my wildest imaginings.

Despite these exciting comforts, my new school lacked the one thing I needed most in those first few weeks. I missed my grandmother's loving gestures and Amma's warm embrace at night as she sang to me, *Mother of sleep come to my child / Dance beside her like a peacock / Give her peaceful slumber.* Now, all I had were dolls to hug and a bed that, at first, was terribly frightening because it seemed so high off the ground.

I remember the fear of that first night very clearly. Ms. Ruth gently showed me how to lie on the bed and cover myself with a neat white sheet, but I couldn't muster the courage to sleep elevated. I staged an instant protest, throwing myself on the floor, thrashing about and screaming while the other girls watched. Unable to bring me under control, Ms. Ruth was left with no choice but to separate me from the others. Perhaps she didn't want my defiance to become contagious. She clasped my hand in hers and led me to a small room with a bed, switched on the lights, and left me alone, closing the door behind her.

I was frightened to be alone, and longed for the security of my mother. I would have given up all the dolls in the world to be with Amma again. I banged my fists against the wooden door and yelled at the top of my lungs, 'Amma! Appa! Get me out. Take me home!' There was only silence from the other side. No one came to open the door.

I kicked the door until my feet hurt and ran to the window and tried to bite into its iron bars. Tears of frustration flowed down my face as I cried out with all my strength. Out the window in the moonlight I could see dark rows of trees and rough, rolling grounds in the distance. No one was out there to save me.

I was exhausted from the day's journey and all the crying, so finally decided to climb onto the bed and give it a try. The feeling was totally different; instead of the hard floor, underneath me was softness and comfort. Instantly, I fell asleep.

My routine in those early days at school was so different from everything I was used to at home. At my new school, I woke up to sparrows chirping outside my window, classical music buzzing from the radio, and the housemother who looked after us in the dorm—we called her 'Aunty'—telling us to get out of bed and go to the bathroom. 'Girls, please get up,' she would say in Kannada and Tamil, walking to each bed, calling our names, and patting us gently.

Until I went to Shanti Bhavan, my childhood was quite similar to that of most girls in Thattaguppe. Each day was the same as the one before. Amma would take me outside the hut as soon as I woke up to clean my face with water from a bucket kept mainly for washing hands after meals. I would watch our neighbor milking her cow and the young women sweeping around their huts and sprinkling water over the ground to settle the dust. My mornings continued with me watching Amma sweep the floor and warm up the previous night's leftovers for breakfast. Then, like the other children in my village, I ran around half-naked, wearing only thin cotton shorts. I bathed in the lake occasionally, and looked forward to the annual village fair where I got to pick a magical number out of an old steel box to win prizes like earrings and rag dolls. When bored and restless, I would sit by the muddy road that ran past our hut and curse passers-by in Kannada, mimicking the foul words Amma and Appa used when they quarreled. Old women warned my mother, 'You look out for that one. Her tongue is too long.' But Amma would laugh and ignore them, masking whatever worries she might have had.

Cursing wasn't the only bad habit I had picked up. Whenever Grandmother took tobacco leaves from the pouch she hid around her waist, I begged her to give me some. She would chew the pungent leaves for a while, then pinch a little from her mouth and place it in mine as a mother-bird would for her chicks. When people came to Grandmother's house to buy liquor, I would chatter away through a mouth dyed red from tobacco, like an all-knowing old woman. It bothered Grandmother.

By afternoon the streets would turn drowsy and still with men grazing cattle in the woods or brewing liquor by the lakeside and women toiling in the landlords' fields. Except for the little ones left running about, playing with insects in the gutters and creating a big nuisance for their grandmothers, nothing would break the dreary rhythm of village life.

Thankfully, as the sun descended over the horizon the village would come alive, taking on a carnival-like atmosphere as men and women returned to their huts along the narrow road, herding cattle or riding on bullock carts. This was when anything could happen; the night offered possibilities for the unexpected. I often saw men brawl, usually over money, and heard loud arguments between drunken husbands and their exasperated wives who begged for some peace at home.

Violence was hardly a stranger in my home, either. Joseph Thatha used to beat Arpuda Ajji almost every other night when he returned from the field. I saw Appa slap my mother whenever he got angry with her. At times Appa came home drunk to his bones with no money left in his pocket to buy vegetables. At first, Amma would fight with him. Then, realizing there was no use quarrelling with a drunken man, Amma would scoop out a handful of ragi from the sack stacked in a corner and boil it into a tasteless porridge. Each morning Amma squeezed the previous night's leftover *ittus*—cooked ragi rolled into a ball—into a liquid concoction, added some onions and chilies, and gave it to me for breakfast. Usually, lunch was no more than rice or ragi served with a watery vegetable curry, and dinner was ittus again. It was much too little for the entire family, especially considering Appa's ravaging appetite. When I whined about food, Amma sternly reminded me that there were times when she had gone hungry all day without even ittus to fill her stomach. Appa never bothered to comfort me, and I didn't question him. From a young age, I was conditioned to think that men knew more about life in general, that they had good reasons for whatever they did, and that a woman's opinion didn't count for much.

Life at my school was so different. Each day we followed a structured routine. Perhaps the biggest change I enjoyed was the food. In my new world, we gathered for breakfast in a nicely decorated room with tiny chairs and tables and were given a variety of Indian dishes, from *idlies* to hot *puris*. Vegetables and tasty curries were served for lunch and dinner, and salt biscuits, fruit salad, or fried groundnuts for snacks in the evening. We would often crowd around the kitchen window, greedily breathing in the warm smell of fresh-baked bread and cookies. After eating the same thing day after day at home, food had suddenly become a joy for me. I was in a wonderland where everything was plentiful.

I recall the first time we were served a dark brown liquid instead of milk for our evening snack. 'Please sit down. You are going to have cocoa,' Ms. Ruth announced. All of us hurried to our seats. Sensing that we were impatient to try the new drink, she quickly poured it into each of our mugs. I tried to say the word 'cocoa,' an unusual English word certainly alien to us. It sounded just as bad as it tasted. From that day onward, cocoa was served every evening. Some of my classmates instantly fell in love with it, but I found the taste strange. Within a few days, however, I too began to like the new drink, and in time, it became one of my favorites.

Food and play were the best parts of our lives. We began our days exercising to nursery rhymes in the early morning sun. Shortly after, we had lessons on alphabets, numbers, and music. In preschool and a year later in kindergarten, we ran around in the gardens, listened to classical music, watched videos about phonetics, and played with toys. I loved to touch the dark nose of my little doll and stare into its glass eyes that always returned my gaze. Playing on the plastic slide and see-saw outside the dorm was always great fun, even if it was the source of many fights among my classmates.

We learnt English, absorbed innumerable words, and listened to stories with pictures. Our first teacher was Mrs. Law, the one who had brought me from my village. She greeted us with a cheerful look and a bright 'Good morning.'

Pretty soon, we learnt to respond, 'Good morning, Mrs. Law' in proper English.

During the first few weeks of class, I pushed past the other children to find a place up front on the floor near Mrs. Law's feet while she sat on a chair and read to us from a picture book. Holding a book in one hand, she read out its title, the author's name, and then started the story. In the beginning we couldn't understand what she was reading, but we followed along. She was speaking the foreign language of our new world. She showed us the pictures and acted like the characters in the book, her gestures exquisitely expressive. We heard with great delight *The Three Little Pigs, Cinderella, Jack and the Beanstalk,* and *Snow White*. I would laugh out loud every time she called out in an eerie voice: 'Rapunzel, Rapunzel, let down your golden hair.'

We tried to imitate her but it took months for the sluggish weight of our Kannada and Tamil accents to wear off. Over the years, my English got more and more polished. Today it has a distinctive character that I am rather proud of—a clear amalgam of Indian and Western accents. Whenever I was back in the village, speaking English commanded respect. No one could understand me, but they were curious to hear me speak the language only important people could. It made me feel rather important too.

Before evening snacks, we quickly changed into play clothes and put on shoes. None of us knew how to tie shoelaces, so the aunties showed us over and over again. We ran around in the small playground behind the dormitory, trying to catch each other.

Heaps of mud collected from the construction projects were our best resource for games. We 'built' the huts we lived in before, and used rocks and coconut shells as cooking fireplaces and pots. I blew into the 'fire' with a stick as if it were the funnel made of a black hollow rod my mother used at home. My imagination ran wild, recreating everything that was our hut except for the roof.

At night we were told to stomp while walking along the pathways to scare off snakes. We looked like the Teenage Mutant Ninja Turtles, well-armed in our warm, full-sleeved shirts, pants, and leather shoes ready to fight off our nocturnal enemies. A slight hissing or a rustle from the bushes would have us screaming, 'Snake! Snake!' Time after time, the security guards came running, only to find their torches shining upon tiny crickets or sleepy toads.

On Saturday afternoons we were taken on nature walks to look for birds. Sparrows, hummingbirds, and kingfishers were common on our grounds. The bird nests appeared so much cozier for their chicks than our dingy village huts filled with smoke. I imagined them singing as they flew to the heavens. I often pictured being a bird, and flapped my arms as if they were wings. 'Next life, if God permits me, I will be a bird,' I'd say to myself.

Sometimes we were taken outside the school gates to the nearby lake that brimmed with water after thunderous monsoon showers. We walked in pairs, holding hands, and watched the migratory birds that skimmed the lake in great flocks. The sight of white, long-necked cranes gracefully wading through shallow waters and picking up small insects in their beaks was thrilling. Avinash, a fair, chubby boy with an unusually large protruding belly, was usually my walking partner. He was quite a clown during these trips, entertaining us with clever tricks and his acting talents. Years later I learnt that his skills were acquired during his early years performing on the street of his village with his father.

We were not allowed to walk where stones protruded from the shallow water in the lake. The aunties told us that these stones marked where bodies were buried, as that section of the lake had been a cemetery for the poor. In the distance, we could see groups of women from nearby villages squatting upon rocks that jutted into the lake, washing clothes in the water, just as my mother did back home.

What was especially heartening about my first year at Shanti Bhavan was the fun in all our daily activities. I looked forward to the next lesson, the next game, the next new flavor. As my new way of life started to set in, I thought less about my parents. I felt safe and protected in my new environment. Like colorless water innocence flowed, blind to where this new life was headed.

As years passed, I often found myself feeling guilt-stricken at how I came to have so much compared to my family. While my father hauled sacks of liquor on his back, I was learning to sit at a table and eat with a spoon. While my mother was alone, with no one to talk to, I was greeting guests to our school with a smile and curious questions. No one in my family could read or write in any language, but I was learning English and how to add numbers. My brother, Francis, and the child my mother was carrying when I left her would live with whatever little they had. I, on the other hand, was learning to long for more of the good things I had already been given.

Chapter Four

Father Figures

The wait was unbearable. Three long months had passed and now I would finally see my parents again. They were coming to Shanti Bhavan along with other parents for an important meeting.

I pressed my face against the window, searching for Amma and Appa among the crowd. The thoughts of being held in my mother's arms, and being carried around by my father on his shoulders were enough to send me jumping about in the dorm with the same excitement I used to feel back home at the village fair. When the time came, we were taken to the dining hall, a large tile-roofed building that was still under construction, for the much awaited moment.

We had been dressed carefully for the occasion—hair combed neatly and faces beaming at a high polish. Wild with excitement, we were finally let loose to run into the gathering of parents. Plenty of confusion erupted since some parents could no longer identify their children. We looked so different to them, dramatically transformed by our clean clothes, full cheeks, haircuts, and huge smiles. Some mothers embarrassed themselves by grabbing the wrong child. Fortunately, the mix-up didn't run both ways; we easily recognized our parents. The aunties and teachers looked on, savoring the moment and laughing their hearts out at the confusion.

I found Appa seated by the hall entrance. Screaming with delight, I ran into his open arms as he effortlessly swept me up from the ground. I held him tight around his tree-trunk neck with a force that surprised him. As always he smelled of sweat, piercing my senses, but it didn't matter. I heard the crackle of a packet of biscuits in his pocket and reached for it. Appa smiled. It wasn't every day he had a few rupees to spare for things like that; this was a special occasion.

My attention quickly turned to the section of the hall where the women were gathered. Dressed in bright saris with jasmine flowers pinned in their braids and red bindis pressed on their foreheads, the mothers looked like a basket of bright marigolds. Amma was amongst them, waiting eagerly for me. She snatched me away from Appa before I could even eat one biscuit, and wetted my face with a string of kisses. 'How are you, Chinna?' she kept asking lovingly, waiting for me to say something to satisfy her. I closed my eyes, enjoying the warmth of her embrace after so long an absence, and took in with all my senses the scent of her hair and the softness of her skin. It was so good to feel loved, to belong to someone who was all mine.

That first visit proved to be momentous in more ways than one. Not only did my parents get to see me again, but they were to meet the man I would later come to think of as Dad—different from father. Even years later, Appa had no difficulty describing that day in vivid detail. After all, it was an unusual experience— the first time he met the man to whom he'd handed over the responsibility of bringing me up.

As the parents settled down, all eyes turned towards the entrance to the dining hall. Those who were chatting were nudged into silence as Mrs. Law made her way down the concrete stairs. Walking beside her was a tall, well-built man whose eyes were hidden behind dark sunglasses, giving him a sophisticated look. Everyone had expected our benefactor to be a fair-skinned foreigner. However, his light brown skin and sharp facial features, not to mention his large ears that stood out prominently, suggested he was of Indian origin. His black hair, sparsely sprinkled with white, was neatly parted to the left. Everyone knew his name was 'Dr. George.'

Except for a few scattered whispers, the gathering of staff and parents was reverently quiet. There was a palpable tension in the room now. This was the moment our parents had been waiting for; they needed answers to the many questions that troubled them. As in our village, suspicious neighbors and landlords everywhere had raised doubts about the true motives of the school and the man behind it.

The stranger greeted the crowd with folded hands and head slightly bent in earnest respect. In a loud, uneven chorus, the parents returned the Namaste with the same adoration they bestowed upon landlords, priests, and moneylenders. But unlike those powerful men who made the families stand for a while whenever they arrived, this man said warmly, in English, 'Please sit. Please sit.'

Seeing a sea of blank looks, he gestured several times with his hands for them to sit down. The stranger couldn't speak any of the local languages, so two staff members sat nearby to translate for him. They repeated his words in Tamil and Kannada, the two languages spoken in the states of Tamil Nadu and nearby Karnataka.

Dr. George told me many years later, 'I knew then that whatever was to happen that day would determine the future of our school.'

Village landlords and leaders of slum communities were already spreading rumors that some children had been killed, their organs removed, and their bodies dumped in remote fields. These power brokers were afraid that their control over the poor would be lost if their children received a good education, obtained high-paying jobs, and transformed the economic conditions of their families. They were determined to undermine the school at any cost.

Dr. George cleared his throat. 'I am very happy to see all of you.' His voice rang out with gentle strength. He appeared relaxed; casually, he crossed his legs.

But things didn't click immediately. I'm sure his addressing the parents in English struck everyone as odd, and the time waiting for translation made it even more unnatural. The parents were just as intrigued by his speaking a foreign language as they were curious about what he might have to say. He countered the intensity of their stares with a smile, not to let their gazes unnerve him.

'It has been twenty-five years since I left India for America,' Dr. George began. 'In my younger days, I was an officer in the Indian army, but I left after suffering a hearing impairment.' Touching his right ear, he said disarmingly, 'I don't hear very well.'

Nobody uttered a word, so he continued.

'After making some money in business, I decided to start a school to educate children from poor families. That's why I am here.'

He waited for the interpreters to do their work.

Dr. George had been moved by the difficult lives led by the Monpa tribes in the Himalayan mountain ranges where he served as a young army officer. The poverty he witnessed during his travels in India inspired him to start the school. He was appalled by the caste discrimination that many endured, and it was his desire for social justice that had brought him back.

He spoke with deliberate seriousness, but emotion lit his face. 'I believe that all children, whether black or white or brown, rich or poor, are equal,' he continued, constantly gesturing with his hands. 'Everyone must have the opportunity to study at a good school.'

He explained how he had assembled a team to make his life's mission a reality. He purchased more than thirty acres of land in this distant village where poverty was rampant. Soon construction began in earnest for this residential school, our school, to be named Shanti Bhavan—Haven of Peace.

It couldn't have been clear to him whether anyone in the audience really understood the meaning of what he had said, but they nodded as if they did and sighed just the same. Using simple language, facial expressions and hand gestures, he tried to make it easy for everyone to grasp what he was saying.

'I live with my family,' he said. 'I have a wife and two grown-up sons.' He paused and added with a mischievous twinkle in his eyes, 'Only one wife.'

The interpreters tried to contain their smiles as they translated. The audience erupted in laughter. It was the kind of joke they enjoyed most. Though relationships involving a man and more than one woman were not uncommon in their communities, his openness about it was hilarious. Where we came from, rich folks seldom joked with the poor.

Appa wondered why this stranger wanted to help his family. He was surprised to hear a man from *phoren* (foreign) say, 'Your children will be tomorrow's leaders. They should study hard in school and college. And when they get good jobs, they will improve your lives.'

It was too farfetched for the parents to think that their children would be able to help them in a big way years later. Moreover, waiting so many years for their children to complete college education was simply beyond their comprehension. They probably didn't have confidence in their children's ability to study beyond a few grades in the local school. What made them suspicious was that he still hadn't asked for anything in return.

Finally, Dr. George asked if there were any questions. A few hands shot up. A young father stood, drawing the attention of the crowd. 'In our village, many people are saying that you will kill our children and take their kidneys and eyes and sell them in America. We are afraid.' Heads nodded in collective assent.

Dr. George chuckled and didn't show so much as a kernel of surprise, since he'd already heard of these rumors. 'I will not take your children's kidneys or eyes. I will give them my heart.'

A soft gasp rippled through the crowd. Some parents whispered amongst themselves, unsure what he had meant.

An elderly man dressed in a simple shirt and a lungi raised his hand. 'Are you planning to convert our children to Christianity?' he asked.

'I am a Christian,' Dr. George answered. 'I am a Hindu. I am a Muslim. I am a Jew. I am all of these.'

Several nodded, impressed. I'm guessing most of the parents found this statement confounding. But a few probably understood the implications of what he was saying, and tried to explain to others.

Dr. George waited patiently.

At last, a young man cut through the chatter. 'Is this all government money?' He pointed to the construction going on outside.

'I have not accepted any financial assistance from the government, nor do I plan to,' Dr. George replied instantly. The crowd was confused. They couldn't understand where the money was coming from. They were accustomed to grabbing whatever the government offered them by way of concessions and food subsidies. It was difficult for them to grasp why anyone would reject government assistance.

'Without basic amenities like electricity, running water, and proper roads, it has been difficult,' Dr. George said, referring to the challenges inherent in constructing a school in a remote village.

We heard more about these early hurdles when we were older, like the day a bulldozer ran into a huge anthill. Out of nowhere, a large cobra sprung up and posed menacingly with its hood spread out. Several more snakes followed, some crawling towards the bulldozer. The driver screamed, completely aghast. The local superstition is that if one killed a cobra, its partner would avenge its death. Afraid that the snakes might creep up to his seat, the driver jumped down and ran away from the vehicle. Mr. Frank, the facilities manager of the school, and two laborers took long sticks to chase the snakes away. The frightened driver watched from a distance, muttering a feverish prayer. Only after being assured that the snakes had been driven out did he return to work.

It was apparent from the start that there was much skepticism among the parents about the motives of rich people. What Dr. George had said sounded just as lofty as all the promises that politicians and landlords often made but failed to keep.

'Why are you doing it for free?' one man asked.

Dr. George answered calmly, 'People like you haven't had the opportunity to overcome poverty. You have been poor since birth, and your ancestors were poor for generations. I believe that educating your children will help your families rise out of poverty.'

Appa did not understand why Dr. George would want to help poor families with his own money, but he wasn't altogether unfamiliar with the generosity of rich people. After every harvest, the landlord in our village would invite his laborers for a meal to be served in the open ground outside his large house. When politicians gave saris to poor women before elections, they asked only for loyalty in return. Occasionally, a few rich folks from the city showed up in their beautiful cars at the village on religious holidays or on their loved ones' death anniversaries. Some considered that their acts of benevolence on auspicious days would be rewarded with God's blessings. My parents along with our neighbors would gather with great anticipation for what was promised by the village leaders—an afternoon meal, clothes for the children, or whatever small gifts that might descend from rich visitors.

Dr. George ended his talk in the same reassuring tone in which it had begun. 'I hope you also have the same dreams for your children as I have. I don't want you to take them out of school and force them to work. Or get the girls married off early.'

His confidence had a positive effect on the audience. Placing his hand on the shoulder of a pleasant-looking man sitting beside him, he said, 'This is Mr. Jude. He is the CEO of this institution, my right-hand man.' Mr. Jude smiled and, like Dr. George before him, joined his hands in Namaste.

Turning to another staff member sitting close to him, Dr. George said, 'This is Mrs. Law, the principal of the school. All the staff here will take good care of your children. From today onward, they are my children too.'

The crowd was now visibly excited and moved by what they had just heard. They rose as one and offered a thunderous ovation. 'We will cooperate, sir,' many in the crowd shouted. 'We will help you.'

Appa, like all the others, stood with his palms joined in respect. Amma, soon to give birth to her third child, my only sister, picked herself up carefully. She joined the others, but I know Dr. George hadn't convinced her. She wanted me home, and there was nothing she could have heard at this gathering that would have changed her mind about that.

As for Dr. George, his mission was slowly beginning to take shape. For Appa, there was now a good future to dream about. Both my father and my father figure came away from this initial meeting with hope in their hearts. Soon, I was busy playing by my mother's side, oblivious to the significance of all that had taken place that day.

It was time for the parents to return home. As they prepared to leave, every child pleaded to go with them. We loved the school, but watching our families walk away was too painful to bear. The aunties had to restrain us, and had no choice but to bolt the dormitory doors. As before, I stamped my feet and screamed, 'I want my Appa. I want Amma!'

Thinking about that day now, I realize how crucial that first meeting was for everyone. If Dr. George hadn't been able to persuade my parents and set their minds at ease, Appa and Amma might have taken me back home with them, closing the doors to the new life that now lies ahead of me. By the same token, it was Appa's unrelenting insistence in the face of nearly unanimous opposition from family and neighbors that gave me a different future. It appears that karma offers just one chance, if any, in one's life for such a transformative prospect. Dr. George often tells others, 'It is hard to truly transform poor people. Money can feed them for a while, but beliefs and mind-sets are very difficult to change.'

After that first session with our parents, every time Dr. George returned from the United States, he would meet with them. Although travelling to Shanti Bhavan always meant rising early and taking several buses, my parents told me they awaited such days eagerly. With the help of his interpreters, Dr. George communicated freely with our families, and they in turn grew more at ease, and even jovial with him. It was clear that Dr. George understood they needed to know what was happening in the school and how their children were faring. Over time, Amma reconciled herself to seeing me only when I returned home for the holidays and during her occasional visits to the school for special events.

While our parents were anxious to hear about our progress, we children looked forward to seeing Dr. George for entirely different reasons. Like Santa Claus, he appeared with a sack full of surprises when he arrived from America. He would smile lovingly at us, his pioneers—the first two groups of children at Shanti Bhavan. 'Hello, children,' he would say in greeting. We would jump all over him, electrified by the sight of colorful lollipops in his hands. The aunties found it hard to keep us under control when he was around. We even had a nickname for him, a private one we used chiefly amongst ourselves: we had christened him, 'DG'.

All of us enjoyed being with DG. Whenever we encountered him, he was playful, asking silly questions and joking with us. He usually ended his conversations with us by enquiring seriously, 'How come you are so smart?' Happy to learn that DG thought of us that way, we smiled and looked at each other to be sure. When I talked to him alone about the books I had read, like *Charlotte's Web* or *Beauty and the Beast*, he often concluded with the question, 'Do you know you are a genius?' I would reply that I didn't think I was, but he confirmed his belief in me anyway, much to my private satisfaction. But his smile would disappear in an instant if he found things amiss. Poor grades or improper behavior would bring out the strict side I dreaded.

Several years would pass before I realized how important DG was to our lives. I will never forget the time we thought we had lost him forever. One morning at assembly Mrs. Law announced, struggling to sound calm, 'Children, Dr. George's office was in one of the twin towers in New York that were destroyed by terrorists. We haven't heard from him yet.'

We stood aghast. I must admit that I felt worried not only at the prospect of losing DG but also about how it would affect us. I had come to enjoy every minute of playing with my friends and eating different foods every day. If Shanti Bhavan closed and we were all returned home, what would our lives be like then?

Two days later, to our great relief, Mrs. Law read aloud an e-mail she had just received. DG had been away in Washington, DC on the day of the attack. No harm had come to him.

A month later DG suddenly walked into our dorm with Mrs. Law, catching us by surprise. Everyone was full of questions. Face beaming with a big mischievous smile, he announced that he had seen us through the window of the airplane he had arrived in and had waved at us, complaining that none of us waved back. He always had something ludicrous to say, and my imagination would soar hearing him and seeing how playful and silly he could be in our presence.

A day or two following his return, DG showed us a video about the World Trade Center attack. For the first time watching it, I felt frightened and insecure. Our good fortunes could disappear in a moment. What happened in a distant land might be enough to end the fairy tale we were living. The worry disappeared when Ms. Ruth called us over to drink cocoa, and we went back to our carefree lives.

Chapter Five

Learning About
My Mother

The holidays were nearing. I was eight years old. The whole school was abuzz with excitement as we stacked our books in large cardboard cartons, packed away our clothes and blankets, and talked nonstop about how we were going to spend the next three weeks with our families. I could hardly wait to tell Amma all about my classmates, our games, our walks, our meals and treats, and everything that had happened since she and I had been apart.

Too restless to sleep, I lay awake the night before going home imagining Amma and Appa smiling as Ms. Ruth told them I had been a good girl in school, that I didn't steal chocolates from her cupboard, or lie like I used to before, and that I was doing well in class. I could almost taste the sweets that Grandmother would make for me—roasted peanuts rolled into balls with melted jaggery.

I was sure my little brother and my sister—now four years old, the age I was when I left home—would be excited to see all the beautiful things I had made in art class. My favorite was the collection of bird feathers gathered during nature walks around the campus and by the lake outside the school gates. The thought of playing in the ragi fields of my village or stealing mangoes from the landlord's garden made my excitement barely controllable.

Now that we were old enough to understand, Mrs. Law had spoken a day earlier to all of us on the dos and don'ts of being home. We were to keep up with our hygiene, bathe regularly, protect ourselves from sexual abuse, be helpful to our siblings and parents, and not interfere if violence broke out within our families. I found it all a little dizzying.

At last, the day arrived. I managed to push my way to a place among my classmates who stood against the dormitory's broad glass windows, trying to spot their parents among the families who were being served breakfast in the dining hall. The dorm doors were locked to stop us from running wildly to our parents before our housemothers and teachers could update them on our performance in school.

'Leelie, I see your mother,' I shouted to a classmate over the noise of the television set and the boisterous chatter of excited children.

'Who else is with her?' she yelled back.

'Your father is with her.' I had just spotted his lean figure by her mother's side.

I scanned the crowd for my parents. They hadn't come. I pulled away from the window. My temples hurt.

Just then I caught sight of Appa's short figure among the group of mothers and fathers who had broken away from the crowd in the dining hall and were sweeping across the lawn to get closer to our dorm. I could almost feel the magnetic pull of their anticipation. Aunty Shalini wouldn't let parents come to the dorms looking for their children, and so she guided them back.

I stepped away and sat on my bed silently. I was troubled to see that Appa was alone.

Just then, one of the housemothers opened the door to let us out of the dorm. All my classmates ran to their parents, but I walked towards my father, crying. Appa tried to calm me when my second-grade teacher, Miss Christina, a tall, fair-skinned Anglo-Indian woman whose gentle nature had won our hearts, joined us. She had nicknamed me the 'fighting hen' because of my reputation as a feisty, hot-tempered girl who constantly got into fights with classmates.

'I don't know where you get all that energy, Shilpa,' she said, smiling at me and greeting my father warmly. 'She's like a volcano.'

I could sense that she was more impressed than disappointed.

Sounding confident despite her difficulty in speaking fluent Kannada, Ms. Christina turned to my father. 'Shilpa is a bright girl. She loves reading and does well in spelling tests. She needs to do better in Mathematics.'

Appa sat smiling as she spoke, nodding as if he understood the difference between spelling and math. He appeared nervous in her presence, as if he didn't quite know how to handle himself in the presence of an educated female. Regardless, he was pleased, and thanked her with his hands folded respectfully in Namaste. I wished Amma were also there to hear the good news from my teachers.

During the three-hour bus ride, I could not stop wondering why Amma hadn't come for me. Every time I asked, Appa simply avoided answering. Finally I stopped asking, but kept thinking of it. When the bus conductor hollered, 'Thattaguppe,' at the end of the journey, Appa lifted me off his lap and stepped out first, turning around to carry me down the bus's rusty steps.

It felt like an eternity since I'd last seen Amma. That had been during the winter vacation nearly six months ago. Unable to control my excitement, I skipped along the road humming my favorite English tune, 'My Bonnie Lies over the Ocean'. I knew she would be delighted to hear me sing English songs. Each time she tried to learn the songs from me, we both ended up laughing at her awkward pronunciations; but, determined to learn, she never gave up.

At a distance, I could see the large cross atop our neighborhood church, towering over the thatched roofs of the huts that bordered the sides of the road and the small shops displaying their wares to tempt the passerby. Carefully dodging clumps of cow-dung and stray dogs running about under the hot sun, I walked past shabbily clad boys playing cricket on the road with coconut tree branches as bats. I couldn't help noticing the rubbish piled alongside the muddy road. The scene was far from glamorous, but it was home.

Just as I was about to hop over the gutter to approach our house, Appa stopped me. 'Shilpa,' he said in a tone that clearly meant *no*, 'Let's first see your grandmother.'

I was just too anxious to see my mother, and nothing else could be more important. The door to our house was locked. I wheeled on my father, 'Appa, where is Amma?'

'She is there,' he said simply, avoiding my eyes and indicating that I follow him. I couldn't understand how Amma could be inside a locked house but I obeyed and kept close to him.

From a distance, I could see my grandmother standing outside her hut waiting for me with my sister in her arms. I yanked my hand from Appa's grip and ran as fast as my chubby legs would take me down the slope towards her.

'Grandma, Grandma!' I shouted. Her face lit up and she quickly put Kavya down by her side.

I clutched her large waist as she bent down and kissed me. Kavya was clapping her hands, repeating, 'Akka has come! Akka has come!' For a moment, I forgot all about Amma. As I struggled to pick up Kavya, she wrapped her small arms around my neck tightly. I smothered her with kisses.

'You have grown dark,' I teased.

'She plays too much in the hot sun,' Grandmother complained. 'She doesn't listen to me at all these days.'

Holding my hand, Grandmother led me into the dark hut, thatched with dried coconut leaves. 'Step in with your right foot. It is good luck,' she reminded me. I slipped out of my rubber shoes and stepped over the clay threshold with my right foot. She walked me to a large, wooden-framed portrait of Jesus that she'd neatly garlanded with purple wildflowers. Drawing the sign of the cross on my forehead, she uttered a prayer under her breath before searching for a matchbox. With a solemn expression, she lighted the shaggy end of a broomstick on fire and swung it three times in front of my face. I recoiled from the burning broom, afraid sparks might fall on my dress. She chanted loudly, 'Let all evil spirits that set their jealous eyes upon you go away. Protect my child in your grace.' I remained still, waiting for something to happen, certain that her prayer would drive away the devil.

I wasn't unfamiliar with rituals like this. My family had been converted to Christianity centuries ago, yet we still clung to age-old Hindu traditions. Church teachings about Christ and Heaven were interspersed with superstitions about spirits and the power that our ancestors hold over us. Grandmother told me that inner peace could be found only if demons were chased away. When I grew older I questioned her beliefs, but she would answer, 'If there is a God, there is a Devil, too.'

The practice I dreaded most was what Grandmother did whenever I fell ill with fever. She would remove a black glass bangle from her wrist, crack it against the wall, place one end of the broken shard in the kerosene flame, and swiftly press it to the back of my head. It was believed that the shock from the sudden burn would chase the evil spirit away and cause the fever to subside. If I continued to cry, Grandmother would sing softly, imploring the moon, 'Chanda mama, be kind to my child.'

Opening her eyes at last, she said, 'Are you hungry?'

'No, Grandma,' I said, my thoughts elsewhere. She sat me down on the floor covered with a fresh coating of cow-dung. It felt cold to my touch. She pulled me onto her lap, pressing me against her comforting breast. Kavya stood against the wall watching me attentively. 'Where is Amma?' I asked for what seemed like the millionth time.

Just like Appa, Grandmother didn't reply immediately. She ran her hand lightly through my short, boyish hair.

Her uncalled-for tenderness made me even more suspicious. 'Where is Amma?'

Her grip on me tightened, she took a deep breath, and sighed. 'Amma's not here, Chinna. She went in a plane to work in a faraway place.' Using words an eight-year-old could understand, Grandmother explained that Amma had travelled to Singapore to take up work as a housemaid.

I didn't understand what a housemaid was. Grandmother explained to me that she washed plates and spoons and cleaned toilets in the homes of rich people. I wondered why Amma would go so far away to do such work. I'd learn later from Amma that she had found it difficult to look after the needs of the family with Appa's meager income from the liquor business. She was sad that she couldn't buy better clothes or give us gifts on special occasions like Christmas and Mother Mary's feast.

I stayed frozen for a moment in my grandmother's lap before bursting into tears. The word *plane* made everything seem so distant. I wanted my Amma, and I couldn't bear not being with her. 'When will she come back?' I asked, shrugging off my grandmother's embrace.

Grandmother started crying as well. Seeing us weeping, Kavya joined in, amplifying the chorus. Kavya was barely four, and with Grandmother always with her, she didn't feel Amma's absence the way I did. She even called Grandmother, 'Amma,' convinced that she was her real mother.

I couldn't understand why my mother had left without telling me. Why couldn't she wait until I returned home from school? Suddenly remembering my father, I turned around to lash out at him, to call him a liar, but he had disappeared. The plastic bag filled with my schoolwork lay abandoned at the doorstep.

Grandmother held me tight, humming a hymn and cradling me in her lap. I used to like the soothing melody but now it brought cold comfort.

From that day on, I stayed with Grandmother when I was home. Appa and his side of the family were nearly invisible. Aunt Margaret and Aunt Rani, Amma's two sisters, had joined the convent, so the house felt lifeless to me. Fortunately, Grandfather and Uncle Naresh showered me with much love and affection.

On warm days, Grandmother would take Kavya, Francis, and me to the lake that lay behind the village. I loved running around in the shallow waters, chasing after white herons that came looking for fish. Whenever I went too far into the deep water, Grandmother would yell at me to get back to shore. 'If anything happens to you, what will I say to your teachers?'

After washing our clothes and laying them out to dry on the wild shrubs that grew everywhere, she would line us up naked on the bank and scrub the dirt off our skin with a stone. 'Ajji, it hurts,' I often screamed, trying to yank myself away from her strong grip as she ran the rough stone over my skin. 'You have so much dirt on you,' she would complain, ignoring the fuss I made. Sometimes, if we were lucky, she would fetch hot water from the liquor brewers for a special bath.

Kavya was always adventurous, chasing little fish into deep waters when she barely knew how to swim. She was my joy. She was everything I could want in a younger sister. I enjoyed playing with her and looking after her. I begged Grandmother to let me bathe her and dress her up, as though she were my doll. In the evenings, as we wandered freely around the village, Kavya would introduce me to her friends as we passed by their houses. 'She's my elder sister. She just returned from school,' she'd say. Everywhere we went young girls and boys stopped to stare at my strange presence by her side. And I was pleased with all the attention, happy to be with my sister without a care in the world.

In the early mornings, when a layer of darkness still coated the sky and long before the rooster crowed, I would take Kavya to the bushes that served as the toilet. It was a good idea to go in the dark; during daylight hours, one risked the embarrassment of being seen by others and, more importantly, being harassed by flies. Even under the thick cover of darkness, I could see people walking towards their habitual spots.

When Kavya was done, we would walk over to the small brook, and I would wash her bottom. Years later, even after a toilet shed was built behind the house, I preferred to go into the woods. The shed smelt horrible even from a distance—just like the ones in bus stops and railway stations. Water had to be carried from the bore-well each time one used the toilet.

As days passed, I turned quiet. I was often immersed in thoughts of Amma, hardly speaking to anyone or asking for anything. The mere mention of my mother's name triggered an immediate burst of anger. Even Kavya, as little as she was, sensed my moods and kept away from me whenever I was upset.

My father's absence didn't help. He was not to be seen most of the time, and whenever he did come to Grandmother's house, his visit was brief. Once I watched, numb, as a landlord punched Appa in the face. Grandmother came running from her house at the commotion on the road. I could see the redness in Appa's eyes shining through like jack-o'-lanterns against his black, shiny skin. He owed the landlord money he had borrowed for his drinks. In many nights to follow, I would wake up suddenly from a nightmare of the landlord punching my father over and over again.

Grandmother tried to keep me engaged with teaching me how to clean rice on a straw pan or draw *rangoli* with colored powder. When no one else was home to help her, she would ask me to rub her back when she took a bath. I was proud when she entrusted me with such a big task. She would sit on a boulder in the small shed adjoining the hut, naked as a new-born, with a bucket of water she had warmed with firewood.

Without turning around, she'd pass me a flat stone the size of the bar of soap I used back in school. I'd rub the stone slowly from top to bottom all along her back, occasionally glancing at her full breasts and big nipples that dripped water like raindrops when she poured it over her head. I found her sagging breasts beautiful and assumed that every mature woman was supposed to look like she did. The sight of her body made me feel very different about my own; I wanted so badly to look just like Grandmother someday.

Grandfather joined us every evening after returning from work, dirty and tired. For a long time, he had been earning just three rupees a day as a laborer in the landlords' fields. He supplemented his income by scavenging twigs and dry branches to sell in the village for a pittance. Later, when several sugarcane factories opened in the area, Grandfather found better work on a plantation, cutting stalks and boiling the liquid that had been pressed out of them in a machine.

Grandfather sometimes took me to the factory and showed me how jaggery was made from sugarcane juice freshly squeezed from the stalks. The sight of the hot, bubbling liquid was nothing like the boiling ragi water spilling over Grandmother's pot. I watched the process in fascination and loved it when Grandfather brought me one of the fresh pieces of jaggery to eat once it had cooled and hardened.

I will never forget those lazy afternoons on the plantation when Grandmother and I would sit in the shade of a tamarind tree, chewing sweet sugarcane sticks cast away by the workers for being too tender or unripe. Occasionally, I would go to the narrow stone canals that provided water to the factories. I loved splashing my feet in the clean water and peering closely in search of tiny fish and frogs I could reach out and catch.

But, like all good things, Grandfather's plantation job didn't last long. When competition from larger mills nearby forced the factory to shut down, he was out of work. Though only a laborer, he had been proud to be a factory employee. It was a step up from working for landlords.

After losing his job, I could see that Grandfather was distressed and worried, hardly talking to anyone for days. Eventually he was able to find employment in a shop that sold grains and spices. With what little the family earned, Grandmother bought ragi and a few vegetables and somehow kept everyone fed.

Grandfather had to work long hours at his new job. I liked to imagine him as the grand master of the shop, ordering others to carry the gunny sacks of rice and ragi. Grandmother later told me that he was just a coolie who did the carrying himself.

As darkness set in, Grandfather would come home exhausted, and could hardly keep his eyes open. After dinner, as Grandmother and I stacked the dirty dishes in the kitchen corner for washing the next morning, Grandfather slept seated on the floor. Mouth wide open and nostrils fluttering with each deep snore, he looked like a giant, drowsy tortoise. Kavya and I couldn't hold our laughter, hearing Francis imitating all those funny sounds coming from Grandfather.

During the rainy season Grandfather often came home fully soaked. In the forested hills of Thattaguppe, long monsoons brought torrential rain. The huts on both sides of the road were built upon slightly elevated land, and when drains overflowed, floodwaters flowed all around the huts, forcing the cowherds to let their cattle inside. Days got harder as the heavy showers made it difficult for anyone to venture outside.

Rain or no rain, life followed a predictable routine. The women of the village rose each morning well before the sun came up and lit cooking fires to warm up left-over ragi paste. Men woke up just in time to begin another day in the landlord's fields or brewing liquor in the forest. Appa would find his way through the woods to his designated spot, well hidden by the bushes, where he brewed liquor. For him, it was like going home. Brewing illicit liquor had been taught to him by Joseph Thatha in his early childhood and now it was a profession that offered him a livelihood and some measure of independence.

In the evenings, Grandmother would boil corn in a small steel pot over the earthen cooking place and make black tea, as milk was expensive. It was her way of keeping us eagerly awaiting the treat instead of running outside to play in the rain. I would beg her to let me out of the house by myself, but she wouldn't allow me to go out without my siblings or cousins.

One evening, when she was busy corralling her chickens safely inside their straw baskets, I ran out onto the road, following the sounds of merriment that came from a small crowd of men gathered outside a neighbor's house. I noticed a tall girl with hair much longer than mine dancing in the center of the crowd. It was Ann-Mary, a ten-year-old, who was once my senior at Shanti Bhavan but had been expelled a few years earlier. She didn't notice me until one of the men called out, 'Shilpa, come in and dance!' I giggled and shook my head *no*.

A few others joined in. 'Shilpa, please dance,' they begged. Finally, sighing, I joined Ann-Mary and danced, shaking my hips and arms in rhythm. I tried to imitate her, but couldn't follow her seductive movements. The cheers from the crowd became deafening, adding to the excitement that filled me from inside. Within a few minutes, several men joined in the dance, their sweating bodies forming a wall around me. I recognized the familiar scent of alcohol that hung in the air in our hut around Grandmother's sarayam customers and whenever Appa came home late at night.

Suddenly, I noticed a ten-rupee note flapping on Ann-Mary's salwar top; someone in the crowd had pinned it on her. I felt a rush of envy, wanting one for myself. Just then, a clean-shaven, middle-aged man sitting atop a stone near the edge of the gutter called out to another man, 'Give this to her.' In no time, a note was pinned to me as well.

Overjoyed at the reward, I danced faster, becoming frenzied as the men laughed at my gyrations. A few minutes later the crowd began to break up. I was staggering with exhaustion and turned to go home.

The man who had given me the note approached and said, 'Come with me. I have some presents for you.' I accepted, not realizing the danger in going with a stranger. Suddenly, it struck me that I was already late. 'I will come later,' I said and ran away.

Grandmother was anxiously awaiting my return. I knew I'd upset her, but was still in a daze from the sound of the crowd clapping, shouting, laughing, and cheering. It rang in my head. But so did Grandmother's frequent references to Ann-Mary as a 'bad girl'. Fearing that Grandmother would take away my reward, I hurried to my place on the floor and lay down on my stomach to conceal it. Come the light of the morning sun, I was relieved to find my precious ten-rupee note still pinned to my dress. The wrinkled note looked fancy to me. For the first time in my life, I had earned money! It was liberating, but I was not entirely comfortable with the way I had earned it.

Years later I would understand why Grandmother didn't want me to associate with Ann-Mary. She was expelled from Shanti Bhavan for repeated thefts and for imitating sexual acts, having often witnessed her mother with men. And now, back in the village, men came to buy liquor from her house and to seek her company, and she, a child of ten, had begun to entertain them.

Into the third week of my holidays, I was beginning to feel more hurt than angry with my mother. I missed her terribly and only talking about her could ease some of the pain. I asked Grandmother to tell me about Amma's past, and she was only too happy to oblige, even if I wouldn't fully understand the importance of some of the stories for several years to come.

According to Grandmother, Amma was barely thirteen when she joined the family's liquor business. She had grown up with three generations of her family packed under the same low roof. Her grandparents would frequently ask Amma and her siblings to fetch alcohol for them. If the children dared to refuse, their grandmother would twitch her puckered mouth and mutter, 'Hope you vomit to death.' The children were afraid of being cursed, so they quickly complied.

The family liquor business goes back generations. My great grandparents were both heavy drinkers who fell asleep in a drunken stupor every night while Grandmother was left alone to sing songs to lull her thirteen siblings to sleep. With no one to pay any attention to the younger ones, Grandmother was forced to leave school at an early age. By the time she got married at sixteen, she was already quite familiar with the duties that came with mothering. Her parents' weakness for sarayam not only made Grandmother a parent before her time, but also shaped her own daughters' destinies.

'I would send your Aunt Maria off with two rupees to the houses that sold cheap liquor,' Grandmother said. 'But Maria didn't always succeed. She was too proud to beg. One day, your mother asked if she could try.'

'What happened?' I asked, anxious to hear every story I could about my amma.

'The very first evening she returned home pleased with a plastic container brimming with two litters of sarayam,' Grandmother said with a smile.

From that day on, Amma became the family's official liquor collector. Every other evening after sunset, she would set out along the dusty road with a lantern to break the impenetrable darkness.

Her persistence with suppliers soon won her the reputation of a big-mouth bully, capable of talking even a forty-year-old man into giving her the liquor she wanted. She refused to allow men to intimidate her, and it was her boldness that drew Appa to her in the first place.

In the mornings, Amma would stay home to cook for Grandmother who worked in the fields like Grandfather, and for her four younger siblings who returned for lunch from the local school. Once they went back to class, she would pack the leftovers in a small steel vessel to take to Grandfather as he worked in the fields. And in the evenings, with Grandmother shouting after her to be careful, Amma departed for the liquor hunt.

Eventually Grandmother decided to get into the liquor business herself. She remembered telling Amma, 'From today onward, we will buy sarayam from suppliers and sell it in our house.' Grandmother was convinced that the business offered the promise of a good return for the family to survive better on the money earned from it. Amma was happy that both mother and daughter were to be at the helm of a business. I too was caught up in the picture Grandmother painted of the family business, even though I knew first-hand that it wasn't always so charming. I could only guess what Amma might have faced haggling for sarayam. After all, what did I know? My ideas of hunting for liquor came from the games of seek and find we played on the pleasant grounds of Shanti Bhavan.

'Each time she went, I would pray to Jesus for forgiveness,' Grandmother told me. 'All my life I have seen what this evil liquid does to people. God, please forgive me.'

Despite her reservations, Grandmother passed on the tricks of the trade to Amma who soon became capable of running the family business on her own, though it was never easy to handle drunkards. Once darkness set in, then as now, customers flocked to her house like ants to sugar. Grandmother would let them in, but seat them close to the entrance door before serving them and collecting money. When buyers consumed too much, they collapsed on the floor and refused to get up. It used to be Amma's job to shake them, and if they still couldn't manage to pick themselves up, she would have her younger brothers drag the drunkards out of the house and leave them outside for their relatives to find. Her resilience against adversity and her fighting spirit probably came from the way she grew up. Having watched Grandmother serving customers and drawing out cash from them, I too was growing familiar with the ways of the business.

Grandmother told me that in the beginning Grandfather worried about the family's safety and reputation. 'This is not good. What will others say?' Grandfather asked one night. 'They will say you are not a proper woman. We have four daughters and anything can happen with those drunkards coming to our house.'

Grandmother nodded, but reminded him, 'We need the money. Things will get better if we continue to sell sarayam. Then you won't have to borrow money to get a haircut.'

Grandfather smiled at the thought of lots of money. That was enough for him to forget his worries. He turned over on the mat, closed his eyes, and was soon fast sleep. Grandmother was assured by her husband's consent. And yet she warned me not to speak to strangers, afraid that I might inadvertently reveal too much and the police would be pulling up in front of our hut. It would not have been the first time a child innocently caused a loved one's arrest.

One afternoon, I asked Grandmother to tell me about how my parents came to be married. 'Was it love-at-first-sight or an arranged marriage?' I asked, remembering the Bollywood films I had seen in school where the hero and heroine instantly fell in love in their first encounter.

'It wasn't either,' she replied. I was confused. There had to be something more between my parents than the frequent fighting I had witnessed. Grandmother began to explain. It was a heavy narration told in bits and pieces over the next few years.

Amma was very attractive as a young woman and accustomed to men staring at her. She was darker than her sisters, earning the pet-name 'Karkie' which meant 'dark girl,' but none of the others had her sharp nose, big mischievous eyes, or smooth skin. Amma told me Appa liked her because she was bold and had a mind of her own, unlike her friends who stayed obediently in their homes, never daring to talk or even make eye contact with men.

This vision of Amma as a young woman was new and exciting to me. I thought of Miss Christina saying I was like a volcano. I thought of my boldness in asking questions in assemblies, asking visitors to the school about their lives. I wanted to be like Amma—daring.

The first time Amma caught Appa's stare, she found him looking at her 'improperly'. She was marching in a procession to the village's old stone church on the day of Aunt Maria's wedding, imagining how she herself would look on her wedding day. Though some men had already asked her parents for her hand, Grandmother had refused them, as tradition dictated her eldest daughter had to be married first.

A few days later, Appa went to Amma's hut. It was the first time she acknowledged his presence, though they lived on the same lane and might often have seen each other. She was seated on a mat on the ground next to her parents when Appa announced, 'I came to ask for your blessings to marry your second daughter.'

Grandmother was furious. For one thing, she had no intention of letting Amma marry a man whose parents were known for being heavy drinkers with a habit of quarrelling nastily with their neighbors.

Appa left that night without success and Amma had nothing to say in the matter. But if anyone had thought of asking her, she might have said she was impressed by the courage of this young man in coming and speaking so politely, bravely, and directly to her parents.

Appa's first visit would not be his last. The next time he came, he found her alone, winnowing rice. The sight of Appa was exciting, but alarming. She begged him to leave. Without being asked, he sat down before her. He placed his hand on the rice and said with a sincere expression, 'Sarophina, I swear I will marry you. I won't leave you.' Amma slid away from him. It was wrong for an unmarried woman to talk or sit so close to a man.

'Please go before Mother comes,' she whispered with a frightened glance towards the door. 'If anyone sees you—'

Appa reached for her hand and placed it on the heap of rice grains she was cleaning, a gesture deemed to be sacred and often an element of Indian wedding ceremonies. His action—so solemn, so intimate—conveyed the most serious of intentions. Amma froze. She didn't know whether it was her fear or the excitement of his touch that overwhelmed her.

Covering her palm with his own hand, he asked, 'Will you marry me?'

It took a minute for Amma to say, softly, 'Yes.'

Appa grinned and, with his mission accomplished, swaggered out onto the lane and into a whole new world.

But Amma was apparently unwelcome as a daughter-in-law because her family could not give a dowry. Appa had chosen her out of love, over his parents' objections, and he would have to face the consequences. Joseph Thatha made it clear Appa was no longer a part of their family.

Grandmother told me she did not fault Appa's family for rejecting her daughter. 'His family was struggling to make ends meet and a handsome sum of money would have been a great benefit. This foolish man got himself in big trouble by going against his father's wishes.'

Disowned by his father, Appa had no place to spend the wedding night other than with Amma's parents. They stayed with her family for the next three months, sleeping near the door, not far from my grandparents. The unmarried girls in the house slept in the next room. It was hardly an ideal situation for newlyweds.

Soon neighbors began to criticize Grandmother for having the young couple spending nights where there was no privacy and with young girls in the hut. Moreover, Appa failed to be faithful from the very beginning of their marriage. Rumors were already circulating in the village that Appa was flirting with a woman who frequented the neighborhood lake to wash clothes and bathe while he brewed liquor in the woods close by. A lot of this Grandmother did not explain to me until I was a teenager. Finally, Grandmother told Appa that she could no longer allow him and Amma to stay in her house.

With a little money he had saved, Appa rented a hut on the same lane that no one else seemed to want. Within its walls a woman had hung herself after her husband committed suicide by drinking poison, unable to repay the money he had borrowed from a landlord for his daughter's dowry and wedding. The family that lived there last had fled, convinced the house was haunted by the troubled souls of the couple. No one else had dared to stay there since. Left with no choice, they lived in that house until one night Amma began to act as if she were possessed by the spirit of the dead man and the priest had to be summoned to cure her.

Before long, Amma became pregnant. When her pregnancy ended in a miscarriage, everyone said she was cursed by ghosts and the wrath of Appa's family. Appa blamed Amma for all his misfortunes and demanded that she follow his every command. Like his father before him, he believed his wife was his property. He did whatever he wanted, and that included heavy drinking, hitting her, and behaving as though it was his right to satisfy his manly needs with other women. Not knowing anything better of men, Amma concluded that he needed other women in his life to be happy, and she was prepared to accept it. After all, there was nothing she could do to stop him.

'Perhaps that was why his desire for your mother became a different thing—not love but possessiveness,' Grandmother said. 'Once she came running to my house in tears. Your father had beaten her in a drunken stupor. It had become a daily ritual. Your mother sobbed in my lap and said, "Why did you marry me to him? I want to die." I had seen this happen to young brides so many times before.'

'What did you tell Amma?' I asked Grandmother.

'I told her this is the fate of women. We have to learn to live with our husbands,' Grandmother said. 'A woman's place is always in the service of her man. I don't want any of my daughters to live disgracefully, away from their husbands.' So Amma returned to the leaky hut.

I was stunned by how subservient Grandmother expected wives to be. There was no one to take Amma's side. When I grew old enough to understand, Amma explained how she coped with all her troubles and managed to fulfill the duties expected of her as a wife, a daughter, and a woman. Her personal desires were of little concern to anyone in the family, so she seldom expressed them. Almost everything she did was dictated by her husband and she never complained about what she lacked. I couldn't understand where she found joy. That was the woman's world in which I began my childhood.

Having learnt more about my parents' life together, I understood why Amma agreed to work so far away for so long. Grandmother was devastated that Amma was not there to bring up her children properly. 'My daughter had to leave because of that cruel father of yours.' She would repeat those words countless times throughout my mother's absence, sowing in me the seeds of strong resentment towards my father.

Chapter Six

The Difficult Days

It was the end of the holidays and time for me to return to school. Appa arrived at Grandmother's hut at four o'clock that morning and knocked on the door so loudly that even Uncle Christraj who could sleep through a storm woke up with a start. 'Can't a poor man at least have his rightful share of a good night's sleep?' Grandfather grumbled. As the knocking continued, he scrambled for a matchbox and lit the kerosene lamp.

Grandmother made her way towards the door, careful not to step on Kavya and Francis who were still fast asleep on the floor. I heard my father shout from the outside, 'Please wake up Shilpa and get her ready. We must leave now or we won't make it to Shanti Bhavan on time.'

I sat up defiantly. 'I want to stay here with you,' I pleaded with Grandmother, burying my head in her bosom. She tried to calm me with kisses.

'Say good-bye to everyone,' Grandmother said after she managed to wash my face and get me into the dress I had worn to come home from Shanti Bhavan. Leading me to the corner of the dark room where two framed photographs of my great-grandparents hung on the mud wall, she said, 'Take their blessings. They are always with you.' I stared at the photos for a minute, unsure what I was to ask of them. Then I prayed to them to grant my wish to stay home with my family. I could not hold back my tears when Grandmother took my hand to draw me away.

My brother and sister were sleeping through the commotion I was creating. Sobbing, I quickly kissed them both on their cheeks, feeling terrible about leaving them. My uncles, Christraj and Naresh, advised me to study well, not get into fights, and obey my elders. I promised them that I would be a good girl, and that was enough to satisfy them.

I was still wailing when Appa picked me up in his arms and walked out of the hut. Grandmother insisted that she accompany us to the bus stop, but Appa said it would make it harder for me to leave. I clenched my fists and hit him hard on his shoulders to free myself but he wouldn't budge. I just couldn't win this battle with him.

I was wailing for Grandmother as we made our way through dark streets thick with morning mist. The shepherd living across the lane was already at work, filling his bullock cart with the cow dung strewn over the road the previous night. He didn't even look up at me to watch a child being carried, screaming through the village streets. No one seemed to notice.

After hours of bumpy travel in the bus, the road smoothed into clean, even tar as we neared the brightly painted signboard that read 'Shanti Bhavan Residential School' in bold blue letters. From a distance, I could see the school's water tower and the red tiled roofs of the dorms rising above a line of tamarind trees. My stomach tightened.

The bus stopped some distance away from the wide gates of the campus. As Appa gripped my hand and led me down its steps, I had no idea this would be the last time he would ever escort me to Shanti Bhavan. Ever afterward, he relinquished that duty to Grandmother; he had no time for me. Appa would slowly recede into a world of his own, making liquor, later chasing wild elephants from sugarcane fields and, in his spare time, running after local women. The distance between us would grow so wide over the years that even during school vacations he would rarely come to see me at Grandmother's house or bring me surprises from the woods like the tiny white birds he had caught or the wild berries I loved so much.

As third graders, we'd moved into a new dorm, the only two-storey building on the campus. It stood like a lighthouse overlooking a sea of green lawns and thick stands of bamboo alongside the winding stone payments. Ms. Ruth who had looked after my class from pre-school through the second grade handed us over to Aunty Shalini and we braced ourselves for changes. I was jealous that Ms. Ruth was now tending a new set of twenty-four children.

Nevertheless, in no time my heart filled with affection for Aunty Shalini. She was a loving young woman in her late twenties with luscious black hair that flowed down her back. A small, maroon bindi always sat perfectly at the center of her forehead, and her eyes sparkled with warmth when she greeted every child. Her skin was lighter than mine and she accented it with a coating of talcum powder every morning after her bath. At times, I thought she was even prettier than Amma. But there was a sad look in her eyes that she tried to conceal behind her cheerful smile. Soon I came to understand why. Though married, she didn't have children of her own.

Aunty Shalini gave us all pet names, usually those of birds and animals, and addressed each of us as 'my child'. As time passed, I came to think of her as our amma in school. Many of my classmates began to call her 'Mummy,' which brought immense satisfaction to her, and she'd respond with a loving kiss or a hug.

In the Big Dorm, life had a new rhythm and new demands on us as slightly older children. We were now expected to follow the set daily schedule without constant reminders and guidance from the aunties. Every morning I woke up at six and went to play soccer, basketball, or baseball on the large field a few yards behind the dorm. In the evenings after bath, Aunty Jyothi, an unmarried woman young enough to still have trouble with pimples, turned on the CD player for us to dance to Tamil and Kannada songs—songs that brought memories of my home. Every Saturday after lunch all the boys and girls gathered in their respective dorms for the hygiene hour. We trimmed our nails, washed our muddy shoes, and dusted cupboards and cots. Old newspapers were laid out on the ground in the small backyard lush with jasmine and tall rose bushes. The aunties called us one by one to comb our hair, letting lice fall onto the newspaper only to squash them instantly with bare fingers. Most of us carried lice from home and whined about how much we itched. I had often complained to Grandmother that sleeping next to Kavya gave me the bugs and tried to get my sister to keep her hair short like mine. But Kavya was proud of her long, thick hair and would not entertain the thought of losing it.

One afternoon as we were singing songs in an animated chorus, Aunty Shalini walked in looking pensive. 'Children, today we have with us a new pre-school boy,' she said. We were all aware that the screening process for selecting the new class of preschoolers had been going on for months. Every now and then Mrs. Law, after returning from her house visits in the villages, would give us an update on how many girls and boys had been selected. This little boy was different. He was handed over to us by a family who had found him in a large garbage ditch and taken him into their care. Having heard about Shanti Bhavan, an elderly woman from that family brought him for admission in the hope that the school would accept him. I couldn't help but compare his fate to mine; I, too, was to be discarded in a pit at birth and was saved only by my grandmother's defiance against the wishes of my father. The girls in my dorm said a special prayer for him that night. We were all glad that he had passed the selection process and was now a part of us.

The next morning Avinash and I ran to the pre-school dorm, anxious to see the boy. It was easy to identify him; he was sitting alone in a corner of the room watching a small group of girls and boys playing with wooden blocks. A couple of children were bringing the roof down with their wails for their mothers and fathers, reminding me of my own first days at Shanti Bhavan. Walking up to the boy, I tried to lift him up and cradle him in my arms, but he stiffened and kicked out at me. Avinash tried to talk to him in Telugu. At first the boy would not speak or even smile but slowly he began responding to Avinash's questions with quick nods. Soon Avinash was able to pick him up and raise him high, and the boy broke into loud laughter. We were just beginning to become friends when he caught sight of the housemother bringing breakfast. He quickly freed himself from us and ran to follow her. From now on he would no longer be hungry, cold, or alone, I thought to myself, happy that he finally had a home. And I saw the children who a moment before had been crying for their parents being gently guided towards their breakfast.

Come evening time, when rains often poured down without warning, the aunties would frantically herd us back to our dorms from the playground. Once inside, we would sit on the concrete veranda encircling the backyard and watch the beauty of the falling water, like little frogs awaiting their chance to jump into the pond. I was confident that nothing could take away the dizzying freedom surrounding me.

Despite all this, I was not doing well in my studies or relationships with friends and teachers. I couldn't stop thinking about my family, especially my mother. Lying awake at night, I'd picture my mother singing lullabies and telling bedtime stories to the children she looked after in Singapore. What language did they speak in that country? What food did Amma eat? What clothes did she wear? I would fall asleep with one question relentlessly chasing another.

There was no one to answer my questions. Amma had left me without a word and she hadn't spoken to me since. I began to doubt whether she loved me anymore. The anger towards her spilled over to everyone around me. I transformed from a cheerful, friendly, and curious girl to an enraged, rebellious, and defiant child. In the dorm, I often fought with other girls over simple matters like having a seat right in front of the television during video classes or insisting that I get to wear every Sunday the clothes I liked best. My temper became impossible. Former friends didn't want me on their soccer teams or in their debate groups. No one did.

Keerthi, an unusually thin and tall girl, was one of the best students in my class and others looked up to her, but I resented her for finding fault with me. 'She's like an animal. So badly behaved,' I once heard her whisper to the others, making sure to speak loudly enough for me to hear. At first I was frightened and confused by my own actions, but with time I accepted what everyone was saying about me—that this was who I really was.

Even as warm and motherly as she naturally was, Aunty Shalini's affection for me was sorely tested and she began to show a much harsher side. What bothered her the most was my habit of striking out and hitting anyone who crossed me. Ms. Ruth was surprised to hear the teachers complaining how difficult I was to control in class. 'She wasn't like this in second grade,' she said. 'She was so obedient and smart.'

Aunty Shalini began to treat me with icy strictness, believing this was the only way to straighten me out. One Saturday, after we finished our lunch, she gathered all the children in my dorm, seated herself on a plastic chair, and looked soberly at us as though something terrible had happened. She ordered me to stand up and face the rest of the children.

Hesitantly, I lifted myself off the floor and turned towards my classmates.

'Starting today, no one is allowed to talk to Shilpa. She is a very bad girl,' Aunty Shalini commanded, her voice stern and her expression grim as she scanned the room. 'I don't want any of you to become like her.'

In years past I had loved being summoned to the front of the class to recite a poem or read a passage during the creative writing period. I was proud to be noticed. But this was different. I was standing exposed before my peers who were watching me with contempt and pity. I felt ashamed of myself and wanted to run away and hide.

That was the beginning of my difficult days. When her temper got the better of her, Aunty Shalini dealt with my bad behavior by slapping me. The official school rules didn't permit staff to hit children, but none of us ever complained, since we were used to our parents beating us with belts and sticks. 'I deserve this,' I told myself every time I received a hard slap on my face or was banned from watching the Sunday night movie.

I must have somehow relished the attention my bad behavior brought. With my mother gone, my need for affection, already enormous, grew even more. I was often seeking affection from the aunties. If Aunty Shalini or Aunty Jyothi ever said a kind word to me, I would clasp my arms around her neck and bury her in kisses, baffling her with my suddenly loving behavior. Lost in self-pity, I wondered why they couldn't always treat me affectionately.

My teachers grew increasingly exasperated. During a math class, I vehemently refused to open my book and work out the problems. My classmates were startled by my defiance. Fed up, my teacher dragged me by the arm and made me stand outside the classroom. Seeing some visitors who were taking a tour of the school building heading in my direction, I felt ashamed and stepped back into the room. The teacher shouted at me to remain outside, but I wouldn't budge. She tried to push me out and I stomped on her foot so hard it caused her toe to bleed.

The teacher cried out for someone to fetch Ms. Nirmala, my class teacher, to come at once to deal with me. Learning what had happened, Ms. Nirmala pinched me hard on my arm as she hauled me off to Aunty Shalini.

But I refused to apologize to anyone.

'I don't know what to do with her,' Aunty Shalini cried in frustration. She raised her hand to slap me.

I flinched, but my fear quickly turned into anger.

'The devil has entered your body,' Aunty Shalini said, for everyone to hear. 'Look at your hair. It is twisted like horns.' She pointed at the uneven edges of my short hair standing up on both sides of my head. It was no fault of mine that my hair stood up at the ends; every morning, I would stand in front of the mirror trying to wet and comb my thick hair down, but with no success. Even the boys made fun of the way my hair stood up.

'If you don't change your behavior, you will be sent away from Shanti Bhavan. Do you want to go back to your village?' Aunty Shalini asked.

This took me by surprise. It had never occurred to me that I could be sent away from school. Until then, I had taken it for granted that I belonged to Shanti Bhavan and it would always be that way. For a moment, as I missed my family so badly, I thought I wouldn't mind leaving the school. But when I thought of Ann-Mary and how Grandmother spoke of her with contempt, I knew it would be a disgrace for all of us.

'Bow your head,' Aunty Shalini shouted. 'How dare you look me in the eye when you have done something wrong? Don't you have any shame?' She turned towards Aunty Jyothi. 'From today, she will clean toilets and sweep the entire dorm during games time. Let her sleep on the floor at night.' Aunty Jyothi nodded.

I was convinced that there was no one in this world to love me. I was angry at everyone—angry with my mother for abandoning me, angry with my classmates, and angry with all these women who, blind to the love I longed to give and receive, failed to see my true nature.

And something that made my resentment towards Aunty Shalini grow stronger was that she was very affectionate towards one of my seniors named Sheena. Unlike me, Sheena had delicate features, accentuated by a black mole above her upper lip that stood out in contrast to her light skin. Her eyes, highlighted with thick black kajol, brightened when she was excited. Aunty Shalini and Mrs. Law showered lots of care and attention on Sheena because she had no parents. 'Why can't they love me too? Don't they know that my mother is not with me?' I would think, feeling sorry for myself.

I learnt from the stories that had spread around the campus that Sheena had lived in three different foster homes before coming to Shanti Bhavan at the age of five. In each of those homes, she was considered more of a servant than a family member. In one, she lived with a woman named Arifa whom she thought of as her mother. But one day Arifa told her that she had bought her from an old woman who couldn't take care of her. Sheena was shattered.

Soon, Sheena found herself with another family—a middle-aged woman named Nela, her husband, and two young children. Sheena said Aunty Nela was very loving and gentle towards her, but Sheena disliked Nela's husband Rafil, a fat, sullen man who never accepted her as part of the family.

It was Aunty Nela who had brought Sheena to Shanti Bhavan for admission. It wasn't clear what Nela's true motives were in giving Sheena away, particularly since she'd initially wanted her as a maid. The truth would forever remain a mystery, as Nela died before Sheena was old enough to ask her.

Knowing her story didn't soften my heart. Aunty Shalini, Mrs. Law, and all the girls in my class gave her special attention. Blind with jealousy, I started a senseless fight with her during a baseball game, and we hadn't spoken since.

April rains drenched the thirsty grounds that hadn't tasted water in more than three months. This was also when snakes came out from between the rocks, seeking the warmth of the morning sun. Scorpions that could be mistaken for small lobsters would appear from nowhere in the soil, as though they had been reborn. In the rain-shadows of the Western Ghats, every drop of water meant life for all creatures. It was time for us to go on our summer holidays.

At times I didn't even care if I were to be sent away from school or asked not to return after the holidays. I was prepared to stay at home with Grandmother and Kavya. At least they wouldn't make me feel like a bad girl.

But this time, no one came to take me home.

With my mother away, Mrs. Law considered it unsafe for me to live in my grandmother's house where liquor was sold, and she didn't think my father was responsible enough to take care of me. Aunty Shalini chose not to explain those reasons to me, though. Instead, she told me that I was being held back as punishment for my bad behavior.

I cried bitterly all morning. Slumped against the main door of the building, I watched the other children wave goodbye to the aunties and walk away holding hands with their smiling parents. I even imagined Amma walking me to the gate, taking my hand and laughing at my chatter. Memories of Amma only brought more tears.

Just when I thought all the others had left, I saw another girl standing alone near an overgrown hibiscus bush. It was Sheena. Wiping away my tears, I slowly approached her. She, too, had tears in her eyes. As I neared, she turned away.

'I'm not going home,' I muttered.

Sheena didn't respond. She turned around and started walking away. I ran to catch up with her.

'Where are we staying?' I asked, studying her weary, tear-stained face.

'We are together with Aunty Shalini in the big dorm,' she managed to say between heavy sobs. She sat down on the concrete doorsteps of the dorm. I joined her and we sat together in silence for a while, not knowing what more to say. The sudden quiet of the campus brought with it a strange, overwhelming feeling of loneliness for us both.

The holiday passed more quickly than I expected and by the end of it Sheena and I had become the best of friends. We were together all the time, taking walks through the lush gardens, playing for hours on the large trampoline that was laid out on the lawn, swimming in the shallow pool, watching television, and sharing our stories during intimate chats after dinner.

At first I found it very intimidating to be around her. Apart from her beauty, there was much more to inspire awe—her graceful dancing, the ease with which she could sketch a scenic view, and her quick memory for the lyrics of the Hindi songs she loved listening to on the radio. But there was also something fragile about her, and the more I got to know her, the more I felt an urgent need to protect her from all that was painful to her. She had gone through enough and I made it my responsibility to see to it that she was happy. And in a strange way, much as I sought to protect her, she offered me a sense of security that my mother could not and a joy that Kavya and I could not share.

Sheena wished she had a home to go to on vacations with her amma or appa, as others did. I could not give her that but by the time this holiday ended we had become inseparable. I even began referring to her as my 'best friend,' a term I had never used before.

Once school reopened, while others ran about or bicycled around the field during evening playtime, Sheena and I would sit under the shade of a neem tree and share our childhood experiences. I always sat next to her while watching movies and demanded that the soccer team captain put us on the same team. On lazy Saturday afternoons, we loved looking at each other's scrapbooks filled with clippings of movie actors and singers.

'You look like Aishwarya Rai, Sheena,' I said, comparing her to the famous Bollywood actress and admiring her light skin and her sharp, delicate features. Sheena brushed off the compliment with a smile but I thought she was secretly pleased. I thought of myself as plain and ordinary, while Sheena was beautiful.

We were an unusual sight. Sheena was popular and beautiful, and I was neither. Sheena would walk confidently ahead of me while I followed along behind her like a loyal bodyguard, making sure she was okay. I could never refuse her or do anything that would hurt or anger her. I was willing to accept a subordinate role if it brought her happiness. She gave me a sense of belonging to someone. With Sheena as my friend, I didn't need anyone else. She always took my side in quarrels with the other girls—no small task considering how much they disliked me for my hot temper and unruliness—and comforted me when I was sad. That was all I asked for. I told myself my mother would soon return, but for Sheena there was no one to call her own. She was an orphan, and even more alone than I was. I resolved never to hurt her.

It was hard not to notice the dark brown scars on her lower lip and arm, left behind by beatings from one of the women she had lived with. Pointing to them one evening under the neem tree, Sheena said, 'I wish these scars would go away.'

I promised her that they would. And she believed me.

Chapter Seven

Rejection

The vineyard stretched for nearly a mile outside my window, wilting in the fiery summer sun. I was as usual slumped on a makeshift cot looking out while the few other girls in the room sat on the floor, engrossed in a game of carrom board. The towering presence of a large anthill in a dry corner of the grounds made me wonder how tall it would grow. My attention turned to the rheumatic screech of a rusty hand-pump that the gardener was desperately trying to start. With plenty of time to spare, I grew lost in the smallest details.

A sudden voice startled me. 'Go to your beds, children. I'll come around to give your medicines,' she said. It was Sister Sheila, a petite, soft-spoken woman in her early forties. I straightened myself out on the cot, slid under the covers, and waited for her.

It had been nearly a week since I was brought to Baldev, a small clinic run by my school. Here, patients with minor ailments come from nearby villages for outpatient care, and sick children from Shanti Bhavan are kept isolated. Uncle Tommy, a young, energetic member of the facility staff, had rushed me to the clinic after I awoke a week before around midnight with raging fever and a fit of uncontrollable shivering.

'It is viral. All of Bangalore has it,' the doctor who periodically visited the hospital confirmed after putting me through a thorough check-up the next morning. I was told not to return to school for at least five days. 'We have this problem during the monsoon season,' the doctor said with a worried look, referring to the recent outbreak of fever that was spreading through Shanti Bhavan.

I spent my days in the clinic sleeping a lot and waking up only for meals—a welcome change from the busy schedule at school. Sister Sheila checked each bed at precise, four-hour intervals, carrying a thermometer and notepad to record every child's temperature. She often lingered a little longer by my bed, asking about my family. She told me I woke from nightmares on several occasions, calling for my mother.

'Where is your mother?' Sister Sheila asked at last. Her voice was gentle and her expression open and concerned.

'She went away in a plane to Singapore.' I said, eager to talk about her. The last time I had seen my mother was three weeks earlier when she came to Shanti Bhavan for the second time in the same month. Before that, she had been gone for over two years.

'What is she doing in such a faraway place?' Sister Sheila asked.

'My grandmother says she cleans toilets and cooks for rich children,' I said flatly. I was used to giving everyone at school the same answer my grandmother had given me. Memories of my mother's recent visits to Shanti Bhavan still haunted me and there was a hunger in me to talk about it to someone, so I slowly spilt the details to Sister Sheila.

One Sunday morning, a month ago, Mrs. Law called me to her table during breakfast. DG was sitting across from her in the dining hall with a group of first graders gathered excitedly around him.

'Good morning, Mrs. Law. Good morning, Dr. George,' I greeted them both respectfully. DG smiled at me but immediately returned to delighting the children with riddles and silliness.

'Shilpa,' Mrs. Law said gently, 'your mother is coming to Shanti Bhavan today to see you.'

I couldn't believe it. 'Mrs. Law! What time will she be here?'

'Calm down, my dear.'

I didn't realize I had jumped out of my chair. 'But when will she come?' Even a moment of delay was intolerable.

'By 11 o'clock,' she replied, putting her arm around my waist and giving me a quick kiss on my cheek. 'Are you excited?'

'Yes, Mrs. Law. Yes.' I answered almost in a scream, unable to control my joy, and thanked her several times before hurrying away. I gobbled down breakfast and ran to my dorm to tell Sheena and the other girls in my class. Even Keerthi hugged me, and Kavina, one of the girls I really liked, said how happy she was for me. Since making friends with Sheena, relations with other classmates had improved a bit. I guess my temper had improved some too.

I sat by the window facing the dining hall and waited eagerly to catch a glimpse of my mother. There was no one in sight except for the kitchen staff who were busy spreading red chilies and spices on large straw mats to dry in the sun. I kept turning impatiently to look at the large rectangular steel clock above the entrance door.

I was strangely nervous. Over and over I asked myself, 'Does she still love me the same way as before?'

An hour later, Aunty Jyothi entered the dorm and instructed me to comb my hair neatly, wear black shoes, and come with her to the dining hall. 'Your mother has arrived,' she said with a smile. I ran to the bathroom and struggled before the mirror to flatten out the edges of my hair. I wanted to look nice for Amma.

I followed Aunty Jyothi across the lawn holding her hand. From a distance I could see a fairly chubby woman seated all by herself at a table facing the entrance to the dining hall. I was looking elsewhere for my mother when suddenly the woman sprang to her feet, knocking over her chair in her haste. I tightened my grip on Aunty Jyothi's hand. The woman ran towards me crying out, 'Shilpa! Shilpa!'

Within seconds she locked me in her arms. She held me close and kissed my cheeks, my lips, and my eyes, calling me her chinna. She held my face between her hands and wept. It was my amma.

When the initial shock of seeing my mother passed, I found myself crying uncontrollably with my face pressed against her chest. I was confused. Her body felt strange against mine. I wiped her tears and she responded with more kisses. 'Please don't cry, Amma. Please don't cry,' I repeated, unable to stop crying myself.

Holding me tight, she took me to her table in the dining hall and seated me on her lap, as though I was a small child. This was the first time I'd seen Amma dressed in something other than the faded saris she always wore. She looked so different now in a tan churidar printed with dark green flowers. Her once protruding collarbones were barely visible, and I found her prettier than before.

Breathlessly, without wasting a moment, I asked the question I had harbored for the past two years, 'Amma, why did you leave without telling me?'

Amma looked away for a moment, struggling to maintain her composure. 'I had to. Everything happened so quickly.' She took a deep breath. 'I wanted to come and see you but your grandparents told me not to because you were too young to understand why I had to leave.'

I wasn't fully satisfied with her answer, but didn't want to press her lest I make her sad. Instead, I began telling her all about the school and my friends. She was overjoyed listening to my chatter and held me tightly in her arms.

'You have grown taller,' Amma said, gently pushing me back to take a good look. I told her that only two girls in my class were shorter than me, so I always stood third in line. She ran her hand through my hair and softly touched my face and arms as though she wanted to be sure I was real. Her tenderness towards me was something I had badly missed, the kind of love only a mother could give.

Aunty Jyothi came over and asked Amma in Kannada if she was hungry. Amma surprised me by replying in English, 'Yes, ma'am. I am hungry.' I couldn't wait to tell the girls in my class that my mother could speak English. I didn't care if I made them jealous.

I stayed with her for the rest of the morning. I had so much to tell her about my days in school and she seemed both eager to hear my excited babble and fascinated by the way I talked. 'You have forgotten how to speak Kannada,' she said, noticing that every line I spoke in Kannada was interspersed with English words.

I nodded in embarrassment, then retorted, 'And you've learnt English,' making her laugh.

'Amma. That is Sheena. She's my best friend,' I said, suddenly catching sight of her seated next to a large, dark man with a rough face. Amma told me not to stare as it was impolite. I looked away, disturbed that I didn't recognize him and wondered how Sheena knew him.

For the next two hours Amma and I talked, or more precisely, I talked and she listened. When it was time for her to leave, Aunty Shalini pulled her aside and they spent several minutes together. I noticed Amma's face growing taut. Aunty Shalini being unhappy with me, I worried what she might be telling Amma. Was she talking about all the trouble I gave my teachers and aunties? But couldn't she see that my behavior had been improving? My fears partly faded when Amma returned, kissed me, and promised to visit me again the following Sunday. We parted in tears but this time we both had something to look forward to.

That evening, as Sheena and I sat watching the boys play basketball, I asked about the man she had been with. 'Was that your uncle?' I asked cautiously, remembering the terrible stories she'd told me about him. She once mentioned that Rafil, Aunty Nela's husband, had fondled her when his wife was not home. 'Why was she seeing him now?' I asked myself.

'Yes,' Sheena replied softly.

My face betrayed me. I didn't like the way he looked. His protruding belly and bloodshot eyes reminded me of the ruthless villains of Kannada movies. I was afraid for her. Sheena didn't look concerned but I couldn't be sure how she really felt.

The week passed almost as quickly as I had hoped it would. My mother was coming to visit me again.

I was overjoyed to see Amma waiting for me in the dining hall. She was seated with my father, Aunty Shalini, and Ms. Nirmala. I rushed down the stairs and ran to her.

Without giving me a kiss or holding my hand she turned to follow Aunty Shalini who led us immediately along the paved pathway to a small garden rich with cherry trees and bright red mayflowers. I walked quietly beside her, overtaken by anxiety. Amma gestured for me to sit beside my father on a stone bench. Aunty Shalini and Ms. Nirmala joined them, seated on another bench facing us.

Amma stared coldly at me. There was no hint of a smile. For a moment, she appeared a stranger. She had definitely heard about me from Aunty Shalini. I didn't dare to lift my head to look her in the eye.

'Shilpa, I heard you are behaving badly in school,' Amma said sternly in Kannada. 'If you are sent away from Shanti Bhavan, I will make you work as a servant and sweep roads in the village. Do you understand?'

I cringed in fear. And remembered Ann-Mary.

Ms. Nirmala joined in, 'Shilpa isn't doing well in class, either.'

'She does not listen to anything we say,' Aunty Shalini added. 'All of us find it so hard to take care of her.'

'You better watch out,' Amma warned, pointing her finger at me. I was afraid she would hit me, but she held back. Parents had been told by school authorities not to beat their children. I kept my head down, ashamed and fearful, concentrating on my falling tears.

Appa suddenly spoke, addressing me first by my sister's name before correcting himself. This slip only confirmed how absent I had been from his consciousness.

Slowly, I lifted my head to look at him.

His eyes were red and his lips parched; I had heard from Amma he had been ill for almost a week. 'What will you do if you are dismissed from Shanti Bhavan? You will have to marry some useless fellow in the village and end up having lots of babies,' he said with tears filling his eyes. Having lived a life of hardship, my father greatly valued education and was upset to find I was taking my good fortune for granted.

I didn't reply. It was hard to believe in the genuineness of his concern for me. Why hadn't he come to visit me in school? Why did he hand me over to Grandmother and ignore me when I was in the village?

He paused. 'Look here.'

I stared through tears as he slowly undid the buttons on his shirt. I screamed at what I saw: all over his chest were big gashes—some healing, others raw and deep.

'I almost died from a tree falling on me,' he said softly.

I covered my mouth with my hands. Aunty Shalini gasped and turned away.

Nobody but Appa spoke, his voice weak. 'If the other woodcutters hadn't come quickly and pulled me from under it, I would have died that day. My chest still feels heavy.'

Angry with myself, I looked down, feeling terrible for being such a disappointment to my parents. The guilt was unbearable.

'Shilpa, do you see how much your parents are suffering?' Aunty Shalini said. 'Your mother has to work as a housemaid far away and had to leave you, your brother, and your sister to earn enough money to take care of the family.'

'Both your parents are hoping you will be able to help when you are older,' Ms. Nirmala added.

Seeing me remorseful, something she thought was rare, Aunty Shalini asked with sudden softness, 'Will you work hard?'

I nodded.

'Will you listen to your elders?' she asked, her voice firmer this time.

'Yes, Aunty.'

'Will you be a good girl?'

'Yes, Ms. Nirmala.'

Everyone appeared satisfied with my answers. 'It is time for your parents to go,' Aunty Shalini announced.

I remained on the bench with my head low, crying, while Appa buttoned his shirt. Both of them stood, and I looked up to find them staring into my tear-streaked face. Appa appeared sad, but Amma was still angry. I badly needed my mother to hug me at least once and kiss me goodbye. I wanted to assure her that I would be good. And I longed to give her farewell kisses. Instead I heard my amma announce coldly, 'We are leaving.'

I stood up, wishing to run to my mother but the look on her face fixed me to my place. 'Amma,' I cried out, still hoping that she would scoop me up in her arms and tell me everything was okay and nothing had changed between us.

'Just go,' she snapped.

'Go to the dorm,' Aunty Shalini ordered.

Rage like I had never felt before surged through me. I had been living without my mother for so long and now Aunty Shalini had succeeded in turning her against me. What kind of lesson was this? She was my worst enemy now, the one who was separating me again from my mother. The remorse and softness I had felt just a few minutes before vanished entirely.

Amma gestured for me to leave with a quick, dismissive motion of her hand. I was wounded by her open indifference towards me and could not make sense of her sudden transformation. What had become of the loving mother who embraced me so warmly only a week ago? The black hole of abandonment took hold of me once again and this time I had no strength left to resist its pull.

Many years would pass before I learnt that she behaved this way to appease Aunty Shalini who had instructed her to treat me the way she did. Amma clearly recognized that my time at Shanti Bhavan would come to an end if my bad behavior continued. She had seen this happen to Ann-Mary, once a schoolgirl like me and now a plaything for men, dancing in the streets of our village.

Amma turned around and walked away with no trace of affection, with Appa following her. I stood transfixed, watching her disappear at the bend in the road marked by the looming presence of a tall tamarind tree. I wheeled and cut across the lawn to my dorm. I didn't want my classmates to see me crying. They were engrossed in watching a movie in the television lounge. Entering the dorm with my head down, I managed to make my way to bed without attracting their attention.

A few girls who entered the dorm to go to the bathroom stopped by and asked what was wrong. I didn't answer.

Leelie sat on the edge of my bed and tried to console me. 'Please don't cry, Shilpa. Shall I ask Sheena to come to see you?' she asked gently.

I snapped at her. 'I don't want to see or speak to anyone.'

By now there was a small group of girls standing around my bed helplessly watching me suffer. Leelie guided them away. 'Best to leave her alone for now,' she whispered. 'Sheena will know what to do.'

They all silently walked away.

That was the last time I would see my mother for the next five years. Grandmother told me that even though Amma wanted to return, Appa was adamant that she remain abroad for a few more years to finish her contract and generate more money. At the time I was certain that she didn't return because of me.

From that day, my nightmares began.

Sister Sheila was silent for a few moments when I ended my story. She studied me, her eyes dark with sadness. 'Shilpa, pray to God every night before you go to sleep. Ask God to look after your mother and you. A child's prayers never go unanswered,' she said, planting a kiss on my forehead.

I didn't believe her. The last time I had earnestly prayed to God was for the rains to stop so I could go swimming in the pool. But heavy showers continued for two more days, turning the weather too cold to swim. I had lost all faith in my prayers.

Sister Sheila tucked me under the warm blanket and I wished her goodnight before she moved on to the next bed. I lay awake thinking of Amma. What was she doing now? Did she tuck in the children she looked after every night? Did she sing lullabies to them or tell them the stories of the Kings of Mysore that she used to share with Kavya and me? I missed her so much.

That she left me again without telling me she loved me was unbearable. All I could conclude was that there was no one in the world who cared for me deeply, except Sheena who was always kind to me.

After a few days, I recovered from the short bout of fever and went back to school. My defiance returned with a vengeance. When slaps and public shaming couldn't get me to surrender to her wishes, Aunty Shalini finally ordered me to pack my clothes and stay with the younger girls who lived downstairs, adding banishment to the usual punishments of sleeping on the floor at night and cleaning the dorm instead of going for games in the evening. Aunty Shalini hoped humiliation could get me to mend my ways.

I returned from evening snacks and flung myself onto my mat on the floor. A hushed silence spread through the dorm; the little girls grew anxious seeing me so disturbed. I hated my life. Why was I even born?

In seventh grade, my body became as stubborn as my personality. My height froze and I didn't grow an inch after that. My small round face with its frame of bouncy, unmanageable, thick, black hair gave me a confused look that accentuated the troubled daze I always seemed to be in. 'Your mind is never in the present,' Aunty Shalini would say and about this she was right.

Adrift in the rough waters of grief, I found myself reliving in my mind every moment from the past—the painful ones and the fleeting moments of tenderness with my mother. Carried away by this sense of utter rejection, I was travelling a self-destructive path that alienated me from my friends, wrecked my relationships, and sealed me in loneliness. I was saved from expulsion only because DG attributed my bad behavior to the absence of my mother. He still seemed to remember the bright, curious girl I once was.

One afternoon when I was in the eighth grade, Aunty Catherine, one of the senior housemothers, came to my classroom and asked the teacher for a word with me. Nervous, I followed Aunty Catherine to a secluded corner of the assembly hall where we took a seat on the cement steps. She opened a brown envelope with a foreign stamp and pulled out a letter written in Kannada.

'Your mother sent you a letter,' Aunty Catherine said. Unable to read Kannada, I waited anxiously for her to share its contents with me. I stared passively at the words scrawled in my mother's disjointed handwriting. Aunty Catherine strained forward, studying the paper, to make sense of what she read. The words she had scribbled resembled what a five-year-old might write.

Amma wrote that she thought of me every day, missed me, and prayed to God to keep me in good health. She also asked me to be a good girl and not give anyone trouble. The letter brought back memories of the last time I had seen her when she had shouted at me and walked away without a kiss.

Much of Amma's letter was about her problems with Appa. She wrote that when she was at home he would come home drunk every other night and beat her. But her biggest complaint against Appa was about his flirtations with other women. Her letters were the beginning of her efforts to create distance between Appa and me. The letters I was to receive from Amma in the years to follow shed light on their turbulent years together. Maybe her marriage was doomed from the start, but I couldn't understand why she wanted me to reject him. I could sense her struggle to reach me through those letters, and yet she made me feel more alone. Her letters brought me more sadness than anything else and I felt humiliated that the aunties discovered through them my family's ugly secrets.

Over time, I saw in Amma's letters some words and sentences written in English. She told me her employer had taught her to write a few English words. I sometimes boasted to my classmates that now my mother not only knew how to speak English but also how to write it. As most of the parents were uneducated, my mother's achievement was something special.

My feelings towards my father were complicated by my knowledge of the many painful incidents between my parents and his flirtations with other women. I couldn't understand how a father could be so indifferent towards his wife and children. I saw him as a cruel man who made my mother abandon me and now he too didn't care about me.

In seventh grade, I stopped hugging Appa. I told myself we were now strangers to each other.

Chapter Eight

A Walk in the Woods

Appa pulled aside the thorny bushes with his rough hands, waiting for me to pass through the narrow track leading into the woods. I was on vacation from school after eighth grade when he had agreed to answer my questions about his life, but preferred the familiar tranquility of the forest where he felt most at home. It was where he could smile freely and laugh at my questions, and open his heart to share his story.

After hearing sometimes more than I cared to know about my father from my mother's letters and Grandmother's stories, I found myself gradually wanting to stop finding fault with Appa. The slightest show of his fondness for me—a visit to my Grandmother's hut when I was there for the school vacation, a gift of fruits or sweets—melted my anger and turned me curious about him. I made up my mind to discover for myself what kind of man he was.

I started with his father. 'Appa, why doesn't Joseph Thatha talk to me?' I asked, unsure why my grandfather stared blankly at me whenever I visited him, with no sign of recognition or warmth.

'He lives in a world that exists only in his head,' Appa replied with some bitterness. 'For him, all that matters is his drink.'

Appa said that as a young boy he once begged his father not to drink. Slapping him hard, his father responded, 'I can leave your mother, but not my drinking. Remember that, boy.'

It was the last time Appa ever questioned his father.

Every man I knew in the village drank regularly. I had seen my father and Joseph Thatha getting together with their friends to talk about liquor—who had the best quality, what was wrong with this one's supply, who had been caught by the police recently, and when they would meet again to drink. I thought drinking was simply part of being a man, until Mrs. Law taught us that drinking in excess is an illness.

The shriek of a jackal broke the quiet. I looked around, startled, unsure whether it was safe to go further. Unconcerned, Appa walked a few yards ahead of me. The forest floor was covered in a blanket of leaves and moss, making it slippery even for the most sure-footed. Anyone else would have tripped over the sharp-edged stones that rose up through the ground cover, but Appa's tread was as practiced and sure as that of a crystal-eyed fox. He took long, impatient strides, hands swinging stiffly by his sides, as though someone were chasing him.

'Why are you walking so fast, Appa? Slow down,' I called out, stopping to catch my breath.

'When an elephant is chasing you, you can't afford to walk. You have to sprint,' he shouted back with laughter in his voice.

I was unsteady in my fancy leather sandals, occasionally tripping on the uneven ground as I struggled to keep up with him. Stopping to write in the small notebook I carried, I reflected on what was around me and stared at the vast stretch of rocky hills that loomed over the trees like an eternal protective wall around the village, I asked, 'Appa, when was the first time you drank?'

'When I was five,' he replied instantly.

'Five?!' I bent over my notebook.

'Yes. My uncle wanted to see me drunk. He promised to give me a piece of jaggery if I gulped down a whole glass,' he said, laughing. 'Your grandmother was shocked to see me lying unconscious on the floor. She tried to hit him with a broom.'

We reached a silent creek that broke across a stony track. Appa simply walked straight into the water. On rainy days he would wade through it, welcoming the soft slush between his toes. I preferred to stay dry, carefully balancing myself on small boulders jutting up from the water and jumping off them to reach the other side.

'Why did you brew liquor?' I asked. He had stopped doing that work recently, choosing to make a living chasing elephants instead.

'That was one of the few occupations in the village. Everyone was either buying or supplying it.' He turned to make sure I was not too far behind.

Appa explained that he preferred to go selling liquor after dark to avoid policemen who were on the lookout during the day. He walked through the forest at night to get to his customers in the nearby villages. 'You had to remember all the turns and twists, or you wouldn't make it out of here before dawn,' he said, pointing to the dense foliage in all directions.

The forest wasn't as much a sanctuary for him as it sometimes appeared. After all, he had to look out for not just wild elephants but also forest guards. Police frequently came searching for illegal liquor-brewers like him. Yet, he preferred the quietness of the woods to the merciless moneylenders from the nearby town who were waiting to catch him and demand repayment of their loans. They would do anything to extract all they could.

Appa knew his way through the woods even where there was no track. I was sure he was familiar with every tree in the forest. They were his most loyal friends, each standing at the same spot, awaiting his arrival. Every time he passed a eucalyptus tree, he pulled off a twig and chewed on it. The potent medicinal taste of the stem seemed to give him a little kick of exhilaration, helping him to relax.

'This is the chakki,' he said, halting abruptly before a tall, broad tree with unusually slender, thorny leaves. Running his hand over its thick bark, he said, 'Of all the trees in the forest, the chakki is the most precious to us. Its bark is the main ingredient in sarayam.'

'How do you use it?' I asked.

'We scrape the trunk with knives and boil the bark with jaggery in a steel barrel for a few hours,' he answered. 'The dark liquid you get is strong enough to intoxicate anyone.' We spent the next hour sitting in the shade of a large tree as he shared his trade secrets, and we laughed at stories about his drunken customers, until it was time to go home for lunch.

The next morning I set out again to learn more about his early life. He wasn't sure why anyone would want to know about someone like him. But his eyes gleamed; I knew he was enjoying the attention.

The thick forest suddenly opened into a small clearing. A middle-aged man sat cross-legged under a tree, filling a gunny sack with tamarind fruits that two young children were gathering from the ground. Tamarind found its way into every curry, and fetched a good price in the village market.

Appa called out, 'Ramanna, this is my daughter. English medium school. She has come home for the holiday.' The man acknowledged my presence with a smile. I could see that Appa was proud of me.

Appa kept walking until we reached a secluded area, dense with tall, thorny brush. He waded into what looked like impenetrable undergrowth and dragged out two rusty old barrels.

'We used these for making liquor,' Appa said, brushing off a layer of dark soil. He seemed to want me to know how he had spent his days working hard at his trade. He boiled jaggery in water with the bark of chakki in the barrels, and left them underground for eight days so the solution could ferment into liquor. On the ninth day, he dug out the barrel and drew the potent substance through a tube running from a hole on one side of the barrel to a large rubber sack. Once the liquid was completely transferred into the sack, he waited until sunset before heading to the neighboring village to sell it.

Appa recalled marching through descending darkness along narrow mud paths with the rubber sack of sarayam on his back. In the forest he usually walked barefoot, wearing nothing but his underwear, as he couldn't afford to get his clothes torn and dirty.

As he went back to hide the barrels in the bushes, I went through the notes I had scribbled. 'Why are you hiding those barrels when you don't use them anymore?' I asked.

'It's an old practice. Nobody leaves his secrets in the open,' he replied. I was fascinated by his answer, not having found any compelling need for his strange habit. I began scribbling again, eagerly recording everything my father said.

Suddenly, Appa turned pensive. He looked down, staring at his own shadow as though he wanted to erase his past. 'I have gone through a lot, my girl. Neither you nor your brother and sister should suffer as I did,' he said, gazing into the distance, his voice soft.

I didn't know how to respond. He was my father but also a stranger. I could appreciate what he wished for Kavya, Francis, and me but I didn't understand his past or how he really felt about us. I didn't know how to comfort him.

Just as swiftly his mood changed again and answer followed answer. 'At the age of seven, I joined your Arpuda Ajji in the landlords' fields pulling weeds. We were paid two to three rupees at day's end, depending on how much we had weeded out,' he said. I couldn't imagine how anyone could do this job from morning till evening, day after day.

The next job was even worse. 'A couple of years later, I started working at a Gunna's home as a servant, cleaning sheds, grazing his cattle, and doing whatever I was told,' Appa said. But it was not a job that paid anything. Grandfather had failed to repay the loan he had taken from the landlord for Aunt Teresa's wedding so he sent Appa to the landlord as a bonded laborer.

Appa was happy to help out his family. It made him feel like a hero. Despite the grueling dawn-to-dusk work, he was satisfied with an occasional good meal with rice and curry when his mother could manage to make it for him, or free time on Sundays to go fishing in the lake with friends. He was young and strong, but no one can work like that forever.

'Not too long afterward, I learnt from my father how to brew sarayam. As the eldest son, I was the first to join your grandfather in the family business. At fifteen, I became his full-time partner.'

Appa went on to talk about how he and the other liquor brewers avoided being caught by police. Because he was involved in an illegal activity some might call him a criminal, but, to me, he was simply making a living in the only profession he could find. 'I didn't have any other choice. There were hardly any other jobs here,' he said.

Families like mine couldn't be faulted for brewing and selling liquor. The land offered nothing to the poor, for they owned hardly any that was cultivable. For women like my mother and grandmother, their meager wages from weeding the landlords' fields contributed very little.

The police sought to catch people like Appa only to extort bribes before letting them go free. Appa told me that usually he carried with him some money to give to policemen, but some of them were too greedy to satisfy; he had to come back with more the next day or risk being imprisoned for a week.

No one in the village was safe from theft or violence. Despite its putatively Christian culture, Thattaguppe still harbored plenty of crime.

'It wasn't hard to find rowdies in the villages willing to do anything,' Appa said.

Generally, a few hundred rupees and a good meal of chicken curry with ragi balls were all that was needed to get a man to eliminate anyone. Even the lane on which Joseph Thatha lived was ruled by a family of criminals—four brothers who disposed of those who displeased them as casually as they discarded cigarette butts. When one brewer refused to sell liquor to them for a lower price, they twisted his arms until they broke. A man suspected of flirting with their sister was beaten to death and left hanging from a tree in front of the church. These thugs controlled everyone, including the police whom they bribed.

'The price of liquor was more than the price of life,' Appa said.

'One afternoon in the forest, as I was emptying jaggery into a steel barrel filled with boiling water, I heard an unfamiliar voice behind me. Before I could react, a policeman lunged forward and pinned me to the ground.' He shook his head at the memory. 'When I tried to free myself, he struck me hard against my face with his fist.' The force of the punch left him dizzy.

The police didn't need courts or judges to enforce liquor laws. They pushed Appa into a jeep and quickly drove off, not stopping until they reached a clearing in the woods where other policemen were waiting. That was where they usually stopped to give criminals like him a good thrashing. Appa finally produced for them his week's earnings to avoid going to jail. They let him go, but not without a stern warning, as though they were genuinely concerned about enforcing the law. As Appa walked home, he comforted himself with the thought that they hadn't taken everything from him; he had hidden some of his week's earnings in his underwear.

As Appa told me this story, I could see from his grin he was proud of the way he handled the police. He knew what they were looking for—not sarayam, but money.

Appa told me how difficult it was for him and his siblings to live in the narrow space of a single-room hut. He described the kitchen as three stones arranged in a triangle at the corner of the hut where meals could simmer above the fire. The walls of the room were covered in so much soot that Appa couldn't remember any color other than the blackness that hugged the walls.

Arpuda Ajji prepared the same meal every day. No one ever complained. Food was a means of survival, not a source of enjoyment. Even so, if Appa so much as uttered the word 'hungry,' Joseph Thatha would smack him with a sturdy stick. If he asked for another ittu, his father would growl, 'What are you grumbling about, you fool? Didn't I just see you eating a man's share?' He was usually too drunk to notice his children's cries for more, and when he did, it infuriated him. Ajji would always try to comfort them with the promise of a good meal the next day, though she could never keep her promise.

Appa told me he was fairly good-looking in his younger days, and his friends referred to him as 'Handsome Anthu'. I was sure this had something to do with how women saw him. Most adults in the village carried a nickname that bore particular significance to their looks, their occupation, or something unusual about them. A notorious liquor supplier who is said to have murdered seven people was known as Murder Nagaraj. My maternal grandfather was Somersault Udayaraj. He was almost killed when his bullock cart rolled over and skidded down a steep hill. Rumor had it that his loud cries of 'Amen' convinced God to save him from falling into the gushing river below.

I learnt that Joseph Thatha was also quite good-looking in his youth, unusually tall for a village man. He always wore a serious expression and seldom showed any affection or happiness as he went about his work from morning till late at night. Tedious hours of laboring in the heat, hacking trees for wood and brewing liquor in the forest, left him hardened like a brick baked in the sun. His drinking habit had turned him into an unpredictable man by the time he married my grandmother, Arpuda.

Arpuda Ajji was given to Joseph in marriage before she turned fifteen. Even at that young age she had large, round breasts and wide hips that drew the attention of many men in the village. Her parents raised buffalos for a living and were looking out for a man who wouldn't ask for a big dowry. They found their affordable match in Joseph, a twenty-four-year-old coolie whose parents didn't demand any dowry because of his bad reputation as a drunkard. Like everyone else in the family, he had not attended school.

In those days Arpuda Ajji carried herself with grace. Her husband's ill-treatment of her did not diminish her determination to carry out her family duties. Even in her forties, my grandmother was a beautiful woman. But wear and tear from years of hard work in the field could be seen on her face. Yet, her eyes displayed strength wrought out of enduring hardship and indignity. She covered up her fears and disappointments with a look of contentment that served as a mask.

Arpuda Ajji, Appa said, never questioned being a so-called 'low caste' woman. She saw no chance for change in her status and didn't think there was any necessity for it. It was her way of recognizing life for what it was and accepting it unconditionally. She believed the prevailing social order was designed by God and it was her duty to live within it. 'One doesn't get to choose one's parents,' she would often say with resignation. As she saw it, sorrow and suffering connected heaven and earth, and there was very little of anything joyful in between. She viewed herself as a prisoner of fate and her goal was the survival of her family--mere survival, nothing more.

Arpuda Ajji was well aware of what her society expected of women. In her world the purpose of her existence was to meet the needs of her husband, to serve his parents, and bring up their children. Her personal desires were of little concern to anyone, so she seldom complained about what she did not have. There was no sympathy for her from her husband or in-laws. Her inner longings for love and companionship as a young woman were suppressed by her daily chores and the demands placed on her by the family.

Neither Arpuda Ajji nor Joseph Thatha truly recognized the importance of educating their children. Now that I had grown up with proper schooling, it bothered me that my father couldn't read or write in any language. When I mustered the courage to ask him why he hadn't studied, he told me simply that his father tried briefly to get him to go to school but he had no interest. As a child, Appa didn't understand why he was sent to school; he couldn't see how getting an education could save him from being a coolie. No one was there to guide or encourage him, and with all the financial pressures at home, he couldn't have remained in school for long, even if he had wanted to.

We had been talking in the little clearing for a long time. Now Appa wanted to know something about me. 'When will you finish your studies?' he asked, looking straight into my eyes.

I didn't want to tell him but after a moment I replied, 'I have six to seven years left, Appa.'

'My God!' He struggled with disappointment. 'When will you start working and making money?'

'When I am ready,' I said, irritated.

'Will you become a doctor or a lawyer?'

'No,' I said.

He didn't ask what I did want to be. There was no chance that he would think, even for a moment, about achievement rather than money. But I also knew he took pride in me for being different from the other girls in the village—dressing in Western clothes, speaking fluent English, walking with confidence. With a broad smile, he would quietly watch me as I spoke to anyone he introduced me to. If he sees me as the one who might save him from misery in his old age, so be it. That is, after all, what I want, too.

The next morning Appa insisted that we go to the forest again despite talk among villagers of elephants being spotted in the area the previous evening. 'Don't you know I am the king of the forest?' he said with a grin. 'Why are you worried when I am here to protect you?' There was no doubt he knew the forest well and wasn't afraid. I gave him a sarcastic look, but was secretly pleased he could protect me, and that he saw himself as a hero.

I was eager to find out why he dropped out of school so early. He told me that when he was six, Joseph Thatha took him to the small school that Father Sigeon had built for the poor, after other relatives insisted that he do his fatherly duty to educate his son at least for a few years. The packed classrooms had no chairs or tables so all the children sat on the floor. On his first day, Sister Clara, the stern-faced, stubby, first-grade teacher, asked him to recite the Kannada alphabet. He would already have learnt it had he attended kindergarten, but he hadn't; Joseph Thatha couldn't afford to pay the fifteen rupees admission fee. Appa mumbled something incoherent, buckling with embarrassment. When he finished, the teacher ordered him to stand up, fold his arms, and try again. When he proceeded to stammer, the other students laughed at him.

'Take a piece of chalk and start practicing the letters on your slate!' the teacher scolded.

He was lucky. Before the government had begun providing slates to schools, children sat outside practicing letters in the dirt until the afternoon sun made it unbearable.

For the rest of the year he repeated alphabets, counted numbers, and sang rhymes. In the second grade he encountered problems with arithmetic. He seemed unable to learn numbers and was often caned for it, each blow cracking his small, tender palms.

Appa would return home by early afternoon, smarting from pain and humiliation. The simple joy of a game of marbles in the evening sun or, better yet, a day off from school, made his childhood bearable. Appa had a way with marbles; he would take aim, squint, and launch straight into a tiny hole in the hard ground. If only numbers had come so easily to him! I can see I am Appa's daughter after all.

But I knew from my own experience that with more patience and encouragement from his elders there was more he might have learnt. I was ashamed Appa couldn't sign his name on official documents when the school authorities asked him to so I tried to teach him, one by one, each letter of his name. His fingers kept shaking and he could barely hold the pen. After the first try he gave up, dropping the pen in exasperation and flinging the piece of paper into my lap. 'Don't give up so easily, Appa,' I said. I waited patiently as he tried again and again until finally he mastered the individual strokes that made up each letter.

The first time he wrote his own name on a piece of paper, I leapt up, delighted. 'Oh, good, Appa. Well done. No more using your thumbprint to sign!' Impulsively, I gave him a quick hug.

He looked up, surprised. I hadn't done that in years. Turning away, he smoothed the paper with both hands.

I didn't know what to say. 'You'll still have to practice, you know.'

He looked at me for a moment as if he wanted to say something, but in the end he just nodded.

Joseph Thatha used to beat him and deprive him of dinner, but failed to motivate him to attend school. Eventually, he gave up on his son. 'I thought when I die my son will sit by my head and read the Bible,' Thatha said. 'But this donkey doesn't want to!' Soon, Appa was put to work as a servant in a Gunna's house.

The next day, on our way back home from the forest, Appa told me what it was like to work for another Gunna. The master, a beefy looking man with a thick moustache and a pink scar on his lower lip, had employed Appa as a servant in exchange for one hundred rupees a month. 'I was amazed to hear how much more I was worth than the two rupees a day I had been making by pulling weeds,' Appa exclaimed.

On the very first day, the landlord sent Appa back home to get his own plate and cup. He and his wife wouldn't let Appa eat or drink from theirs in the kitchen. Appa was not allowed to enter any of the rooms in the house, except for the entrance veranda where he slept and the cow shed where he worked to clear the dung while the cattle grazed in the fields. He didn't question his living arrangement.

Revulsion at the thought of Appa being so ill-treated consumed me. 'There is no such thing as low or high caste. Castes are meaningless!'

'That may be true in your textbooks. Not here.'

There was no point in arguing because I knew he was right. I hid my anger. I wondered what would have become of a child as hot-tempered and rebellious as I was in the world my father grew up in. Or I too might have become submissive.

I wondered what my father craved as a young man. Did he dream of cars and places to visit, or did he have nightmares of being locked up in jail? I sensed his dreams were very different from mine.

Everything Appa learnt was self-taught. He moved about in the forest listening to its silence and watching the shadows. He fished in the lake with his bare hands. He gathered wild berries and wood apples (locally known as vilam palam) by throwing stones at them.

We walked home that evening in silence. Appa's pace was unusually slow, as if he were weighed down by the painful memories he had dredged up in the past few days.

Until then, I had thought of my father as a cruel and uncaring person, unfaithful to my mother and indifferent to me. He had spoken to me with affection, letting me know that he cared. He was not simply the harsh man that Grandmother and Amma made him out to be. I saw in him an intelligent man with considerable foresight—a man who learned from his own failures, one who understood a lot more about the world than his father. At the very least, he was wise enough to send me away to get an education despite the family's objections.

I was thankful my life so far seemed to be headed in a very different direction from that of the women in the village. Yet, even with my Shanti Bhavan upbringing, I was not sure I had completely outwitted my fate, or whether my karma might still undo me in the end. As an 'untouchable,' will I someday be punished for reasons I can't now comprehend?

I saw Kavya running towards us as we entered the lane where we lived. In no time, she was in my arms in a tight embrace.

'What stories did Appa tell you?' she asked eagerly.

'I'll tell you after dinner,' I replied. And I kept my promise.

Chapter Nine

The Elephant Chase

With no visible signs to distinguish summer from winter or autumn from spring, I relied on school activities to tell me what season we were in. Nap time on hot afternoons, swimming in the pool in the evenings, and eating chocolate banana popsicles for snacks meant Grandmother would soon come to take me home for summer vacation. We had no snowmen in winter; colorful paper wrappings, green and red ribbons, and sprigs of mistletoe-like plants plucked from the gardens signaled the arrival of our Christmas.

I had survived my first semester of ninth grade with perhaps a bit less drama and better grades. After the summer vacation spent getting to know my father, I was again home for Christmas vacation. Seeing me in the distance, Kavya and Francis raced each other down the slope, screaming, 'Akka! Akka!'

Overjoyed, I hugged my sister tightly and reached out to pat my brother as he danced around us. 'How are you?' I asked, 'How are you?' as I turned from one to the other.

Kavya began to tell me all about her friends, the stray kitten she had adopted, and how often Francis got a beating from Appa for not finishing his homework. I turned to scold Francis but he had disappeared.

I caught sight of him running to announce my arrival to everyone in the family. I felt like a celebrity. As he returned, I noticed several pink scars on his cheeks, and turned to ask Grandmother about them. She replied casually that my sister and brother often fought with each other, and those marks were from her pinches and scratches.

'They must hate each other,' I said.

She laughed. 'Small children always quarrel. Don't worry.'

I nodded.

'Your brother loves your sister so much he can't do without her.'

Suddenly I felt a pang of jealousy; I knew they didn't feel the same way about me.

News of my arrival spread fast, and by the time Grandmother and I had finished praying before the framed picture of Jesus, a few neighbors had arrived to see me. Everyone had something to say about my appearance.

One woman didn't approve of my short hair which stopped a few inches above my shoulders. 'Don't they allow you to grow your hair?' she asked, explaining that long hair gave women beauty.

Another woman was curious to know whether there were boys in the school. When I said that there were, she turned to my grandmother with distaste. 'In our day, we were not even allowed to look at boys. My mother told me to keep my eyes down when I passed them on the street.' She looked straight at me. 'How times have changed!'

I was irritated but remained quiet, remembering my teachers' admonitions not to argue.

But not all of the comments were negative. A few neighbors said I looked very smart, fashionable and, more importantly, had become a quieter person—a quality admired in young women as being one likely to attract husbands. Most men in the village preferred obedient, dutiful wives.

Appa arrived. He had developed a slight pot belly and his hair had thinned since the last time I saw him. He smiled at me. 'Have you been studying well?'

I was glad to see him. 'Have you practiced your writing?'

He laughed and took the glass of plain, black tea Grandmother offered him.

'Appa, has Amma called you?' I was eager for any news of my mother.

'Yes, she calls at least once a month.'

'Does she send you money?'

He waited for a moment before replying, 'Yes.'

Part of me wanted to take back the question, realizing I had probably insulted him by questioning him so directly about money in front of everyone. I wanted to ask him what he did with the money but refrained. Grandmother told me later that he spent it on drinks and women.

'Do you know when she'll be coming back?' I asked, more softly, sadness welling up inside me.

Appa kept silent, staring at the floor. Then, instructing me to send for him if I needed anything, he left. I didn't see him again for several days.

The next few days were spent playing on the improvised rope-swing that hung from the tamarind tree at the end of the lane, and accompanying Aunt Maria to the lake where she washed her clothes. I enjoyed spending time with Kavya and her friends who were busy with their make-believe games. On most evenings I visited the market with Kavya or my cousin, Devya, to run errands for Grandmother or to escape the boredom at home.

One evening we were on our usual visit to the market. Devya couldn't join us because Aunt Maria was down with some sort of illness and needed her help preparing dinner. I preferred Devya's company to Kavya's because we were the same age and had a lot more to talk about, especially her interest in a young man who lived close by. I sensed my little sister had become resentful of my closeness to Devya. Kavya accused us of keeping secrets from her.

Once when she demanded we reveal what we were whispering about, I snapped at her. 'Behave yourself. Don't ask questions about adults.' I was taken aback by the sharpness in my tone and so was Kavya.

She stuck her tongue out at me and ran away crying.

I felt bad about scolding my sister, but I couldn't trust Kavya not to tell Grandmother and, if the family found out, Devya wouldn't be let out of the house.

'My father will take me out of school to stop me from meeting him,' Devya said. She often met the boy on the bus on her way to school. I didn't think there was anything wrong in her liking a boy. She was a bright girl who deserved a lot more than what the village could offer.

I wished both my siblings and Devya could also have the opportunity to live and study with me and enjoy the freedom I often took for granted. I feared they would one day resent me for my luck. It seemed a terrible shame that Shanti Bhavan could take only one child from each family.

In the market that evening, the blend of different smells from fried snacks—delicious bondas, freshly baked egg puffs, crisp dosas, and spicy kababs—filled my senses as I sank into the market's contagious energy and spirit. I couldn't resist buying the bondas that were sizzling in the oil pan at a roadside shop. Kavya gobbled hers while I ate mine slowly, thoroughly savoring its crunch.

Then I heard someone call out to Kavya, and turned to see two men seated on the wooden step of a grocery shop, smoking cigarettes. They looked familiar; I was certain I'd seen them before but couldn't remember where. Both were probably in their twenties, one younger than the other, and their disheveled hair and the glittery, thick, gold-plated chains around their necks gave them the look of village louts. One glance and I was sure they were trouble. It was clear they were not to be trusted, and I felt uncomfortable even making eye contact with them.

The older man grinned at Kavya and nodded towards me. 'Who is she?'

'She's my sister,' Kavya muttered. I felt her tugging at my sleeve. We hurried to merge into the busy crowd of the evening market. I was afraid they were following us; I turned to look but they were nowhere to be seen.

I didn't tell Grandmother or Appa. They wouldn't have allowed me to step outside again. But my encounter with the two men continued to disturb me. Little did I know then that they would pursue Kavya and me, and my family would face a terrible tragedy at their hands.

Two days later, a new worry replaced that uneasiness. A neighbor came running to Grandmother's house saying Appa had been caught with a woman near the water mill in the neighboring village. Upon hearing that they were having frequent trysts, her husband hired some local ruffians to thrash Appa. I hadn't seen or heard from him since the evening of my arrival and now hearing what he had been up to filled me with rage. I was old enough to understand that he was probably having an 'affair.'

I remembered my classmate Kavina once telling us that her father was in a relationship with her mother's younger sister. 'He's having an affair,' she said, and I looked it up in the dictionary, wanting to know exactly what it meant. I loved learning new words.

'That man will never change. What to do now?' Grandmother called out to my uncles to find Appa and bring him back. I was angry with him and worried, not knowing what would have happened to him. I began to cry.

'Stop that,' Grandmother said sternly. 'Women must stay strong in times of trouble, or the home will fall apart.' She continued her household work as though this were nothing out of the ordinary, but from the way she was chopping vegetables, I could see she too was tense.

After a few minutes, unable to restrain herself any longer, she burst into a long, vehement tirade about how Appa was constantly bringing shame to the family. 'By tomorrow morning, this news will have spread like wildfire. You just watch how happy they are going to be,' she mumbled, referring to the women with whom she fought over almost everything—who stole someone's chickens, whose daughter would get a rich husband, and other petty village rivalries.

An hour had passed and still there was no sign of Appa. Restless, I went to sit by the roadside, closely watching every passing vehicle. Grandmother spotted two of her friends emerging from a neighboring house. She went to them, perhaps seeking consolation from other women who had faced similar problems.

'Poor Sarophina,' one remarked bitterly. 'This man has a wife and a daughter who has already come of age, ready for a family of her own. Still he is behaving like this.' The way she casually referred to my having gotten my period as a sign that I was ready to have a family angered me.

Ever since I started my periods, I had been treated differently. Grandfather instructed Grandmother to set aside a glass of milk occasionally, as he strongly believed that girls who had come of age needed to be strong and healthy. Grandmother, on the other hand, had gone extreme; she had taken it upon herself to be my personal guard, accompanying me herself whenever she could and otherwise making sure my siblings or cousins were with me.

'You must be careful now. Those vultures out there are waiting to catch innocent chicks like you,' she warned whenever I stepped out of the house. She often overwhelmed me with her protective instinct, but it made me feel special.

Kavya resented it. 'I want to get my periods too,' she often protested, bursting into angry sobs. She refused to believe me when I tried to explain that she would, too, in a few years.

'When his wife isn't there to keep him happy, what else can he do?' the second woman retorted. I was repulsed, but didn't have the courage to speak up, afraid it would upset Grandmother.

A short time later, a police vehicle pulled up in front of my parents' house. Appa staggered out of the jeep, favoring his ankle. Grandmother went back inside, sighing in relief that her son-in-law was still alive and hadn't left her daughter a widow.

Kavya, Francis, and I ran towards Appa. Ignoring us, he slowly limped into his hut, pulled out a straw mat, and lay down. I grabbed the half-empty bottle of liquor he was carrying, and thrust it into my brother's hands. 'Go throw this in the garbage pit,' I ordered, my words mirroring the first moments of my life. When Francis hesitated, Kavya barked at him and he took off. I took Kavya's hand for a moment, grateful for her support. She stood staring at Appa and squeezing my hand.

'Get the balm,' Appa groaned, avoiding my eyes. I retrieved the small bottle of ointment from the cupboard, and sat down on the mat beside him to rub it over his back and shoulders. He moaned in pain each time I pressed hard. When Francis returned he sat quietly on the doorstep watching us and soon Kavya went to sit with him.

The neighbors who watched the scene unfold looked at us with pity. I could see they were touched by our apparent devotion to our injured father. In reality, I was simply doing my duty as a daughter, and my touch was devoid of affection. I kept looking at Francis and Kavya huddled in the doorway. This was the life they had to endure, all the time.

I knew it was easier for me. But sometimes, even at school Appa managed to bring the humiliating side of our family's life with him. At a parent-teacher meeting the year before, I noticed Kavina hiding from someone. In a confused whisper she told me, 'Your father is looking at me strangely. I feel awkward.' I turned just in time to catch him staring at her, like he did at the young women who passed by our house on their way to and from work. I felt terribly ashamed of him and wanted to vanish from the room. I begged Kavina not to tell any of our classmates, fearing that I would be ridiculed. From the way I behaved towards Appa for the rest of the afternoon, I was sure he understood that I had noticed, but he didn't seem to care. But no matter how I distanced myself from my father or tried to think of him as a stranger, I was still tied to him emotionally.

An hour passed. Appa couldn't bear the pain from the beating and began to moan in anguish. Grandfather had to take him to the village medicine man who lived in a shack on top of the hill. By the time he came back late that night, I was lying down with a bad fever. My blurred vision of Appa, returning exhausted and tearful, entered my dreams.

That night I dreamt of ruffians entering our house, throwing plates and pots out onto the road, and scattering Amma's saris all over the floor. I woke up screaming, and Grandmother had to hug me tight and place a wet cloth on my forehead to cool my fever.

The very next morning, Muniappa, a village landlord, and two rough-looking men turned up in front of my father's house. I had gone there to check on Appa, although I wasn't feeling very well myself. He was sleeping, trying to recover from the damage done to him the previous day, and couldn't hear them shouting for him. I came out of the house quickly to find out what they wanted. I was sure they had heard what had happened to Appa the previous evening, and considered it an opportune time to pressure him for whatever they wanted. When it rains it pours, I thought.

'Where is your father?' one of the men asked in Kannada. His tone of expectation easily revealed his authority over Appa.

Trying to act bold and wanting to impress them, I replied in English, 'He is resting inside.'

By then Appa had struggled out of the hut, and greeted the landlord respectfully, 'Namaste.' He turned his gaze in my direction and gestured to me to go inside. I could see fear written all over his face.

I obeyed him and he pulled the door shut behind me. I heard the men yelling at Appa, followed by the sounds of a struggle. Unable to bear it, I opened the door to see the two men viciously beating Appa.

'Appa! Appa!' I cried out and rushed towards him.

Blood was gushing from his nose.

Suddenly Kavya and Francis were there and screaming, 'Stop! Stop!'

'Kavya,' I called, 'Fetch Grandmother. Run.'

And she ran.

'Stop hitting my father,' I screamed at the two men.

'Shut up,' the landlord shouted back. I could feel the flood of warm tears running down my cheeks. By then, a large crowd of neighbors had gathered around.

An elderly man bravely stepped forward to question the landlord. I recognized him as the one who rang the church bell every day. Now he was risking getting beaten too. But the landlord seemed to be listening to him—maybe the landlord respected his elders, maybe he feared this man's connections to the church, or maybe it was yet another thing I didn't understand about the workings of my village.

The landlord turned to his thugs and said something I couldn't hear. The men stopped hitting Appa.

'You better pay soon,' the landlord ordered Appa. 'In the meantime, your English daughter can live with me.'

I instinctively grabbed Appa's shirt. He pulled me by the arm and stepped in front of me.

'I will bring the money as soon as I can,' Appa responded firmly. He didn't want the landlord to think he was weak.

'You have said that before,' one of the men replied. 'Next time, we will not wait. We will take her with us,' he added, pointing a warning finger at me.

They left and Appa escorted me into the house. He wouldn't look at me.

'You aren't going to send me away, are you?' I asked, wiping away tears.

Appa slowly raised his head, looking at me sadly. I could tell he was terribly worried. Seeing him helpless, I was worried too.

I had heard of daughters and even wives of men who had failed to repay their debts being taken to work as servants in the landlords' homes. No one in the village dared to challenge that practice. Only last summer, Appa told me a little about being a 'slave' in the same Gunna's house when he was a young boy. His father had put his son there when he couldn't repay a loan and several years passed before Joseph Thatha got Appa out. I couldn't even begin to comprehend something like that happening to me.

'Shilpa, stop crying. I will pay him,' Appa said.

Kavya had returned and came to sit by my side on the floor. She reached out to dry my tears. 'Don't worry, Akka. Nothing will happen to you.'

I took her hand gently. 'You don't know that.' Turning to Appa, I said, 'Take me back to Shanti Bhavan.' I didn't have anything more to say and my silence spoke for me.

From that day on, even with Grandmother or Francis escorting me, I didn't feel safe. I just wanted Appa to tell me he had repaid the debt.

After the incident at the water mill, we grew even more suspicious of Appa whenever he disappeared for days on end. It was a complete surprise then when one day Appa sauntered into Grandmother's house with the long stride of a proud man. He settled down on the floor with a big smile as though preparing to announce something very important. Uncle Christraj and Uncle Naresh leaned against the door and stared at him with disdain. Neither was fond of Appa. They blamed him for my mother's absence and neither had forgiven him for the incident at the mill.

I wanted Appa to announce that he had repaid the loan but instead, after capturing everyone's attention, he revealed that he had gotten himself a government job chasing elephants from sugarcane fields. As part of the arrangement, at night he would have to stay in a makeshift hut close to the forest. 'My boss will come to check whether we are vigilant.'

Grandmother was aghast. 'You leave that job right now. I don't want my daughter to become a widow and these three little ones to be fatherless. Do you understand?'

Unlike her, I was actually excited at the news and amazed at the thought of anyone chasing elephants for a living. It may not have been the news I wanted to hear but I still couldn't resist the sense of adventure.

Within a few short weeks, Appa had accumulated a horde of crazy tales from his new job. Francis and Kavya sat close to him and listened attentively, not wanting to miss a single word. I sat on the wooden cot a little distance away and pretended I wasn't interested. I wasn't ready to forgive him for cheating on my mother and bringing disgrace to the family, but I loved his stories.

We knew elephants loved snacking on sugarcane, their voracious appetites often destroying whole harvests. 'During the day, we inspect the fields next to the forest searching for any signs of elephants the night before and decide whether they might come back,' Appa began.

'What are the signs?' I asked, unable to hide my interest. I had loved hearing my classmate, Avinash, talk about animals and the snakes he had caught on several occasions. I couldn't wait to tell him about Appa's new job.

'Often, you see large clumps of dung and deep footprints. At night, we carry firecrackers to scare the elephants away from the fields back into the forest.' Appa opened a green cardboard box he had brought with him, filled to the brim with the small, round fireworks.

Just a month before, some villagers had tried to chase the elephants away from the fields, but the animals attacked them, stomping two men to death. Since then, the government had added more men to the team of elephant chasers and ordered that some animals be caught, if possible, for a nearby zoo.

A renowned forest ranger, Narayananna, was appointed by the government to lead a group of men on an expedition. Narayananna and the group veterinarian rode atop tamed elephants, while forest guards and their officers followed in a jeep. Appa and some others travelled on foot, working tirelessly under the hot sun to clear a path for the jeep by breaking or pushing aside tree branches and thick bushes with their bare hands.

Not long after they entered the forest, the team spotted a herd of elephants a little distance away. Narayananna brought his elephant closer to the herd, and fired his tranquilizer gun. Thinking he had missed the target, he reloaded the gun and fired again. After allowing a moment for the tranquilizer to take effect, they rushed forward to assess the condition of the animal.

'A young elephant was lying in a shallow depression with its neck tilted in an unnatural position, gasping for breath. It had two tranquilizer darts, one in its rear leg and one in its neck, and appeared nearly unconscious,' Appa said, his voice strained with emotion.

Appa saw the vet dismount from his elephant and run to the injured one on the ground. He frantically tried to feed the fallen elephant glucose through a long tube. 'But by that time, the elephant was already dead,' Appa said.

It surprised me to see him struggling with the memory.

Some discussion followed between the vet and others, and an officer said they had to investigate why the elephant had died. Appa suspected everyone knew that an overdose of tranquilizer had killed it. Nevertheless, two officers began to cut up the elephant while Appa and his partners hastily dug a pit for the animal's corpse. The officers sliced into the elephant's head and removed its small tusks.

The herd stood at a distance, looking on and making low, mournful trumpeting sounds. 'I will never forget how much the elephant herd cared about one of their own, even when they were scared,' Appa said, turning his gaze deliberately upon me. 'Unlike us humans, even in danger they stay together.' I averted my eyes.

Appa kept his focus on me for a moment before continuing. One of the officers was sent to fetch a local pujari—a temple priest—from the nearby village to bless the body before burial. The pujari lit incense sticks, placed them at one end of the pit, and slowly poured milk onto the dead elephant's body. All the while, he chanted a holy hymn in Sanskrit that no one could understand.

'When we die, no pujari comes near us,' Appa murmured. 'The elephant must have belonged to a high caste.' Such rituals were done to receive blessings or deflect harm brought about by angry spirits. Unholy *untouchables* had no need for any such rituals. They couldn't please the Gods in any case.

Appa's story ended there that night, but it embedded itself in my memory. Since that day, whenever I hear the sound of firecrackers exploding in the distance on festive nights, I think of my father and the fallen elephant.

Appa had led an adventurous life since childhood, yet his new occupation as an elephant chaser was even more dangerous. Strangely, he didn't seem concerned about his safety. He was proud of his official job, and often joked that for once he was working for, and not against, the government. 'In our family, I am the first one to have a government job,' he would often declare with pride, irking other members of the family. He reminded everyone that if he were to be killed, the government would give his family one lakh rupees—a very large sum by his standards. This was no comfort to me.

Villagers held government employees in high esteem as they could earn plenty of money one way or another. Bribes made up the bulk of their monthly income. I didn't know much about Appa's salary, but I was reasonably sure the elephants didn't give him anything extra on the side.

Each evening, Kavya and I would wait for Appa to wish us goodnight before he left for work. He would be dressed in dark green pants and a green shirt to camouflage himself in the forest. I would picture him moving about at night, his ears attentive to every rustle of leaves and to each hoot of invisible owls. I liked to think of him as our soldier, protecting our family from the elephant threat. More than anything else, for the first time in my life, I felt proud of him.

Appa often glanced at me to see if I was noticing him dressed in his uniform. I could tell that he wished I could like him and respect him. One evening, he produced a gunny sack filled with several large wood apples and wild berries. I avoided eye contact with him, but secretly enjoyed his show of interest in us. He cracked one wood apple open on the doorstep and handed it to me before he gave any to Kavya and Francis. I was touched, but hoped Kavya and Francis hadn't noticed. Crude as his ways were, those simple gestures were worth much more than the expensive gifts he wished he could give us.

Occasionally, I would go with Appa to buy beef from a butcher. Until recently, nobody sold beef in the village, as the higher caste people did not permit cows to be slaughtered openly. Gunnas sold their cows to the poor when the animals got too old to give milk. The coolies butchered the cows far away in the fields and sold the meat there. Everyone, including the Gunnas, knew of this practice.

Meat was piled up in clumps on fresh banana leaves. For twenty rupees one could buy a hefty kilo of fresh beef. Everyone bargained with the butcher for a little more. Those who could not pay stood to the side looking longingly at the red meat. 'Please, *Anna*, I will give you money later. Just give me a little,' a sorry-looking mother pleaded, her two little daughters watching hopefully from behind.

The bald butcher barked at her and gestured for her to leave. 'You said the same thing last week. Go from here.'

The butcher weighed the beef using a stone he claimed was a kilo. He had stones for other weights as well. Whenever customers complained the weights were incorrect, he would respond, 'These stones are heavier. My price is for my kilo, not someone else's.' No one could argue with that.

The cooked beef was as tough as leather, but we found our fun in the endless chewing. My siblings and I often bargained with each other for better pieces without bones. For us, the meat offered an irresistible, magical taste.

We knew this was our rare treat. There were no others. But Kavya longed for good clothes and trips to the theatre, and Francis wished he could eat something different from time to time.

Appa once remarked that I looked like him. In a way, I was glad that he seemed to want me to, but I wasn't happy to think I might resemble him. His sunburned face was almost as dark as charcoal and his moustache was even darker. At just over five feet tall, Appa had passed on to me his short stature. But his arms were strong and hard, and he often asked me to check his muscles, which he told me were made of rocks. The roughness of his hands resembled his feet, broken nails sticking out from an array of cuts. I would stare at his legs, especially at his dry, patchy skin that was visibly peeling in many spots. When I asked him why his skin wasn't smooth like mine, he replied with a mischievous smile, 'I shed my scales from time to time, like a snake.'

Seeing how hard my father was trying to make me happy confused me. He was an enigma to me. He was domineering with my mother and mostly absent for Kavya, Francis, and me, but subservient in the presence of Gunnas. Though uneducated, he was smart enough to escape the clutches of the police and the landlords, and win over the women he secretly courted. There could be no doubt that he was also one of the best elephant chasers in the village.

Not all of Appa's stories were sad. Some were funny and others scary, like the one he told us about other elephant chasers who thought they saw ghosts in the woods and ran away. Appa was skilled enough to distinguish shadows and silhouettes from real creatures, and wasn't easily scared. 'I'm more frightened of humans than spirits,' he once said with a chuckle.

Kavya was afraid of ghosts; Grandmother used to tell her spooky tales to stop her from leaving the house at night to play with friends. 'Just wait and watch,' she said. 'The drunken fool who hanged himself across the street is going to catch you one night,' she would say to my sister.

I didn't need ghosts to frighten me. Just a few days later, I saw the same two rowdies from the market in front of grandmother's house on a motorbike, stopping to stare into our hut. They wouldn't dare come inside the house, I told myself. I searched for Kavya to warn her, but she was nowhere to be found.

Even though Grandmother was strict about my sister and me staying at home after darkness set in, she couldn't control Kavya, however hard she tried. Eventually she gave up, comforting herself in the thought that Kavya was used to the ways of the village and was smart enough to handle any dangerous situation. Despite Grandmother's confidence, I was growing more and more concerned about Kavya's increasing defiance of her elders and the restrictions placed on her. Why wasn't anyone taking strict measures to set her right? Or was I expecting too much from her at eleven? And why was Kavya's rebelliousness a matter of such concern to me while I remained blind to the reasons for my own willfulness at school?

After a restless night spent worrying about Kavya, I woke up early, feeling unsettled and in need of a walk. My wayward sister was fast asleep on the cot we shared, her face peaceful and innocent. A surge of love filled my heart, and I kissed her gently on her forehead. I wished she would wake up, but she didn't.

With a heavy heart, I stepped out into the misty air.

Chapter Ten

Talk of Marriage

For some strange reason, I had turned to the tranquility of the village for comfort that morning. But peace was fleeting with the sounds of the village hurrying to life rose with the dawn. People were rushing to work in the fields and elsewhere on foot, bicycles, and bullock carts. Those struggling to make a living couldn't afford to stay home once the sun came up.

Early on the last evening of my vacation, Grandmother called me over for a private conversation by the kitchen. To my surprise, Grandfather was also there. He usually returned only after sunset but today he was home before dark. It had to be something important.

Patting the ground near him, he signaled me to sit facing them. 'What is it, Thatha?' I asked, plucking nervously at a knot in my hair.

They glanced at each other like children hiding secrets from their parents. Grandmother, as usual, was the one to break the silence. Making no effort to hide her excitement, she blurted out, 'Shilpa, after you finish tenth grade, you will marry your Naresh mama.'

'Marry Naresh Mama?' I exclaimed, the weight of her words failing to sink in.

'Yes, Shilpa.' Grandmother raised her eyebrows at my look of confusion.

I laughed, certain they could not really be serious. The thought of me marrying my uncle was as revolting as Grandfather slaughtering a hen we had raised since it was a chick.

But Grandmother was persistent. 'Your mother wants you to marry him. Thatha and I spoke to her.' She relayed this information with the casual tone of a teacher announcing weekly test results. Still, there was urgency in her voice. 'She asked us not to wait any longer to tell you.' They were studying my face intensely.

I realized with dread that my grandparents were not joking. 'Grandmother, what are you saying? You know I can't marry my uncle.'

Maybe she had imagined I would jump with joy and hug her. She knew I was fond of her youngest son and preferred his company to my other uncles who often scolded me for being too talkative. She was certain I would consent and had been looking forward to announcing the happy news to her son and the rest of the family.

Turning to Grandfather, she snapped angrily, 'How dare she talk like this?' Without waiting for him to reply, she returned to me. 'Shilpa, it was decided before you were born that the first granddaughter in the family would marry my youngest son.' She looked straight into my eyes. 'He loves you more than he ever loved any other girl in the village.'

Nothing she said made sense to me. Desperately seeking support, I turned to Grandfather. 'Thatha, how can I marry Naresh Mama?' Mrs. Law's face flashed before my eyes, and DG's voice telling us to stand up to our families when they were wrong rang in my head. I wished they were here to protect me from my own family. 'It is bad. How can I marry a close relative? We learnt in school that marrying a family member will cause health problems for the babies.' I must have sounded like a doctor counseling a patient. I was tense, struggling to appear respectful.

Grandmother was not impressed. 'In our village, many have married within their families, and their babies are not missing an eye or a leg, like you say.'

My world was spinning out of control. I wanted to run out of the room, but felt rooted in place. Why were my grandparents asking me to do something that was harmful to my future? I had my own fantasies and dreams about marriage.

All the girls in my class often talked about dating and marrying our heroes in movies. Sheena wanted her wedding ceremony on a grand ship. For a long time, I had a crush on a volunteer from America who taught us math and computer science; I cried bitterly upon his departure. As young girls, every time a kissing scene appeared on the screen, we would erupt in screams of conflicted disapproval: 'Fast forward! Fast forward!' It was embarrassing, especially in the company of boys. Marriage was just a farfetched fantasy for us, not something immediate. I had never given it a serious thought, until now.

I was struggling, unsure of everything. I clung to DG's words about the importance of not letting anyone dictate what your life should be.

My grandparents were waiting. I leaned towards them eagerly. 'I want to become a journalist. I want to travel the world when I grow up. My principal always tells me I will make a good reporter.'

The blank expressions on my grandparents' faces told me they were far from enthralled by my ambition. It was also clear they didn't know what a journalist or a reporter was.

I described it to them with hand gestures that they would have seen on television—young women speaking into microphones. 'I want to write about what is happening in the world and speak on TV.' Biting my lip, I waited for the storm to hit.

Grandmother reacted with a look of sheer disgust, as though she were ready to spit in my face. She didn't understand that I could have a happy, successful life and a good career outside of Thattaguppe. I wanted her to see that a world of surprises and opportunity existed for me out there. But how could I get her to believe me when neither she nor any of the other women in our family had ever experienced that world for themselves?

Resentment burned in her eyes as she turned to Grandfather. 'She doesn't want to marry our Naresh!'

Grandfather couldn't be caught standing by while his wife was being insulted by a family member so young. Shaking a threatening finger in my face, he warned, 'You look here, girl. You can't step into our house if you marry someone against our wishes.'

I gasped. This couldn't be happening. How could my grandparents threaten to abandon me, especially when Amma was away? Did they not care about me and my happiness? Did they not want to be part of my dreams of a better life for all of us? I could see that Grandfather meant every word he had uttered. And there was no reason to believe my mother would come to my defense, either. She too, I knew, would give in to the societal expectations of obeying elders. After all, if she didn't, she faced the risk of abandonment by her own parents.

The thought that I should have a say in my own marriage didn't seem to cross my grandparents' minds. It was all about what they wanted—what was good for them, and I was obligated to abide by it. Nothing else seemed to count.

Grandfather pulled out a tiny steel box containing snuff, something he often did when he needed to calm down. He dipped in the tip of his thumb and index finger to pinch a little powder, and then brought it to his nose for a greedy, deep inhale. Drops of powder clung to his moustache like stranded grains of white pollen.

My vehemence shocked my grandmother who had made a concerted effort to remain reasonably composed. But now she raised her arms into the air in a gesture of helpless supplication and looked up high as if she were praying to God to put some sense into me. Finally she stared straight at me and angrily demanded that I follow my elders' wishes. 'This is the way of our family and every family in the village. Every girl must follow it,' Grandmother intoned, as if she were trying to educate me, as if these were things I had failed to learn, having left home at the age of four.

I stared furiously at the two people I had loved so dearly. They were parents to me in Appa's and Amma's absence. But now, they didn't seem to care. My feelings of disconnect from my family grew piercing.

But I refused to give up. 'Aunt Maria married the man you chose for her, and look what happened.' I barreled onward without stopping to catch my breath. 'So many times she has come running here after getting beaten up by her husband. She tried to hang herself. Is that what you want for me?'

My voice betrayed my desperation. I chose my words as carefully as possible and kept my head bowed submissively but I knew I didn't sound respectful enough. In a world where grandparents deserved nothing short of reverence, girls just couldn't talk like this. My spirits continued to sink.

'Yes, we were the ones who chose her partner,' Grandfather said. 'And because she obeyed us, we are always there for her.'

'Every time your aunt is beaten,' Grandmother added, 'we take her into our house and comfort her. Because she listened to us and married according to our wishes, we will never abandon her.'

'I don't want to marry Mama, or any other man.' I was feeling trapped and afraid. 'I see Amma and Appa fighting every day. I hate it.'

'Just because they fight doesn't mean everybody does. Do Thatha and I fight?'

I thought for a moment. My grandparents hardly ever fought, except when they argued about surmounting debts.

Suddenly Grandmother softened. 'You are special. You are different. I always thought you would be the lamp to brighten my dark house.'

I was moved by her kind words, but already knew my family saw me differently from other girls in the village. Her praise did little to change my mind.

Hearing my grandparents talk about marrying me off to my uncle as casually as they would discuss a sudden rise in vegetable prices in the market made it clear my education meant nothing to them. They couldn't see its value, especially since I was a girl. In their view, family responsibilities as a wife and a mother were more important than the free, unchained life I wanted to create for myself out of my education.

With forced politeness I excused myself and struggled out of the room. The fresh air outside was a relief from the suffocating feeling inside. I stood for a few moments watching the sun set behind the dark hills, leaving a vanishing film of bright colors. I wanted to return to the safety of the life I had beyond those hills.

'Akka, come here,' Kavya called out, yanking me back to the present. She and Devya were gathering into a bucket cakes of cow dung that had been strewn on the road. I went to her struggling to mask my distress with a smile. I yearned to confide in her, but knew she was too young to understand.

Devya was busy pouring water into the bucket Kavya had brought to her, stirring the fresh dung with her bare hands before splashing it onto the ground. It was the way floors were disinfected in village huts. I sat by the roadside on a boulder and watched them enjoy the simple pleasures of village life. Kavya found joy in almost everything she did: chasing dragonflies by the lake, learning how to drape a sari, or playing 'Mother' to the little children who lived on our lane. Humor was always a part of her, her musical laughter ringing out everywhere, delighting everyone.

Once the initial shock wore off, I began to look at this marriage proposal with detachment. Marrying me to my uncle involved no dowry from the girl's family. I would be anchored at home to look after others in their old age, and my children would grow up with not just the care and love of their parents, but also that of their grandparents and great-grandparents. My mother might have feared that, just as I had left her at the age of four to go to school, I would once again go off on a path of my own, away from her and the rest of the family. Marriage within the family could ensure that I would remain with her for the rest of her life.

'Will you take care of me when I'm old?' I remembered Grandmother asking me once. I didn't realize then that she was asking whether I would fulfill my expected role—not just as a granddaughter, but as her future daughter-in-law too.

I had replied confidently, 'Of course, I will. You have nothing to fear.'

She was very pleased and gave me a kiss on my forehead.

Now, I understood clearly what she was expecting. The thought of living with the family and taking care of her in her old age in that way had not previously crossed my mind. I had, of course, often looked forward to a time when I could take care of my grandmother, but my plans had not included spending my entire life in the village.

I had always known that, in villages, girls typically end their educations early to get married. Because every family struggles economically, strong financial pressure exists to give girls away as soon as possible to men who take over the responsibility of supporting them. Having a grown-up girl sitting idle at home only invites unwanted rumors and the attention of undesirable men. Even talking to a boy in the neighborhood was viewed poorly. Every time an unwelcome incident took place, the girl was labeled as promiscuous and loose, and was blamed for bringing dishonor to the family. Marriage, especially for girls, is something parents and grandparents decide. If ever a girl went against their wishes, she wouldn't have a place in the family.

Though the idea of marrying someone so closely related was appalling to my schoolmates and me, it was hardly unheard of. Several of my classmates had been subjected to similar arrangements in their own families. During vacation from school, Sunita, then only nine years old, was told by her family that she was to marry her cousin Ram. Child marriage was not unusual in poor villages. The school intervened, and Ms. Ruth assured her that a school official would speak to her parents. She would not have to get married so early, and not to a close relative.

In another instance, one of the senior girls was often left alone at home with her slightly older cousin during vacations. When she complained the cousin was making sexual advances, her mother dismissed it, saying, 'Why does it matter? He is the one who is going to marry you.' Unable to receive help from anyone in her own family, this girl told Mrs. Law, and someone from the school's management immediately called her parents and spoke to them. The thought that I, too, was now facing a similar situation frightened and embarrassed me.

Aunt Maria stopped by the house that evening to talk to me. She tried to soothe me, saying, 'We always thought our niece would become our sister-in-law and stay with us instead of leaving after marriage.' It was clear my grandparents had already spoken to her about my reaction.

I shook my head and replied with teenage intransigence, 'I don't want to marry anyone. I want to study.'

I was not hungry that night. I took a small serving of rice and curry, unlike my usual large helpings, and ate in silence. My stomach knotted in anger and resentment when Uncle Naresh settled down next to me and tried to make small talk as usual.

Until now I had not minded his attentiveness but that night I wished he would disappear from my life. Seeing that he seemed his usual happy self, I knew my grandparents hadn't told him about our conversation. Probably they were afraid of hurting him, especially since they were the ones who had planted the idea of this marriage in his head. I dreaded how he would react when he heard what had transpired that day.

I lay awake for a long time that night. Grandmother's presence beside me was no comfort. I didn't put my arm around her and hug her tightly as I usually did. Instead, I lay listening to the sounds around me: Grandfather's funny-sounding snores, a lonely donkey braying outside, the clinking of bangles around Kavya's wrists, and all the familiar noises that wove into the calm of the night.

Not too long after this day, I was sitting on the floor with my back against the foot of the wooden cot upon which my uncle was lying. We were watching television together. Uncle Christraj had only recently purchased the set from his first month's salary for his work as a car mechanic in a shop outside the village.

There was no one in the house except the two of us. Grandmother was outside having one of her regular gossip sessions with the village midwife who lived across the road. Grandfather and Uncle Christraj had not yet returned from work. Kavya and Francis were away at play.

Suddenly, the power went out and the room went dark. Hardly a minute had passed before I felt strong hands press down on my collarbones in a tightening grip. I felt my uncle's cheek gently rubbing against mine. His moustache tickled me as he slowly traced the side of my face with his lips. I then felt his lips moving from my cheek to my mouth. I froze. Again, his hands squeezed my shoulders as though to prevent me from moving as he placed a warm kiss on the corner of my mouth.

My body turned numb. The sound of his heavy breathing overtook all my senses. I couldn't think.

Suddenly a streak of light shot through the room. He quickly pulled away and settled in his original position on the cot. I looked up to see Devya standing at the door with a kerosene lamp in her hand.

I exhaled with relief. I didn't know whether I was more anxious or ashamed. For the moment, I just hoped Devya hadn't seen us. I didn't know what she would think.

Scrambling up from the floor, I darted into the kitchen where Devya had already started cutting vegetables for dinner. Not able to handle the knife, I gave up trying to help her. I sat staring blankly into space, my heart pounding and my mind racing.

I was scared to tell Grandmother, knowing she would scold me for spinning stories about her favorite son. Talking about him behind his back would be a form of betrayal in her eyes. Family secrets were family secrets.

To add to my troubles at home, I had been feeling unsafe out in the village. Each time I went to the market with Kavya, the two men I had previously seen hanging around would follow us. They would find a moment to come close and try to strike up a conversation. Sometimes they offered to buy me good clothes if I went with them. I would immediately turn away and race back home, afraid of what they might do.

Everything in the village now felt uncertain and dangerous, and I couldn't wait to return to the sanctity of my school.

I don't know when I fell asleep on the last night of the holidays, but I was glad to wake up to Grandmother's call to get dressed quickly or we'd miss the early morning bus to Shanti Bhavan.

Chapter Eleven

The Price of Betrayal

Grandmother stared out the bus window, silent on the long ride back to school. It was very unlike her, but things had turned icy between us and we both felt it. I was relieved when the bus slowed abruptly as it reached the sharp bend leading to Shanti Bhavan. I put my head out the window and drew in a deep breath of the morning air.

The summer heat had been hard that year, turning fields and grounds into dry wasteland. Except for scanty patches of grass on which cattle were feeding, there was very little sign of life. Even the lake that usually filled with the monsoons was empty of water.

Grandmother and I got out of the bus along with a few other families who were also returning to Shanti Bhavan. We walked through the gates and headed straight to the dining hall. On the way, I looked up to stare at the line of colorful flags with the Shanti Bhavan emblem swaying in the breeze. The flags had been hoisted as a proud 'welcome back'.

I caught sight of Aunty Shalini moving among the crowd of parents, trying hard to give equal attention to all those who were swarming around her eager to update her on how things were at home and to thank her for looking after their children. While Grandmother joined the crowd, I sat quietly at a table, playing idly with my spoon.

The hall was now filled with the sound of crying children begging to be taken home, and anxious parents explaining that they would be back soon. By now I had figured out the trick of the grown-ups—making promises not meant to be kept.

Just then Aunty Shalini and Grandmother walked over to my table. 'How are you, Mummy?' I asked, standing up instantly and giving Aunty Shalini a kiss on her cheek.

'I am fine, darling,' she replied warmly.

This one word of affection from her made me forgive every instance of harshness with which she had treated me in the past. She had some sort of power over me, and as hard as I tried, I couldn't resist it.

'How are you? How were your holidays?' Aunty Shalini enquired in Kannada.

In Grandmother's powerful presence I knew better than to burst out with everything that had happened over summer break.

'She was very happy at home, Madam. We had no problem. She didn't fall sick,' Grandmother answered for me.

'Did she stay with you for the entire time? How are her parents?' Aunty Shalini asked.

'Her grandfather and I looked after her for the summer. Her mother calls once a month and her father comes to see the children whenever he can.'

Aunty Shalini seemed pleased. She told Grandmother to advise me to work hard and be respectful to my elders. 'Last semester she was better, but she can still improve,' Aunty Shalini said, referring to recent moderations in my temperament. All the aunties seemed to have noticed that my stubbornness and aggression had mellowed.

After Aunty Shalini moved on to the next parent, Grandmother turned to me. 'I don't want them complaining about you anymore. Be a good girl. Pray to Jesus and he will guide you.'

I assured her I would. 'Grandmother, tell Kavya and Devya that I will be home soon,' I said. 'Please tell Francis to study hard.' I felt terribly sad about having come away without saying goodbye. They were fast asleep when I left home that morning, and all I could do was pray silently to God to look after them. For some reason, I felt sad for them.

I kissed Grandmother on both cheeks and she drew the sign of the cross on my forehead with a slow movement of her hand, reciting a prayer under her breath. For the first time, my eyes were dry as I watched her walk away.

I felt relieved to be free of everyone in my family, and there was nothing more important now than to find my best friend Sheena. It took me a while, but I finally caught sight of her talking to her classmate, Avnith, and his parents who were seated on the lawn outside. She was laughing at something Avnith's father was saying. She seemed to have moved on from being consumed by self-pity. And instead of staying back in the dorm and crying when we all returned with our parents, she was mingling with her friends and their families. I knew how hard those moments might have been for her, but I was glad that she had turned strong enough to cope with them.

'Why didn't I get a family like you?' Sheena had once asked me. I had no answer. I couldn't explain why some were born rich and others poor and hungry or why children like Sheena had to grow up alone, never knowing why they had been abandoned.

I called out to Sheena. Catching sight of me, she waved excitedly. I made my way quickly through the crowd. 'Sheena!' I squealed as we embraced each other tightly. 'How are you?'

'I am well. I missed you so much,' she said.

I couldn't control my tears. The joy of being back at school with my best friend was overwhelming. Sheena mistook my tears for homesickness and hugged me again. I collected myself and calmed down.

I wanted to hear about her holiday and the trips she had made to the city with the staff, but I couldn't wait to tell her my news first. As we walked towards our dorm, I turned to her. 'Sheena, I don't know what to do. I am so scared. My family wants me to marry my uncle after I finish tenth grade.'

'*Your uncle?*' Sheena said, shocked but retaining her characteristic calm. 'That's crazy.' Even in challenging moments, she always managed to rise above while I sank into a bundle of nerves. 'You have to tell Aunty Shalini and Mrs. Law immediately.'

We entered the dorm and sat down on her bed. She turned to me seriously. 'You know Shanti Bhavan won't let that happen.'

I nodded, remembering how she herself had been saved.

Almost a year ago, Rafil had come to Shanti Bhavan to take Sheena home to get her ears pierced. Despite her apprehensions about sending her to her foster family in his care, Mrs. Law was prepared to accept the contention that piercing a girl's ears and nose was a special event in most South Indian families. Mrs. Law consented on the strict condition that she be brought back in two days without fail. To Sheena she said, 'Let's talk before you go.'

Sheena received counseling on how to protect herself. No one had forgotten what kind of man Rafil was.

I was relieved when he kept his word and Sheena returned with a tiny gold stud that accentuated the sharpness of her nose. Everyone was excited and showered her with compliments on how pretty and traditional she looked.

The next day, on my way to the chemistry lab, I caught sight of Sheena emerging from Mrs. Law's office. I was surprised and wondered what was wrong. I concluded that even the principal might have wanted to inspect Sheena's new piercings up close. I waited to ask her about it during our evening snack break.

Little did I know Sheena had met with Mrs. Law to confide in her a story that would leave me convinced that all men were bad and not to be trusted. As Sheena soon told me, on the second night of her stay at home, she woke up to a rough hand caressing her breasts. Startled, she sat upright. In the dim glow of the kerosene lamp, she saw that it was 'Uncle' Rafil. His children who had been sleeping next to Sheena were no longer beside her. Rafil had moved them to the corner of the room so he could be alone with her.

Sheena didn't want to look at him. She ran to the next room where Aunty Nela was sleeping and lay down next to her, trying to lull herself back to sleep. All through that night she kept waking up, afraid that Rafil would try to touch her again.

During that visit, Rafil had noticed how attractive Sheena was with her fair skin, dark shiny hair, petite frame, and chiseled features. She was turning out to be a lot more beautiful than he had imagined. He hatched a plan to get her back from Shanti Bhavan at any cost. There was no line he would not cross, even going so far as to threaten the lives of Mrs. Law and the senior staff, anyone who refused to hand Sheena back to him.

Soon the school authorities found out from Mr. Jude that Rafil wanted to sell Sheena for a handsome sum to a rich man living abroad. DG immediately arranged to file a case against Rafil for sexual abuse of a child. Eventually Rafil settled the matter and promised to leave Sheena alone if he was given some 'compensation'. This arrangement kept Rafil at bay and Sheena hasn't seen him since.

DG also knew how much Sheena longed for a family of her own. Each time he came to Shanti Bhavan from America, he made it a point to call her to the principal's office. 'My family and I will always be there for you. You are our daughter,' he assured her. I could see she trusted him not to abandon her and that he gave her a sense of belonging. With time, like me, she began to look up to DG as a father. For now, both Sheena and I had found our comfort in Shanti Bhavan.

Classes began in earnest. My life was now dictated by tests, projects, assignments, and activities like dance and music lessons. I signed up to learn the piano but dropped out, dejected, realizing I simply lacked the talent for it. Then, I joined hip-hop dance classes that were being conducted by professional artists from America. I couldn't stop admiring how well Kavina and Avinash danced. I, on the other hand, ended up making a laughing stock of myself. My deliberate Indian classical dance moves were at odds with their quick contemporary steps.

Fortunately, I soon discovered a place where I could thrive. I loved public speaking and editing stories for the school newsletter. Mrs. Law noticed and appointed me editor-in-chief. For the first time, I was in charge of something, and for days I went about with an air of newfound confidence. I grew to realize how much I enjoyed working with words, and as time went on, expressed my voice through writing.

My favorite part of school life in the summer was swimming in the afternoons in the giant tank that stored water to irrigate the banana plantation. Aunty Shalini instructed all the girls to wear tights under our swimsuits to avoid revealing our legs as she was concerned about what the workers on the farm would think of us. Being terribly conscious of my heavy thighs, I had no objection. I dreaded getting my period, as it meant I couldn't go swimming. I had heard of a solution to this problem in the health classes conducted by volunteers—tampons—but we didn't have any.

I was heavier than my classmates, and they called me names like 'Fatty' and 'Hippopotamus'. Every morning before class, I would stand in front of a full-length mirror to see if I appeared any thinner than the previous day. Whether I was in a skirt, trousers, or *salwar*, and whatever pose I tried, I would end up frowning at my reflection. I just wasn't as pretty or slender as the other girls. My bright smile which everyone said lit up my eyes and created a small dimple on my cheeks was the only consolation.

I often wore long, loose shirts to conceal the layer of fat around my waist. As I put on more weight, the school staff began to keep track of whether I was exercising enough. Whenever I asked for a second helping at lunch or dinner, my classmates would warn, 'Don't eat too much rice. You will get fatter.' I'd snap at them to mind their own business.

My frustration with weight even made it difficult to look at the few pictures I had of Amma in her youth. She was slim and pretty, her hair full and longer than mine. The girls in my class said I had my mother's sharp nose and narrow chin but not her tall, lean figure. Instead, unfortunately, I had inherited my father's short, broad frame.

My mind was never at ease. Even when I should have been relaxing in the dorm at night, I was thinking of one thing or another and bustling with energy. I couldn't bring myself to sleep, and would stir restlessly until late at night. Seeing me awake, some of the girls would ask me to tell them stories and I would narrate from the Nancy Drew Mysteries and Goosebumps series that they loved. Others would join in too, often sharing their family tales on their lives back home. The girls thought I was too serious because I preferred those stories, the real life stories however raw and sad, to fairy-tales of magic and make-believe that I quickly lost interest in.

Leelie used to describe to us about going fishing with her brother, sneaking off to play cricket with the village boys when her parents were not watching, and pulling pranks on her alcoholic maternal grandmother. We often begged her to tell us about her sister who caught their neighbor stealing cow dung from their shed. The little girl yelled at the woman as she was running off, 'How dare you steal our cow dung? We work so hard to feed the cow, and you take all its dung away?'

Leelie's life was so different from mine, even though we came from the same village. She made everything about her family sound exciting and funny, but I grew to understand it wasn't all easy for her. Her days in the village were harsh as she had to work long hours alongside her mother in the hot sun, plucking beans, harvesting corn, and sowing rice in the small plot of land they owned beside the lake. She learnt how to turn even upsetting events in her family, such as fights between her parents over debts, into something humorous. Perhaps her wit was a way of handling the pain.

One night Kavina told us about her early childhood. Her family hailed from Andhra Pradesh, a state not too far from Shanti Bhavan, where they had lived and worked for generations as daily laborers. In the beginning, they were too poor to rent a place and ended up living on the streets. Her young mother used to take Kavina and her two older siblings to look for shelter for the night, often winding up on the doorsteps of strangers. Her father had abandoned the family after a tense affair with her mother's sister. Her mother begged on the streets with her children during the day, desperate for money.

But Kavina's revelation of her past didn't make us think any less of her. We saw in her the girl she was in the present and she had a lot we envied. All the girls were jealous of her slender figure, plump shapely lips that she loved pouting as we'd seen film actresses do, and elegant dancing style, all of which attracted many boys. She was smart and witty, and often talked about her dream of one-day studying dance and drama at Julliard in New York City. A beautiful, distant ambition!

The close friendships we formed were on full display during festive times. Halloween, Diwali, and Christmas came in quick succession, bringing forth days of laughter and fun, colors, and lights. But the sweet surprises and earnest joys of this special world were not always ours to keep. The conflicts and troubles from our lives outside the school refused to be exorcized.

One morning, I noticed the boys in my class talking in hushed tones. One of my classmates, Keerthi, asked, 'What happened?'

'Ravi's mother died last night,' Avinash said. 'His father arrived this morning to take him home for the funeral.'

A wave of sadness hit me. We were aware that his mother had been ill for a long time but it was only years later that we learnt she had died from AIDS.

Ravi was shorter than most of the other boys. When he laughed, he squinted so hard that his eyes were almost invisible through the lenses of his eyeglasses. He didn't speak much to anyone, especially not to girls, unless the topic was cars or scientific discoveries. It was easy to forget his presence among us, but on that day I couldn't shake him from my mind.

Returning to school a week later, Ravi was even quieter than usual. He hardly ever disclosed his feelings about anything, least of all about his relationship with his father. I wondered if his father ever beat his mother, like mine did. When his father remarried a few months later, Ravi's relationship with him became further strained. Yet, however hard life was, Ravi longed to return home for the holidays. This was not unusual among us, and it was something the staff struggled to understand.

For Ashok, another boy in my class, tragedy seemed relentless. A few days after Ravi returned, Ashok's father was stabbed to death by his wife and she disappeared to escape getting caught by the police. The day before, he had murdered their only daughter for refusing to give him money to buy alcohol. After beating her unconscious and fearing she was dead, he poured kerosene on her and set her on fire to make it look like a kitchen accident. The police were investigating but we sometimes felt that these tragic events were treated as though they were ordinary occurrences in the villages and not something to be taken seriously. I often wondered if Ashok's mother ever thought of what would happen to her son now that he was without her. The gruesome killings dominated our conversation for days.

For two months after his return, Ashok took to sitting in the last row of the classroom. He barely spoke to anyone and did not join us in our pranks, like plucking coconuts from the gardens or sneaking into the kitchen to savor peanut butter. I had been close to him but now I hesitated to approach him, afraid of his newly developed short temper.

But one day, he took me by surprise by showing me his late sister's photograph. I stared into the dark face of a girl who wore pink lipstick, a red bindi on her forehead, and a string of jasmine flowers hanging from the long braid over her shoulder. Her small, bright eyes were just like Ashok's. 'She's beautiful,' I whispered. He was silent then, but later told me he had no regrets about his father's death. Ashok's story would haunt me for years.

Despite these tragedies and almost without recognizing it, I had begun to take my studies and other school activities seriously. Mathematics and science were still tough for me, but I did well in my favorite subjects—English, history, and environmental education. The daily schedule kept me so busy that my mind was fully occupied. I began to feel there were some things I was good at and no longer chafed at Aunty Shalini's control over me nor felt crushed by the pressure from my family. I felt confident that things would turn out right and there was nothing for me to fear. Little did I know how wrong I was.

The parent-teacher meeting at the end of my ninth grade year marked a sharp change in my life. DG had arrived from America a few days earlier than usual and was slated to address the parents. Mrs. Law had already briefed him on a number of sexual incidents that several girls had encountered while home for the holidays. By then, I had informed Mrs. Law of my grandmother's wishes for my future, just as Sheena had advised me to do.

During the parent meeting, DG addressed the issue of marriage. Speaking firmly, he said, 'I don't want you to distract your children with talk of marriage at this age. We want them to be well educated and then they will go on to college for further studies.' He waited to let this sink in. 'They should aspire to higher things.'

The parents nodded as if in agreement.

'We are not bringing up the children in Shanti Bhavan so you can marry them off early to someone in the village,' DG said in some irritation. It was with difficulty that he waited for the translations to conclude. There was another matter of equal concern to him. 'If I hear you are allowing men to make sexual advances towards your children, I will have you arrested. You are responsible for looking after your children, and these sorts of things can't go on. This has to stop.'

By now, the parents knew DG well and trusted whatever he had to say about their children. They wouldn't show any disrespect towards the man, no matter what he said. Crowding around him to express their gratitude, they often embarrassed him by touching his feet and kissing his hands.

After the meeting, the blind parents of a little pre-school boy were carefully escorted to DG by a residential staff member. Everyone watched attentively as the father said, his voice cracking, 'We have never seen our child but now we see him through your eyes.'

Holding back tears, DG reached out to hold the man's hands. 'One day you will see light through your son.'

Tears filled my eyes as I watched them.

DG went around amongst the parents reassuring them that their children were growing up smart and that they would succeed in life.

The parents filed out of the school building and clustered

together in a flurry of tense whispering. DG's warnings were not new to them, but there was a feeling of collective guilt and some resentment after being openly reprimanded. Everyone then went to the dining hall for a quick lunch before meeting with their children.

A short while later, Aunty Shalini instructed me to go to my classroom because my grandmother was waiting there. She assured me she would speak to Grandmother about forcing me to marry my uncle.

When I got to see my grandmother, I greeted her respectfully, but she was stony-faced. 'How are you, Grandmother?' I asked, anxious to break the tension.

She nodded, her coldness towards me clearly visible.

Aunty Shalini and other staff members seated themselves at the large table facing us both.

'Shilpa came back from home and told us you want her to marry your son,' Aunty Shalini said politely in Kannada. I struggled to keep my eyes down and still see Grandmother's reaction.

I stole a quick glance. To me, the expression on her face read, *What is the problem? What wrong have I done?* Whatever her thoughts were, she sat straight-faced while Aunty Shalini told her everything I had said and everything I wanted her to hear.

I fidgeted with my hands in my lap and listened to Grandmother relate how affectionately she had looked after me for the many years my mother was away. But she still hadn't replied to the question.

Aunt Shalini said, 'We feel it is much too soon for Shilpa to think of marriage. You mustn't force—'

'What? I have never spoken of marriage to her. Never,' Grandmother said.

I was shocked. 'Grandma, don't you remember that day in the house when you and Grandfather told me you wanted me to marry Naresh Mama?' My fidgeting was becoming uncontrollable.

'I don't know why this ungrateful child is lying to you. She is going to break my heart.'

'Grandmother! You know you—'

'Shut your mouth.'

With unflinching certainty, Grandmother again denied ever having spoken about marriage. I couldn't understand how she could be so blatantly deceitful. But I didn't dare to speak further, afraid to contradict her. Having long been taught in school to be truthful and face the consequences of my mistakes, it baffled me to see Grandmother spouting lies.

The aunties seemed baffled by the contradictory information. They left us alone in the room to spend time together—something I was not looking forward to. I sat silently biting my nails, fearing what my grandmother might say. I was in no mood to listen to her and wanted to leave the room.

'Why did you tell them that *mama* kissed you?' she asked angrily, referring to Uncle Naresh, breaking the heavy silence between us. 'Is he your *mama* or some stranger on the road?'

Grandmother's face was full of fury. It was clear she felt insulted. Trying to regain her composure, she wiped away tears with her sari. She got up from her seat, turned around, and left the room without even saying goodbye, much less kissing me.

I wanted to run to Grandmother and tell her I would stay with her forever and look after her, yet I couldn't move. That was certainly not the life I preferred, I knew. I sat there alone, ashamed that I had betrayed her but unsure whether I had done anything wrong. *Could truth be less important than loyalty?*

I raced back to the dorm, tears streaming down.

Some parents perched on the pathway looked up, confused to see me crying on this happy day. I was ignoring Grandmother's words that a girl must always hide her weakness in the presence of others. I didn't want to think about her anymore, and I certainly didn't want to abide by any rule she had taught me.

That night I wept for a long time, devastated at having caused so much unhappiness for Grandmother and feeling terribly lonely myself. I was the betrayer in her eyes, who had shamed the family and presented her as a liar. But I felt betrayed by her too—a family member I considered a hero. We had parted as enemies and she might never want me to stay with her again. Since that day, whenever I thought of home, I felt no one there really cared about me. My grandparents had become indignant towards me, my father had mostly been indifferent, my mother had been so far away for so long she seemed unreal, and my sister was off in her own world filled with dark secrets. I wanted to live like Sheena who didn't have to face the burdens of an unstable home.

The two worlds I lived in had become overwhelmingly irreconcilable. I found myself stuck between them, tossed mercilessly from one to the other. When one set of values and traditions confronted the other, a meeting of the minds was out of the question. The values with which I was being brought up at school—truth, honesty, and a strong sense of right and wrong—were drawing me away from the very people who had the most natural claims on my affections.

Nothing seemed right. Everyone in my family, including myself, was betraying another, and there was a huge price to pay for it. The nights were the hardest. Thoughts of Amma, Grandmother, and everyone else made it impossible to sleep. I'd lie awake crying softly under the blanket. At times Amuda, the classmate who slept in the bed next to mine, would wake up hearing me cry, and would come over to my bed and be with me.

Like my mother, I desperately wanted to escape. When she was very depressed, she tried to kill herself. The first time I felt the blade against my own wrist, the pain was quick but sharp. The sight of blood felt real and something in me began to feel real too. I wanted more, but was frightened.

Many times, I breathlessly climbed the huge rocks on the hill facing the ravine, or the water tower standing several stories high, and wished to jump—to feel what it meant to fly. I imagined wind rushing up under my wings, ripping away my troubles as I sailed over everything beneath me, unshackled. I wanted to touch the sky but my feet were chained to the reality of the ground.

Just like Amma, I never found the strength to carry out my fantasies. Probably there was still a part of me that hoped for some meaning, some purpose, to my life.

I just had to find it.

Chapter Twelve

The Unexpected

I recognized it as soon as I saw it on Mrs. Law's face. Her usual composure was absent, leaving her stiff, as if frozen. Her thoughts seemed to be elsewhere as she stood in silence, waiting for everyone to settle down at the morning assembly.

It was fear, no doubt. It couldn't be anything else. I knew that look well by now, having seen it on my father's face when the landlord arrived to collect his dues, and in my grandmother's eyes when Grandfather was out of work for days.

Mrs. Law was fighting whatever was on her mind, struggling to keep her small figure tall in front of us on the stage. 'Children and staff, I have very bad news,' she began, straining to hide the distinct quiver in her voice. 'There is a possibility that Shanti Bhavan will shut down.'

A collective gasp of disbelief and cries of shock shook the room.

'A few days ago I received news from Dr. George that he has encountered severe financial setbacks back in the U.S. Supporting Shanti Bhavan has become difficult for him,' she said, ignoring the raised hands that instantly sprouted in the audience. 'Dr. George has asked that you go home for a longer vacation so the staff can have sufficient time to think over this situation.'

I tried to break the numbness in my body by shifting my position on the floor. It wasn't the kind of bad news we had heard on several occasions in the past—like water shortage or prolonged power cuts. We were used to being told whatever affected us; transparency was fundamental, even if it meant making us upset or frightened. But this was different. This felt like the end.

'If, by luck, Shanti Bhavan is able to continue, we may have to cut the eleventh and twelfth grades to save money.'

I immediately turned around to look at Sheena who was sitting two rows behind me, palm clamped over her mouth. Our eyes met in disbelief and I saw the same fear overtake her too. She was in eleventh grade waiting to continue into twelfth, just as I had been excited to enter the eleventh grade after the holidays. The thought that we could soon be separated was unbearably painful. *How could DG do this to us?* Would she be given away to another family? Would Rafil control her life again?

No one had expected anything like this. Aunty Shalini and Mrs. Ruth were openly sobbing, covering their eyes with their sari pallus. Shanti Bhavan had been their home too.

Mrs. Law waited for the commotion to die down. Taking a deep breath, she explained that Dr. George, upon arriving from America in a few weeks, would be discussing many options with her and other senior staff. We wanted to believe he might have some solution and that, no matter what happened, the school doors would not be slammed shut behind us.

Now, after upsetting Grandmother, I didn't even know if I would be welcome in my own home. Even worse, the idea of living permanently with my family was simply frightening. I wasn't familiar with rural life, nor was I fit to marry anyone from the village. I didn't know how to cook, wash, or serve a man. I had been taught to read, write, distinguish right from wrong, and form my own opinions—skills not valued in village life and unheard of in girls. There was no future to dream of. I felt cheated.

And what would happen to my classmates? After Sheena, my next thoughts went to Keerthi who competed with me when it came to writing English essays. I was secretly resentful of her writing skills and confidence in public speaking classes. But now, I would sacrifice anything to keep her in my life. I had seen her mother several times when she came to take Keerthi home for the holidays. She had worked in a quarry since she was young, cracking granite stones with a heavy hammer. Difficult circumstances had ground her down to a frail, gaunt figure. She had long been waiting for the day when her daughter would pull her out of her misery.

'Children, we are doing our best to find a solution,' said Mrs. Law, stemming my rush of concerns. Her assurance comforted me a little. The younger children seemed perfectly calm. Their chatter was all eagerness and enthusiasm, just as it would be on any other day. They hadn't understood anything except that they were going home for a longer holiday. The older ones filed out of the assembly hall wearing cloaks of silence, walking up the concrete stairs with eyes fixed dead ahead.

Until that moment, Shanti Bhavan had provided an oasis for us. We had taken it for granted; it was our place, our home, and our life. Now, without warning, our perfect world seemed set to shatter. I felt lost in what I couldn't comprehend.

The night before we left for home, Sheena and I sat outside our dorm on the cement rim of the pool. We didn't say very much to each other; I really didn't know what to say, and I sensed that Sheena didn't either. When it was time for us to go to sleep, I turned to her and forced a smile, 'Have fun in Kerala. Take care of yourself.'

Sheena turned and gave a brief nod, saying nothing. As she had nowhere else to go, it had been decided by Mrs. Law and the staff that Sheena would spend the vacation with Ms. Beena, the vice principal, at her home in Kerala.

'Do you think we'll come back?' I asked, twirling a long strand of hair that had come loose.

'I don't know,' she answered softly, refusing to meet my eyes.

'Will we see each other again?'

'I don't know.'

The next morning, we parted in tears. The children hugged each other and cried in an endless stream of goodbyes. All of us had shared our lives together from the age of four and, despite our silly quarrels, our bonds were very close. The thought that we might not see each other again was unbearable. We were afraid the holidays would bring news none of us wanted to hear.

My father came to pick me up, something he hadn't done in many years. He was in a somber mood and chose not to speak to me nor any of the other parents, all of whom had been briefed on Shanti Bhavan's financial crisis. He stood for a moment by my side, not meeting my eyes, stretching out the silence until it was vast enough to swallow the campus. Then we turned towards the gate.

The bus ride was painfully long. Appa didn't ask me any questions, as though somehow I were at fault for what was happening. All I could think about was what I would be doing in the village if I couldn't return to school.

As I got off the bus and walked home, the familiar sights and smells of my village—women carrying large pots of water on their hips, cooking smells and smoke escaping through the narrow windows of huts, and much more—did not bring the happy flutter it used to. I had not been home since my feud with Grandmother, and the thought of having to face her didn't do my nerves much good either. Appa simply left me outside my grandmother's house and walked away. He didn't even bother to talk to them or tell them the news about Shanti Bhavan. With Amma still away, I had no choice but to stay with Grandmother again. Living with Appa was not an option. I stood at the doorstep to her hut waiting for the next thing to happen.

Grandmother stood in the doorway, almost blocking it with her broad figure. 'I never want you to step foot in this house again. I was the one who brought you up and you did this to me?'

I tried not to cry, but tears ran down my cheeks.

I reached forward to hold her hand in mine in a gesture of reconciliation, but she pushed it away. 'Don't touch me.'

I knew I was expected to display remorse, but couldn't force myself to say I was wrong. I stood facing her silently for a while, then leaned forward to try again to take her hand.

She drew back instantly, her hand in the air. 'I want to slap you!'

I flinched. A hurricane was in the making, with dark clouds all around, but somehow it didn't break over my head. At last she sighed and dropped her hand to her side. Knowing there was no other choice, Grandmother gave in, and I stepped into her house.

Neighbors dropped by on their way to graze their cattle or work in the fields to find out if the rumors were true. The news had already spread among the villagers, and they wanted to know about the school's fate. Some comforted my father saying, 'God will not desert good people who are serving the poor.'

But others reiterated the foolishness of sending me away in the care of strangers. 'Didn't we tell you from the beginning this was a bad decision?'

I wanted to talk to Kavya, but she was too busy playing or stitching clothes for her plastic dolls. And even if I had, she would more than likely have laughed it off, happy I would no longer be the family's pride. There was no one else I felt comfortable confiding in.

As the days passed, my relationship with Grandmother thawed gradually. But there wasn't the same warmth as before. When Uncle Naresh was home, she treated me as if I were a nuisance and a traitor. Her son's presence constantly reminded her of the humiliation I had put her through.

Once when my uncle returned home drunk, Grandmother snapped angrily, 'This is your fault. He began to drink because of you.'

I was stunned. I wanted to shout back, but couldn't find my voice. My body tensed and a heavy guilt quickly overtook my anger.

'If you hadn't turned him away, he would have never gone to that ugly, dark Prema,' she continued, referring to a girl my uncle had taken a liking to, despite my grandmother's disapproval. Grandfather, on the other hand, was not bothered. Prema's family had cows and land and was prepared to give a small dowry.

'She is as black as that dog,' Grandmother spat, pointing at a stray that often roamed in front of the house. I hated the thought that someone could be ridiculed for a dark complexion. I had been taught at school never to treat anyone differently because of the color of their skin.

As it turned out, Prema's family soon heard about Naresh's drinking and disapproved the marriage. But that didn't help my situation with Grandmother. She constantly reminded me of the shame I had brought to her at Shanti Bhavan. 'You went running to them and where are they now?'

I remained silent, powerless to counter the bitter truth.

I kept my distance from Uncle Naresh and refused to be concerned about his feelings towards me. When he tried to create any intimacy, I ignored him, just as Sheena had advised me to.

As the threat of closure became more vivid, my chances of completing high school and going on to college were shrinking. Appa was terribly disheartened knowing he didn't have the means to educate me elsewhere. He rarely came looking for me or brought fruit from the woods, and stopped sending my brother to ask if I wanted anything. I sensed he was trying to avoid me.

'What will we do with her?' I overhead Appa saying to Grandfather, 'She doesn't even know enough Kannada to join the school here.'

Grandfather assured him they could talk to the priest and get me a job in the local school as an English teacher. 'She knows such good English,' he said, comforting Appa.

A few days into the vacation, I went to Appa before he left home to ask something that had been weighing on my mind for days, 'What will I do if they come for me?' I was referring to Muniappa's men who had threatened to take me away if Appa failed to repay the debt soon.

Since at this point I doubted whether Appa cared what happened to me, I wasn't sure he would even reply. He surprised me by responding with a confident smile, 'Do you think I would let them?'

I wasn't as confident as he sounded. 'Did you give them the money?' I asked.

He looked triumphant. 'Yes! The entire loan is repaid.' The debt had multiplied now to three times what Appa had borrowed nearly a year ago. I knew the interest was high but didn't realize how much debt had accumulated.

When I told Grandmother the good news, instead of being happy or at least relieved, she turned furious. 'Do you think he would give anything to save you?' she asked in disgust. 'I spoke to your mother, and she sent us the money. Your grandfather went with Appa to Gunna's house and repaid the debt.'

Relieved of the danger of being taken away, I roamed with my escorts more freely in the evenings. Until now, I had been just a visitor to my village, not having to live through much of what others endured every day. Walking along the muddy road that bore no name, and observing the lives of those who lived in the shabby huts on either side, a sense of my own insignificance overwhelmed me. My parents gave life to me in hardship, and now years later, not much had changed for them. If I were to go back to my roots, to look for anything redeeming, I would find only the painful providence that had engulfed my family from the beginning. Now, without Shanti Bhavan, that was likely to continue for me as well.

I felt aloof and lonely as the days dragged on. Most of the time I kept to myself in the hut, barely speaking because I didn't feel close enough to anyone to confide in them and my lack of fluency in Kannada made it a struggle to articulate my thoughts.

One afternoon when Grandmother had gone out and I was home alone watching television, the two men who had earlier approached me in the market appeared in an auto rickshaw. One of them came rushing into the hut and, without a word, caught hold of my arm and tried to drag me out. I struggled as hard as I could and screamed loudly enough for the neighbors to hear. The midwife who lived across the street heard my cry for help and came out shouting. The man quickly dropped his hold on my arm and fled in the auto rickshaw. Terrified, I collapsed on the ground, my hands trembling uncontrollably. The woman who rescued me helped me back inside and calmed me down, as I tried to explain through my tears what had happened. After she left, I locked the door from inside and sat against it, afraid they might return and try to break it open.

That evening when I told Appa what happened, he said, 'I will kill them.' He headed straight for the shop where the two men were often found.

I didn't want Appa to get into a fight. I wanted him to warn them to keep away or file a complaint with the police. I waited anxiously for Appa to return and, when he did, he told me they were hoodlums from the neighboring village and I would no longer see them around because he had scared them to death. 'I warned them. Remember, if I can chase elephants, I can chase human beings too,' he said, laughing.

I felt slightly reassured.

'Always keep the door locked from the inside whenever you are alone,' he said and left me.

The weight of a long month of anxious waiting was crushing me, and I began to feel like a groundhog in hibernation. I kept myself busy, helping Grandmother cut vegetables, sweeping the floor and washing vessels. She tried to teach me how to cook rice and ragi, as if I were being trained for a life in the village. I cleaned the grain on a straw tray, carefully removing tiny stones and black insects from it. But when I stirred the thick ragi paste with a heavy ladle, the pot threatened to overturn. Watching my clumsy housework, Grandmother shook her head and said, 'What will you do after you marry?' I was useless as a girl.

I'd never stayed at home for more than a month at a time, and now found it difficult to adjust to my siblings. I couldn't bear to see Francis coming home after play and digging his hands straight into his dinner. When I complained to Grandmother that he hadn't washed his hands, she replied with a passive smile, 'Let him eat. He is a hungry boy.'

As if his uncleanliness wasn't enough, I had to sit next to him at every meal and listen to the awful sounds he made chewing with his mouth wide open. Once, unable to control my temper, I pushed my plate away and stormed off. I am not sure whether it was disgust or arrogance that made me so rude.

On happier days, Kavya would sit by my side and patiently teach me how to braid my hair into straight plaits or make flower garlands, even though I couldn't master the art of threading them properly. In the mornings, Kavya and Francis would take me along the mud track between the sugarcane fields as if I were a tourist in their village. While my siblings were quite comfortable walking barefoot, I was afraid of dirtying my sandals by inadvertently stepping on what had been left behind by early risers who had made the most of the unripe dawn.

I did relish the simplicity around me: bullock carts rumbling along the dusty road, frightened chickens fluttering away to a safer distance, young boys trying to collect honey from beehives using a flaming stick, and all those quiet details I hadn't fully appreciated. Stray dogs were everywhere, scavenging the litter thrown on the roadside the previous night. I was surprised to see women already at work in the fields, hunched over like four-legged animals, uprooting the weeds and throwing them into heaps. I stopped to listen to the folksongs they sang as they moved from one corner of the field to another, clearing all the weeds in their path. It was the common trait in these women that amazed me—their fierce unity in times of hardship, their relentless fighting spirit, and their humble acceptance of what little life had to offer them. I was discovering my village anew.

Despite the fun we sometimes had together, my siblings continued to treat me as an unwelcome visitor. When we fought over the TV remote or when I complained to Appa that Kavya wasn't doing her homework, my siblings would tell me to go back to my special school and leave them alone. Though I knew they didn't mean it, I couldn't help seeing myself as an outsider and that realization made me terribly sad. How would I ever fit in to a permanent life in the village? How would I find in myself the qualities those women in the fields had found?

When Uncle Christraj returned from work, he expected Grandmother to be at the door immediately to receive him. She would run around like a busy hen, fetching water for him to wash his hands before dashing to serve him dinner. Without a word, she would hand Kavya a small vessel filled with water for him to drink.

'Food!' he would bellow with the arrogance of a landlord, drawing Grandmother to his service like a magnet. There was no time to chat or rest; Uncle Christraj always returned home in a ravenous state, so food was to be served as soon as he walked in. He sat alone on the floor with the steel plate in front of him, hardly ever looking up.

I was no help when it came to serving him. 'What will she do in her husband's house?' he muttered, as I stood idly by.

Grandmother nodded in agreement and asked me to place the steel plate in front of him. I obeyed.

'She's pathetic,' he grumbled, just loud enough for me to hear.

Grandmother laughed. 'I guess she'll have to marry someone from America.'

The trouble was I knew they were right. Whether it was serving food or washing clothes and pressing them with the coal iron Grandmother and Kavya used expertly, I was of no use.

There was one thing I could do. In the mornings, I would walk Kavya and Francis to school, hurrying to get them there before the final bell. I would wait until my sister disappeared through the packed school entrance. I wanted Kavya to know I cared about her. It didn't occur to me then that she wasn't happy with the way things were for her. I had rationalized that since I was older than she was, it was my privilege to be first in everything, but lately I was beginning to see the unfairness. I resolved to look after her when I started earning, and I told her so but she didn't react. She would never sacrifice her pride to accept my help. But sometimes after school I would tell her stories of people and places I had read about in books and seen in movies, and her eyes would light up with pleasure.

With both our parents away at work and Grandmother busy with household chores, I once attended, as Kavya's guardian, a parent-teacher meeting at her school. Young as I was, no one took me seriously at first, but when I conversed with the teacher in fluent English, I drew surprised looks from everyone in the room. My sister's face was aglow and I knew that, at least in that one moment, she couldn't have been happier with me and was thankful for my schooling at Shanti Bhavan.

Unlike me, Kavya was popular in school and with the neighborhood children. She loved joking with them and playing tricks to make them laugh. Often, she'd bring little children to our house and serve them the food prepared for us that morning. I'd scold her for being so generous, saying that there wasn't enough in the house to feed the whole village, but she'd ignore me and walk away as though she hadn't heard me. Often neighbors called her to their homes to sing songs from Kannada films. She had a sweet, high-pitched voice that charmed even the most critical listener.

As days turned into weeks with no word from Shanti Bhavan, I lost myself in an imminent celebration in the village. A neighbor and friend from childhood, Sudha, was getting married. I hadn't attended a marriage before, so was fascinated. But there was nothing much for me to do except watch the commotion created by the villagers who attended—the men who stood around joking with each other, and the women who went about cooking, cleaning, and decorating.

'What work does he do?' I heard someone ask about the bridegroom.

'He is a painter,' another replied. 'He paints rich people's homes.'

'Why did you agree to give her to him?' one woman asked Sudha's mother.

'Both he and his mother came to our house and made the proposal,' she replied.

Another woman whispered to her friend, 'The whole village knows he already has a married woman as a mistress.'

'His parents didn't ask for a dowry,' Sudha's mother explained defensively. 'He is our distant relative. His parents are very thankful.'

I watched the bridegroom sitting on a stool in his underwear outside the hut, surrounded by older relatives rubbing turmeric onto his hands and legs as his father looked on proudly. It was a custom to put turmeric all over the bride and groom on the eve of their wedding.

The painter is being painted, I thought.

Meanwhile, Sudha sat in the next room waiting for a group of women to cover her with the yellow paste. She was stripped down to an inner skirt tied just above her breasts. Her long, thick braid had been rolled into a high bun. I looked on from a distance as women dipped their hands in the turmeric paste and rubbed it onto her gentle face.

As her parents exchanged plates of tobacco leaves and fruit with the groom's family, Sudha stared shyly at her husband-to-be and then quickly lowered her gaze. They were about to be married, but she hadn't really met or spoken to him.

'I was only sixteen,' an elderly relative remarked to me. 'Your grandmother was fourteen when she got married.'

'Oh, look how shy she is,' one woman said, nudging another. Sudha looked embarrassed—how could she not be? She was sitting, with lowered eyes and tight lips, almost naked in front of all these staring women and worse, was going to be married to a man who was a complete stranger to her.

As for me, I found the thought of being the center of attention exciting. Now that my dreams of a fancy wedding to an educated man were fading, I imagined Amma and Grandmother tearfully dressing me up in a grand sari for my wedding, which would be held in the old stone church. It probably wouldn't even matter whether I loved the groom, I thought; the exciting part of marriage was its ritual.

Sudha's wedding was a temporary respite, but once the ceremony was over, I struggled. I kept myself busy teaching English to my siblings, and they in turn taught me Kannada. Kavya helped me brush up on the slang and profanity that were once a part of my vocabulary. It made us both laugh. Apart from the household chores I had by now learnt to do, like cutting vegetables and fetching water from the bore well, I didn't have much to occupy my time.

I once again began to enjoy Uncle Naresh's company. I would run into him frequently in the evenings when he returned from work, and gradually began to see in him a good friend, someone to whom I could express my feelings, someone who would listen. We often sat side by side outside the house, talking late into the evening.

Even in the midst of wondering whether I would ever see Shanti Bhavan again, or perhaps because of it, I found particular pleasure in describing my school life, and Uncle Naresh let me talk. I tried to make him see what it was like watching the performances of the Broadway artists who frequently visited us. I told him about the Western movies I had seen recently, *My Fair Lady* and the *Harry Potter* movies, and recounted stories from the novels I had read. It was always the adventures of my many heroes that interested him most. I hummed the songs I had learnt in the choir, tried to describe the tribal Indian folk dances we performed, and excitedly told him about the treats the school offered on special occasions: like macaroni and cheese for dinner. I told him that for a long time I had been preparing for a good college education and a financially independent future. For some reason, I wanted him to understand the world I had been living in, a place difficult for him even to imagine.

I talked to him about wanting to go to college, to travel to America, and one day perhaps to study at Harvard or Oxford. Those names meant nothing to him, but they were my dreams, and I wanted him to know why, despite my genuine affection for him, I could not embrace a village life as his wife. I expressed my fears about losing what I had come to love most. He always listened quietly and always seemed to feel empathy for my concerns. Even though I had rejected him and hurt him, he was the only one in my family who understood how frightened I was.

Once, in a spontaneous outpouring, I began to describe the kind of man I desired as a husband and father for my children. I expected to be able to select the man I would marry, one who would be compatible with my personality. 'He must be well educated. He shouldn't be into any bad habits like drinking—' I stopped abruptly, chagrined, realizing I was describing someone who was everything he wasn't.

Grandmother kept expecting me to have a change of heart. One day she exploded, 'You will marry him, or I will haunt you as a ghost after I die! You will never escape my curse for seven generations of your rebirths.' I flinched at the sharpness of her words and the fury in her voice, but refused to give in. Seeing no fear on my face, she slowly began to shrink, resigned, before bitterly declaring to Grandfather, who was equally unhappy with me, 'Leave it to God. If He has written it on their foreheads, then they will marry.'

Grandmother's words terrified me. I was afraid of my destiny. With no news from school, I began to lose hope that Shanti Bhavan would survive. Some evenings I'd sit in silence alone by the tamarind tree and think about my classmates and friends, especially Sheena and Keerthi, wondering how they were dealing with the uncertainty about our future. My mind took me beyond the dark hills in the distance, bringing joyful reminders of my school that was now only a beautiful dream. Sometimes I wondered if Shanti Bhavan had really existed. It seemed so translucent, distant, and now quickly tumbling out of reach. I tried to clutch it to my chest, but it only slipped away faster, like dry sand running through a child's fingers. This was a storm I could not brave, and there was no shore in sight.

If I were to resign myself to a life in the village, I would have to make peace with Grandmother and marry her son. There was nothing else I could do. Life had come to a standstill. Without knowing what to expect from marriage, I tried to convince myself it might not be so bad after all. I resolved to reconcile myself to this future, as fate might have inscribed it.

Chapter Thirteen

A Family Affair

My hands would turn damp and clammy by morning, sticky with sweat from another night spent reliving the same nightmare: the tall gates to my school closing for the last time; the security guard clamping the heavy lock into place. The days spin fast, and even though I'm not there, I can feel the ending—rust steadily creeping into the dark iron, eating away at the majestic entrance. Reddish-brown dust blows through the empty classrooms, blanketing the very chairs I had sat on. I watch helplessly, rooted to the spot. The stillness of the place is all that is left. I wake up panting, eyes wide open. I find myself in my grandmother's hut, staring at the familiar patterns of coconut leaves on the ceiling. I wipe the sweat from my brow and inhale deeply.

When days had turned into weeks and still there was no news to give me the slightest hope of returning to Shanti Bhavan, I slowly resigned myself to accept the only choice left—what my family offered me. One afternoon when no one was at home except Grandmother who was taking her usual mid-day rest, I looked at her, frightened, longing for an expression of kindness. Mustering my courage, I sat beside her mat and said simply, 'I will marry Naresh Mama when I turn eighteen.' My voice was soft; there was no exuberance, only submission.

At first she was shocked, then suspicious. She sat upright and exclaimed, 'I can't trust you. You change your color like a chameleon.'

Of course there was no reason why Grandmother should understand my sudden change of heart; I didn't understand it myself. I had rejected her wishes and shamed her before the school authorities. I begged her forgiveness without really meaning it, just as my father often did when a moneylender demanded that he repay a debt. I sat with my head bent, silent, as she showered me with a torrent of insults.

Until now, Shanti Bhavan had been there to save me, but now, without it, I was at the mercy of my family and, if I was to live among them, I simply had to accept whatever life they would let me have. That evening when no one was watching, I slipped away to the nearby fields to be alone. Perched on a tall haystack in the middle of a field, I took in the stillness of the landscape around me. It didn't offer me any tranquility; even the gentle breeze blowing against my cheek couldn't bring comfort. I did not feel the breeze on my skin. My mind was elsewhere. I was hearing the sounds I had grown up with in the world of Shanti Bhavan—lively music from the radio in the morning, happy chatter after classes, and Sheena's shrill laughter as I chased her around the playground in games of tag. How was I to silence those sounds that were so much a part of me?

I knew I could not be content living with Uncle Naresh in the village but I was determined to go ahead and marry him if that was the only option left for me now. Torn between despair and anger, I tried to tell myself I was not to be blamed for my change of mind.

The shrinking sun in the west signaled it was time to return home before someone panicked and rounded up others to look for me. The last thing I wanted was for neighbors to think I was a problem for my grandparents who did so much to look after me. I carefully slid down the haystack, and walked back towards the brightly lit village.

I told myself my uncle had always been sweet to me, and tried to believe he would remain so after our marriage. I pictured him in the role of my husband—physically strong to protect the family, playful with my future children, loving and kind to me.

I wanted to make a beginning to the new life. I would stand by the door and watch the road like a dutiful wife, waiting for Uncle Naresh to arrive in the evening after work. I would hand him a steel pitcher of water to wash his hands and feet before stepping into the house. During meals, to everyone's surprise, I would be the one to serve him, sitting by his side to attend to his orders for a second helping. Grandmother couldn't have missed any of my gestures towards him; she took notice of everything I did and, in her own way, communicated that she was pleased. Both my grandparents were in good spirits when we all ate our dinner together. When the family gathered for an evening prayer in front of the portraits of Jesus and Mother Mary, Grandmother once again gave me a kiss on my forehead. By the gentleness in his eyes and the slight smile that tugged the corner of his mouth, I knew my uncle, too, was pleased. Our family was united and happy at last.

Not long after, my mother returned from Singapore to attend to Kavya's first Holy Communion. After the church ceremony, I spent time in the company of my uncle, taking a walk along the paddy fields. He seemed happy to have me around him and patient with my excited chatter.

The next day, my mother asked me to join her at my grandmother's house to meet some guests—two women and a young girl—who had come to visit the family. I found them seated on a mat spread on the floor, with a plate filled with tobacco leaves and bananas set out before them. Uncle Naresh was seated next to my grandmother while I settled in a corner. I had never seen these two people before and wondered why they were here.

The girl appeared no older than fourteen. She appeared frightened and looked up to make eye contact with my grandmother only when she was addressed. She seemed lost among this gathering of adults whispering to each other about apparently serious matters. At first it seemed neither she nor I had anything to contribute to the discussion that was taking place until, as the conversation between the elders progressed, it became clear she was being considered as a wife for Uncle Naresh!

I couldn't understand why my family was thinking of her when I had told Grandmother I would marry him. Perhaps they thought I didn't mean it or might change my mind. I didn't dare to clarify myself.

A fierce brew of jealousy and anger surged in my bloodstream. *How can he live with a stranger?* I recalled the good times we had shared: the jokes he told me, his loving smile, and the run-and-catch we played around the house. Now, after wanting to marry me, he was considering another girl!

I couldn't bear the idea of this girl lying beside him every night, being touched by him, calling herself his wife, and having his children. The jealousy I felt towards her consumed me, but I didn't want to show it. Accepting my indifferent look as reflective of my true feelings, Amma turned to me and whispered, 'She hasn't gotten her period yet. As soon as she does, she'll marry your mama.' The casual way in which she spoke about his marriage to the innocent girl only deepened my irritation. It angered me that no one asked the girl if she wanted this marriage. Clearly she did not have a say in a matter as important as her own marriage.

Glancing at my uncle, I caught his eye and frowned at him. He sat with his head bowed as though he were going through some sort of punishment. I was waiting for him to sit up and announce that he loved me and wanted to marry me. Instead he remained motionless, not giving me the luxury of knowing his thoughts.

As the smiling guests drifted off, Grandmother was telling everyone how good the girl's family was, as though they had known each other for years. 'The father had a good job,' Grandmother explained. 'He was a mason, but went away with another woman.'

Meeting this new girl made my skin crawl and triggered an intense yearning in me. I wanted my uncle to tell me how badly he needed me, and to assure me that I was more important to him than the girl he had just met.

At last the night fell silent. I knew for certain that everyone was asleep. I sat up, trying to muster courage, preparing to move to the next room where Uncle Naresh was lying. My legs felt weak struck by a sudden fear, but I needed to be sure of him. I craved intimacy with him, to let him touch my body and make me feel special. I needed a sign from him that he still loved me and not the girl my grandparents had chosen for him. After all, I was prepared to marry him.

The sound of my own breathing broke the silence. Kavya shifted in her sleep. I waited a minute, careful to make sure she didn't sense an abrupt emptiness beside her. Still terrified, I made my way over the pillow and across the mat.

Knowing old people's sleep to be as fragile as thin glass, I looked in my grandparents' direction. I saw no movement, so assured myself they hadn't heard me. I bent down and, with shaking hands, tried to remove the anklets that clinked as I walked. But untying them in the darkness turned out to be impossible. I stood up and tiptoed slowly ahead, counting each step and making sure I didn't bump into anything.

I slipped into the next room where my uncle was sleeping. It was gently illuminated by a tiny bulb over the portrait of Jesus. I could vaguely make out Naresh lying on his stomach. I didn't know what it would be like being alone with him in his bed.

I made my way to his cot and sat down beside him, remaining still for a moment to catch my breath before gently touching his feet to rouse him from sleep. Opening his eyes with a baffled expression, he sat up. Even in the near darkness, I could see his surprised look. We stared at each other, afraid. Then he whispered, 'Go back.'

I didn't move. I wanted to obey and not obey at the same time.

He gestured for me to leave. 'You are not in my heart,' he said softly, placing his hand on his chest and shaking his head. The sound of his heavy breathing echoed in my ears.

I didn't want to believe him. *He is lying,* I thought. I was sure of it. I lay down on one side of the cot. In a moment he turned his back to me. Silence was broken only by the sound of our breathing. *Will he push me out? Doesn't he want me?*

Suddenly he turned to me and kissed me. I put my arms around his neck. His tongue pried my mouth open. Gently pressing my shoulders down, he rolled onto me. I had expected his weight to crush me, but it did not. I was overjoyed that he wanted me and didn't think about what might happen next.

His lips stayed on mine as his hand softly sought my body in the dark. He lifted my salwar top and bra, and caressed my breasts. My anklets clinked against each other once, freezing me again, but the sensation of his touch overwhelmed me.

I closed my eyes and held my breath as his lips trailed downward. He kissed the hollow of my neck, and then the wide gap between my small breasts. The sensation was intoxicating.

He stopped.

I tensed as his fingers slid down to remove the string knot fastening my salwar pant. No man had ever touched me there, and I realized in that moment I couldn't allow him to either. Despite the overpowering sensation and the intense anticipation I felt, a feeling of guilt consumed me, turning my body numb. I secured the knot with one hand, refusing to let him loosen it, and held his hand tightly with the other.

I could tell he was aroused and wanted more. He tried to free his hand from my grip, but I clamped down tighter. I knew it was wrong to go further. He pulled his hand away and sat up on the edge of the cot.

In the dim light, I could see him removing his pants. I quickly adjusted the bra over my breasts and pulled my salwar top down. Fully clothed and fully covered, I felt safer. And then he climbed on top of me again. I closed my eyes and held him tight against my body, not letting him move and not wanting to let go. Though afraid, a part of me was happy to feel how badly he needed me.

I let him remain on top of me and that was all I was going to allow him. I assured myself there was nothing wrong with what I had done. After all, Uncle Naresh was the one my family had initially chosen for me to marry, and no one would object to our intimacy.

But then he began again to try to push my hand away, struggling to untie the knot to my pant string. I struggled to resist him.

Suddenly, a small boy appeared at the doorway, crying. A relative living nearby had left her two-year-old son Dinesh with my grandmother that night. Each time her husband returned home drunk, she would bring the child to us where he would be safe from the inevitable violence in her home.

I jumped up.

Panicked, my uncle hissed, 'Go, quickly.'

I was certain my grandparents would wake up to the sound of the little boy crying for his mother. I straightened my salwar, fearing the boy might have seen something he shouldn't have.

'I want my amma,' the little boy wailed sleepily. I rushed to pick him up in my arms. My heart raced in fear but I tried to calm myself with the thought that if anyone were to wake up to see me in my uncle's room they would think that I had awakened to comfort Dinesh. To my surprise, however, no one even noticed. I couldn't understand how Grandmother wouldn't have heard the child's cry, and wondered if they were only pretending to be asleep.

I carried the boy outdoors, deciding to drop him off at his house, a few yards away. All was quiet outside except for a group of men who had gathered to purchase liquor outside Ann-Mary's shop. I snuck through the shadows on the road, hastily crossing the gutter to get to the boy's one-room hut and banging on the door to wake his parents. I didn't wait to answer their questions. I left the boy with them, stepped into the darkness of the night, and ran. Re-entering Uncle Naresh's part of the house, I stopped by his cot, trying to decide whether I should go back to him.

I could still feel the sensation of his urgent touch. I stood still, watching him.

He was fast asleep, sprawled on his stomach as though nothing had happened.

In a moment, I retreated. Walking on my toes like a thief, I reached my spot on the mat next to Kavya and quickly lay there almost lifeless. I couldn't control the pounding of my heart.

So much had happened in such a short time. I grew worried that my grandparents would shout at me for taking the boy home without informing them, so I woke Grandmother up and whispered, 'I took Dinesh to his house. He was crying for his mother.'

Grandmother rose, rubbed the sleep from her eyes, and surveyed the room. The disturbance awakened Grandfather as well. Both went over to Uncle Naresh's room to make sure the little boy was not there.

'I took him home,' I repeated.

'Who asked you to leave the house at this hour?' Grandmother asked sharply.

My uncle appeared to be fast asleep, but I could tell he was pretending.

I was about to return to my room when Grandfather bent down to pick up something. 'Whose chain is this?' he asked, holding up an anklet that had been lying near Uncle Naresh's feet. My hand sprang to my left ankle; it was bare. Trying to be casual, I answered, 'It's mine, Thatha.' I prayed Grandmother had not noticed the nervous quiver in my voice. 'Kavya and I were sitting on the cot earlier. It must have fallen off then.'

Not waiting for my grandparents to question me further, I quickly turned around and returned to my place on the floor. With my back to my grandparents, I pretended to fall into a deep sleep.

Come daylight, my eyes burned and my head ached. My innocence seemed lost forever, and I dreaded to see myself in the mirror. The pleasure I experienced in the night quickly mutated into crippling guilt and fear.

Unable to bear the suspicious looks Grandmother was casting my way, I quickly folded the mat, picked up the pillow, stacked them near the door, and rushed outside. I was just about to reach the road when the very last person I wanted to see came running after me.

'Well, girl, what happened last night?' Uncle Naresh teased. His words made me feel dirty, and I couldn't look at him. I hurried away towards my mother's house. He wanted me badly, I was sure, and suddenly there was an excruciating, half-formed thought in my head that that was probably all I had wanted to know. I was certain that I didn't want him that way anymore.

It was strange to see that everything around me was the same as always when I felt that everything had changed. The milk boy was already on his usual morning rounds. A man was herding his cows towards the fields. A little girl was sitting on her doorstep waiting for her mother to walk her to the woods that served as the toilet. Ann-Mary stood outside her house, her seven-month-old daughter nestled against her sagging breasts. Her first daughter, now old enough to walk on her own, was playing near her mother's feet. I remembered the sight of the men gathered around her house the night before. There she was, once a schoolgirl, then a street urchin dancing for men, now an unwed mother feeding her children by selling alcohol to drunkards. Suddenly, it hit me that I too could end up like her—bulging belly visible above her sari, two daughters to care for with very little money at hand, and no one to turn to but gawking drunkards.

What are you doing with your life, Shilpa? I couldn't muster the strength to answer.

I didn't know myself any more. All I wanted was to return to school and re-enter a world where there was always hope for redemption even for a sinner like me. Here, it was a comfortless existence, an illusion.

The men outnumbered the women among the small groups of families moving in a slow march towards the towering hills in the distance. The women carried on their heads bulging bundles containing a few items of clothing and cooked food wrapped in paper. They walked behind their husbands and other male members of the family who took the lead. An unusual silence and a strange sense of solidarity surrounded them. I watched in awe as their figures soon turned into one blurry silhouette, making their way towards whatever they were in search of, guided by an unknown power.

Amazed, I asked Aunt Maria where the groups were headed. She explained that this was a pilgrimage the villagers made every year to a holy site in Northern Karnataka where, hundreds of years ago, a poor farmer digging in his fields stumbled upon a statue of Mother Mary. After the discovery, the deity is said to have appeared to him in a dream and instructed him to construct a church on the site. Since then, Christians from all across South India flock to this place in the months of April and May to seek the goddess's blessings, make offerings, and pray for miracles. Some say those prayers come true.

'The journey is always difficult but our faith keeps us going,' Grandmother interjected, referring to the four days and nights of heat and rain the pilgrims endured as they travelled on foot through rough, dry terrain and thickly forested areas where there was always a danger of being attacked by wild animals. 'Your grandfather and I made the trip together in the first year of our marriage. When your mother was suffering with appendicitis, your grandfather went to that church and prayed to Our Lady. Otherwise, your mother would have died,' Grandmother said, her voice suddenly choked.

Until this moment I had not had a very clearly formed belief in the existence of invisible powers, but now, something about the rigid piousness of the people of my village made me wonder. Grandmother said that all her happiness in life came from blessings she received from that pilgrimage. She had wanted to make the journey again, but was forced to stay home and look after her young children.

I had been avoiding Grandmother since that night with Uncle Naresh, but now the desire to connect with her and seek her affection filled me again. 'Who is going from our family this year?' I asked.

'Your grandfather and Naresh Mama will be leaving with another group tomorrow,' she replied.

The thought that Uncle Naresh was also going made me pause. I wanted to avoid him but I too wished to go. 'May I go with them, Grandmother?' I asked. This sacred adventure was something I wanted to experience but I had no point of reference, no idea what it would be like. It reminded me of the trips to the zoo we had taken during my childhood days at school.

Grandmother scowled at me. 'You're not used to sleeping in forests at night or walking long distances in the hot sun.'

'I'm a big girl. I can take care of myself.'

'Shilpa, you aren't strong like us. You get a cold with the slightest change in the weather and you complain each time the food has a little extra chili powder in it. Do you really think you can tolerate this journey?'

I remained silent as her words hit a deep chord. Yes, she was right. I lacked the toughness and the innate resilience that every other member of the family possessed. I felt threatened by their strength and my undeniable vulnerability. The thought that I wasn't prepared for a life in the village scared me; for a moment, running away from home seemed the only option left.

Early the next morning, Grandfather and Uncle Naresh bid us goodbye at the wooden doorstep to the house. It made me nervous to picture them trekking through forests and running into wild boars, angry elephants, and poisonous snakes. Grandfather chuckled and said I was being dramatic. Grandmother handed them a bundle each containing all the food supplies and clothing they would need, and drew the sign of the cross on their foreheads.

'Please pray for me,' I whispered, giving Grandfather a tight hug and not telling him what I wanted him to pray for, knowing that he would not wish the same for me. I longed to return to Shanti Bhavan, to see Sheena and my classmates once again, and to feel at peace.

Grandfather kissed my cheek and nodded that he would. 'I will pray for the happiness of the entire family,' he said.

'A good idea,' I said and thanked him.

As I watched them walk away, little did I know my life was once again going to change in ways I had no control over.

A week later, Appa came running into Grandmother's hut calling my name. He had received a call from Aunty Shalini to bring me back to Shanti Bhavan that Sunday. I gasped in shock, closed my eyes tightly, and joined my palms in my lap, saying, 'Thank you, God!' over and over again. I was sure Grandfather had prayed for me on his pilgrimage. Was this really a miracle? Or would there be bad news waiting?

On the day of my departure, Grandmother seemed confused, her face unusually stiff. Believing the school to be permanently closed, she had not anticipated my going. She might have been thinking what was on my mind too: *Would Shanti Bhavan indeed survive or would I be sent home permanently?*

The bus sped past the church gate and the village graveyard. I put my head out the window and stared at the hills. They did not beckon to me, nor did I feel drawn to them. Everything that had happened during my long holiday seemed like a bad, ugly dream. A slight smile began to dawn as I set out upon my own pilgrimage of a very different kind.

On the bus, Appa seemed tense. 'Shilpa, will Shanti Bhavan be able to go on?' he asked. I didn't have an answer. I wanted to give us both hope, but I was just as anxious as he was.

Back on campus, all the staff, children, and parents were instructed by Ms. Nirmala and Ms. Ruth to gather in the school building. The fact that a special assembly was being held with everyone in attendance was in itself very alarming. When the chatter settled down, Aunty Shalini announced that Dr. George had arrived from America a few days before and wanted to address us all. She said nothing about the future of Shanti Bhavan.

Minutes later, DG walked through the main door with Mrs. Law and Mr. Jude. His footsteps, unlike before, were slow and unsteady. The parents rose immediately as a sign of respect as they always did. Embarrassed, he quickly gestured to them to sit down. Eager for the meeting to begin, everyone quickly settled down on the floor which was covered with thick hand-woven mats.

Ignoring the large armchair placed for him in the center of the stage, DG sat down on the concrete step in front of us. 'Hello, everyone. I am very happy to see all the parents. Hello, children.'

'Hello, Dr. George,' we answered in a lively chorus. Our voices were bright, but strained.

From my place in the corner of the hall, I watched DG closely, looking for clues about what he was going to tell us. There was no frown, nor any glimmer of tears, to give me a sense of what he was thinking and feeling.

His voice sounded the same as always but something was clearly amiss. He appeared to have aged considerably since the last time I had seen him. Bright streaks of grey in his hair and dark circles under his eyes gave him a sad, withdrawn look.

'I know what is on your minds. I must talk to you openly about what has transpired.' I leaned forward, not wanting to miss a word. This was the moment I had waited for all summer.

'In addition to my father's death, the past year has been difficult for other reasons,' he said. He had been in the States looking after his ninety-seven-year-old father who had recently passed away. He explained that, during this period, global stock markets had fallen suddenly and the price of houses in America had drastically gone down. 'I met with serious financial losses,' he said, then paused for a few moments to let the two staff members translate what was said into Tamil and Kannada for the benefit of nervous parents. I noticed heads nodding as though in understanding.

After waiting for the crowd to quiet down, DG continued, 'I am finding it difficult to meet all the needs of Shanti Bhavan. The school cannot be run as before.' My stomach knotted in fear. Wiping the sweat from his forehead, he said, 'My family has made some hard decisions.'

I held my breath. Was DG going to announce that the school was being closed immediately and our parents were to take us home after the meeting?

'You all know my eldest son, Ajit, right?' DG asked.

All the children answered in one voice: 'Yes, Dr. George.' I remembered spending time with Ajit when I was in the second grade during his short visit to Shanti Bhavan. I remember him as a big man, much taller than everyone else in the school, like the giant in *Jack and the Bean Stalk*.

'Well, he was working on a book, but decided to stop writing and start fundraising for Shanti Bhavan. We are reaching out to possible donors—relatives, friends, and well-wishers,' DG explained. 'Hopefully, this effort will succeed.' DG said plans were also underway to solicit the help of wealthy people in Bangalore and from other parts of the country.

The possibility of donors, though it was new to us, seemed encouraging.

'I have asked Vivek to shut down the vineyard and clear the banana farm within a week. We cannot afford to run it any longer.' Vivek, DG's second son, had been overseeing the farm adjoining Shanti Bhavan for the past fifteen months, having taken time off before his graduate studies.

The farm employed many families that had previously served landlords as bonded laborers. The workers were paid good wages and offered benefits to help them become independent and self-supporting. However, with high labor costs, the farm was far from profitable. The plan to close down something we had all enjoyed was sad, but I understood that it was necessary.

'It's a wise move to cut costs without delay,' DG said. 'I have borrowed a substantial amount of money from some of my close friends to keep things going for the time being. We must also try to reduce expenses. There are many things all of us can do, like turning off lights and not wasting water.'

My mind quickly began to run through more possibilities, a glimmer of hope dawning.

The meeting helped to raise everyone's spirits, and when it was over, I found Sheena and we embraced tightly. 'I was praying to God through the entire holiday to bring us back,' I whispered.

Over the next month or so, we saw and heard from DG at our daily assemblies and learnt more about the perilous financial situation of the school and how he was coping with the difficulties. Even though he put up a brave front, he couldn't fully hide his worries. When I was older, he told me that it was not the money he had lost in the financial crisis that hurt him most, but the thought of shattering our hopes for the kind of future he had promised us.

If we ever saw him tense or troubled, we too would grow anxious; he was our mirror for what lay ahead. For the most part, however, he managed to appear calm when he spoke to us, careful to shield us from his concerns.

At one of the assemblies, DG told us he was contacting many wealthy industrialists in the area to see if any of them would partner with him to run Shanti Bhavan. But all of us were worried about bringing in industrialists. Would they care about us the way DG always had?

A group of business executives from an organization in Hyderabad arrived the following Sunday. Staring out our dorm windows, we saw several serious-looking men being escorted around the campus. DG introduced us with pride to every visitor we encountered, always referring to us as 'my children.'

A few days later, word spread quickly that DG had returned from Hyderabad after another meeting with the industrialists and had called for an assembly that evening. As we walked down the stairs to the assembly hall we feared he was going to announce that Shanti Bhavan would be sold.

To our great surprise, DG informed us the school would not be partnering with the industrialists. Instead of feeling sad at not receiving their assistance, we felt relieved that Shanti Bhavan wouldn't be taken over by those who might not embrace the school's mission and who would, instead, simply view it as an investment. He told us that volunteers from abroad who had served in Shanti Bhavan in the past had mobilized some funds to supplement what the school already had from other sources—a contribution from DG's mother of all her life savings, loans from friends and relatives, and what remained of DG's own financial resources. The challenge now was to carry the momentum forward and win the support of many more donors. To this end, Ajit and his fundraising team would promote the school through its new website, newsletters, and events. For now, Shanti Bhavan would continue, but not without difficulty.

Our happiness and security hinged on money, and children and staff spent many a long evening discussing how we could cut expenses. If a child let the ceiling fan run too fast, others would remind him about the electricity bill. In time, no lights were left burning unless they were needed, water was used sparingly to reduce well-pumping time, and every pencil and scrap of paper was utilized to the fullest. At night classrooms were lit with candles, and we sat huddled close to each other, reading by dim, flickering lights.

On Sunday afternoons, we did community service: cleaning the grounds, washing our own clothes, pulling weeds, and sorting out storerooms. The number of garden staff had been reduced to cut labor costs, and it was decided that the children should take part in looking after the grounds. The boys would level the road after heavy rain that washed away top soil into the narrow gutters on both sides. Groups of children took turns to help wash dishes. Higher grade girls were moved to the dorm that housed small children so they could help the aunties in the evenings. With these and other minor adjustments, the school was able to carry on with a reduced support staff.

Each morning before self-study classes at 6:30 a.m., Aunty Shalini gathered all the upper-grade children outside the classrooms to pray together. Although most children were Hindu, there were also Christians and Muslims among us, but these differences didn't matter. None of us worshipped any particular God out loud when we said our prayers to save Shanti Bhavan; but, remembering the holy pilgrimage, I always prayed to Mother Mary, begging her to take care of DG and save Shanti Bhavan.

Our lives had changed in some ways with the uncertainty about our future. We were suddenly conscious of the cost of every resource. Yet, even with all our lingering fears, we were happier than ever before, united in doing whatever we could to save our school. As days passed and some sort of normalcy set in, I felt a glimmer of hope.

As for DG, he never let us see him looking sad, even on the day his father's ashes were buried. DG had returned to Shanti Bhavan carrying with him his father's remains in a box that seemed much too small for its burden, to be buried according to his father's last wishes, in a plot near the campus prayer hall. I wondered if he ever allowed himself to shed tears.

Chapter Fourteen

Reformation

'Discern,' she said. 'Stanza three, line six. Who can tell us what *discern* means?'

English literature was my favorite subject and Mrs. Law my favorite teacher. Normally, I seated myself in the front row, eager to get her attention. I relished her challenging questions and the thrill of receiving her compliments when my responses merited them. I worried that Mrs. Law thought Keerthi was a better student than I was.

But on this day, I sat quietly in the corner, not able to concentrate. My mind wandered over my time at home with Uncle Naresh and how I had succumbed to the pressures of my family. Every image was clear and every word fresh, plunging me back into the darkness of our hut and the stealthy steps I took that night—my anklets ringing as loudly as church-bells in my memory. There was no way I could overcome the shame I felt.

I had not yet revealed to anyone the ugly secrets of my vacation break. Even Sheena couldn't bring down the wall I put up. I avoided my classmates, keeping uncharacteristically quiet, feeling safer that way.

So when Sheena's boyfriend, Ajay, began to show an interest in me, it wasn't difficult initially to rebuff him. Of course I would never do anything to hurt Sheena. Still, he would greet me with a smile whenever he saw me, tell me how pretty I looked, and strike up conversations with me on trivial subjects like the weather and food.

And then, in the classroom one evening after the others had left for dinner, I let Ajay kiss me passionately. Only the sound of approaching footsteps forced me to pull away.

My heart raced in panic. My knees buckled at the thought of a staff member catching us together in the dark room. I knew I would be taken to Mrs. Law and DG, and the news would spread throughout the campus within hours. What frightened me most was the thought that Appa and Grandmother would somehow learn about it. Once again, in pursuit of affection and attention, I had allowed an impulse of the moment to land me in an untenable situation. To my relief, the footsteps faded away and I darted to the dorm without saying a word to Ajay, leaving him confused and disappointed.

The next morning, I was hyper alert, anxiously observing how everyone behaved towards me. I watched intently, scanning for quiet whispers or subtle glances across the classroom. After a while, nothing seemed amiss and I felt assured that Ajay had not told anyone and it would remain our secret. Yet, when I ran into Sheena in the dining hall, I couldn't bring myself to talk to her or even look her in the eye. The stinging realization that I had betrayed my best friend paralyzed me.

That evening I dressed up in an attractive skirt with a colorful flowery print to watch a play about our lives back at home that the children were putting up for a group of visiting British teachers. Ajay's performance as an alcoholic husband was impressive, and I sat in the audience staring at him with admiration. The memory of the previous evening was still fresh in my mind. When the play ended, I clapped till my hands hurt.

My excitement about Ajay was too big to put down. I rushed to talk to him backstage. 'Ajay, you were amazing,' I gushed. But, to my dismay, he passed me without so much as a glance. I stared as he headed straight to Sheena who was standing alone, waiting to go on stage. From her happy glow, I presumed he was telling her how beautiful she looked in the sari she was wearing as her costume for a dance.

Searing, irrational rage overtook me and, in that moment, I couldn't have despised anyone more. I felt terribly jealous of Sheena. Why did she always have everything that I didn't—the attention of a popular boy like Ajay, the entire staff's sympathy and love, and enviable beauty on top of it? Ajay was accustomed to girls falling for him easily, so what happened between us meant nothing. He probably didn't think I was pretty enough to pursue. My interest in him fused into intense loathing.

Now, back in class, Mrs. Law was staring at me as if she could see through me, bringing me back to the present with a jolt. I straightened myself in my chair. Fortunately, she didn't call on me for an explanation of the word 'discern'. She slowly shifted her gaze around the room, explaining, '*Discernment* is good judgment. Here, Browning distinguishes between true love and infatuation.'

Mrs. Law's description struck something deep in me. I didn't seem to have learnt any lessons from my past mistakes and I was continuing to bring shame upon myself. Certainly, I had not shown any discernment in being drawn to my uncle for the wrong reasons nor in cheating on my best friend. I had been behaving recklessly, with no regard for the consequences. I couldn't understand where I got the boldness to do such senseless things.

At that moment, a part of me wanted to burst out and tell everyone what I had done. The weight of my secrets hung like a millstone around my neck. My life had turned into a drama of lies and deception. But there was no way I could safely share my secrets with my classmates and Mrs. Law. I was afraid my friends would shun me, and Mrs. Law might decide that my promiscuous ways were a bad influence on the other girls and send me away from school.

My body felt dirty in the company of my classmates who had never been intimate with men, except for Kavina and Amuda who had shared kisses with their boyfriends. Unable to deal with my inner turmoil, I mustered the courage to confess to Sheena, bracing to face whatever was to come. I saw this as my only path to absolution, though I didn't have the slightest hope of forgiveness.

We arranged for a moment to talk alone that evening before dinner. The guilt was eating me alive. I found her waiting for me near the tall hibiscus bush by the steps to the dining hall, and I told her what I had done. 'Sheena, please forgive me. I am so sorry.'

I'll never forget her stunned look, her eyes wide in disbelief. She stepped back as if my presence repulsed her. I leaned forward to take her hand, but she shrugged me off.

'Sheena, please don't. It just happened. I'm sorry,' I begged, desperate with remorse. And then, without meaning to, I blurted out all the embarrassing details of the night I went to my uncle's cot and how out of control and miserable I felt later. 'I don't know what I'm doing. The last thing I want is to hurt you!'

The glow of the street lamp lit her face. She was crying. 'How could you?'

I tried to say something, but no words came quickly enough. She turned swiftly and was gone, not waiting to hear any more. I knelt on the stone pathway and dissolved into tears, not taking my eyes off my friend as she walked away. *What had I done?*

Suddenly, I saw her returning. I wiped my tears and stood up. She stopped in front of me, her face a crumpled mask of disgust. '*You* can do things with village boys, but *I* do things with boys in Shanti Bhavan.' She chose her words carefully, knowing that each one was like a hammer, shattering me.

Before I could ask her what she meant, she turned and walked away. *What is the difference? Am I good enough only for the village boys?*

The next morning as I was walking to my classroom after breakfast, I ran into a group of boys in the corridor chattering and laughing. I kept my head down. Suddenly one of the boys from Sheena's class called out, 'Shilpa, I'm impatient. When can *we?*'

The air rushed out of my lungs, my legs went weak, and my cheeks turned scarlet. *How could a boy say something like that to me?* Everyone within earshot seemed to understand what he meant and erupted in laughter. It was worse knowing I had brought it upon myself and now had to face not only Sheena's wrath but also this humiliation. But there was no point fighting back.

It was not much different with the girls. They aimed their cold stares at me with surgical precision throughout the day. They knew. Everyone was supportive of Sheena, taking pity on her for the double betrayal she had suffered from both her boyfriend and her best friend.

With each passing day, there was less hope of reconciliation and forgiveness from Sheena. Whenever we met, she would walk past without the slightest acknowledgment of my presence.

It was not a surprise that soon Aunty Shalini came to know the full story from Sheena, including everything about my uncle. I could barely keep pace with Aunty Shalini as she led me up the stairs to Mrs. Law's office. I followed her like a prisoner approaching her execution.

We arrived at a small room at the end of the corridor on the first floor of the school building. DG and Ms. Denny were waiting for me. 'Take your seat,' DG said, gesturing to the red-cushioned chair on his right. I hesitated never having sat next to him, but Ms. Denny's stern nod left me no option. I took my seat, burying my trembling hands in my lap. Ms. Beena walked in apologizing for being late.

'Shilpa, from the time you all were little, I have told you there is nothing wrong in liking a boy, or in a boy liking a girl.' DG's brow was deeply furrowed. I hung my head in shame.

DG leaned forward. 'Look up, girl. Look at me. Always look a person talking to you straight in the eye.'

I glanced at Aunty Shalini as if she could focus my eyes for me. Ever since I was a child I had been taught by her to put my head down while being corrected by an adult. Why was DG now telling me to do the opposite? I hesitated before looking up awkwardly, fighting hard not to return my gaze to the floor.

'How many times have I told all of you that you must wait a few more years before entering into any serious relationship? This is not the time for such things!' DG rarely shouted at us but when he did we trembled. He sighed and spread his arms wide in exasperation. 'Darling, you will completely ruin your life if you continue the affair with your uncle,' he said, his voice turning gentle and concerned.

I burned with shame. *How much did he know?* It scared me when he raised his voice but, even more, I dreaded DG's calm voice when I was in the wrong; I wanted him to shout at me. I couldn't help but remember when Appa would sigh in frustration and sit alone on the doorstep after heated arguments with Amma. His depressed appearance terrified me even more than his anger.

Why wasn't DG angry? Had he lost all trust in me? Was he now convinced that trying to bring me back on track was a waste of his time? I felt terribly sad that I had disappointed him.

Mrs. Law, who had so far remained silent, spoke up. 'Shilpa, all of you, both boys and girls, should first complete your studies at Shanti Bhavan and at college and land a good job. Then you can marry the person of your choice. But if you want to destroy your own chances for success, no one can save you.'

I nodded. Handing me a tissue to wipe my face and patting my back, Ms. Denny advised me to have self-control and strength—two essential qualities for every girl. 'A woman is the backbone of every family, Shilpa. And her reputation is her greatest strength. If she's proper in her ways, no one can hurt her family,' she said. I had received the same message from my grandmother. Ms. Beena joined in, reminding me I was too young to get into a serious relationship.

Despite the concern being shown, I was convinced that everyone thought less of me. 'Everyone will .... I should never have.... I'm not a bad—'

DG interrupted me before I could finish a thought. 'Look, everyone makes mistakes. If you choose to beat yourself up instead of focusing on what you can do to change, nothing good will come of it.'

I was taken aback.

Silence spread through the room, seeping into every corner, hanging thick like a fog. No one said a word for a minute or two. Then the clear ring of DG's voice cut through the haze. 'Shilpa, darling, you are young,' he said, taking my shaking hand in his. 'We too were young once upon a time, with the same feelings and desires as yours.' He offered an embarrassed smile and Ms. Denny laughed. I was sure there was no way DG could have ever made the same mistakes I had. 'And what happened between you and Ajay doesn't make you a bad girl.'

Until then, he hadn't mentioned Ajay. I could hardly bear to look at him.

'But what took place with your uncle is something you cannot allow to continue. You escaped once. You mustn't play with your life again.'

I found my voice at last. 'I will not.'

He held my gaze for a second longer; but where I expected anger, there was only kindness. 'So, you hold your head up. Do you understand?'

I nodded. 'I promise I won't get distracted from my studies, I won't get involved in any relationships, and I won't lose self-control.'

Everyone appeared pleased.

But the most important assurance DG gave me was that my parents and grandmother wouldn't be informed of what had happened. Appa would have called me a *sulay*—a prostitute—as he had shouted at Kavya when he discovered she liked Prashanth. Amma, for her part, would have wept as if the world had come to an end. And though Grandmother might not scold me outright, her silence would testify to her disappointment and shame.

During the next vacation, months later, Appa startled me by saying, 'Shilpa, you can do anything you want in your life. Your mother and I will not stop you. You marry the boy Dr. George approves of. But one thing I ask is that you do not run away with a boy and disgrace the family.' His request stunned me. Never before had he said anything like this. Was it his concern for my happiness or the family's honor?

'No, Appa. I will never do that,' I said. But deep inside, I was filled with self-doubt. I wasn't confident I would be able to live up to my family's expectations. How could I be certain of always being a 'good girl'?

I stayed awake for a long time that night with my father's words echoing in my head. I had heard stories of young girls running away from homes and returning pregnant. For those girls' parents, the disgrace made attracting suitable husbands for their other daughters almost impossible. Village gossip and contemptuous stares from neighbors were hard to ignore. All Appa really owned was his family, and my honor was of the utmost importance to him. I also had Kavya to consider; I didn't want my reputation ever to hurt her chances.

Once, Grandfather's brother Chauraj had lured a twelve-year-old school girl into the fields with promises of sweets and was caught fondling her behind a bush. This dreadful incident was hard to forget. The news spread quickly, and the village wasn't about to ignore it.

It was not the first time Chauraj had been caught fondling young girls. Grandmother remembered the night long ago when the rains had flooded her hut and she had sought refuge in her brother-in-law's place. In the middle of the night she woke up to find her youngest daughter, Rani, asleep in his lap, his hands groping her daughter's thighs.

'You bastard,' Grandmother screamed, snatching her daughter away. She picked up a stick used to chase cattle and beat him until he begged her to stop. 'You have a daughter. Would you do this to her?' She spat at him and vowed never to step into his house again.

This time, however, it was a matter involving someone outside our family, and a minor. There was going to be some sort of public retribution. Chauraj was dragged in front of the ten-member panchayat, the village's self-governing body. The witness to the alleged crime, a Gunna's wife, was credible enough that the panchayat sought no further evidence. Only the question of punishment remained.

By the time we got to the small granary where the panchayat was meeting, an agitated crowd had already gathered. Men were seated on the ground in front, except for the landlords and panchayat members who had positioned themselves upon colorful plastic chairs. Women sat on the ground in their separate places under a nearby banyan tree. Over the heads of gawking laborers, I could see my great-uncle standing with his head down, a broken man at the mercy of those who were to decide his fate. His cotton vest was torn in places and his khaki shorts were muddy from being dragged across the field.

The air was choked with tension. The panchayat chairman, a wealthy owner of a sugarcane plantation, listened to what others in the crowd had to say and scratched his head in contemplation.

The girl's mother, a stout vegetable shop owner, stepped forward and spat in the accused's frightened face. Another woman shouted, 'Ammun dunga! Sulaymaganai!' which means 'motherfucker' and 'son of a whore'. Grandmother clapped her hands over my ears.

After a brief discussion among the panchayat members, its chairman ordered that my great-uncle be taken into one of the rooms where grain sacks were unloaded before distribution as rations to the poor. Everyone except me knew what the landlord had in mind as punishment. The murmuring of the crowd made it look like a single organism, rippling with satisfaction. Four rough-looking men led the offender into the room and bolted the door behind them.

'What are they doing?' I asked Grandmother. Grandmother didn't reply. No one explained what was happening behind that door.

Half an hour passed but the door didn't open. I could see Grandfather growing restless and worried, but no one else seemed to be in any hurry.

Grandfather stood up and shouted, 'This has gone on too long.' He pointed towards the door, shaking in anger. 'Why do you have to bash him so much, sir?' Grandfather pleaded with the chairman, his whole body trembling. 'Please let him go. It won't happen again.'

The chairman sniffed, irked that a laborer would question him. He turned to two hefty men behind him and ordered that Grandfather be given a few lashings.

'Grandfather! Grandfather!' I called out frantically.

Other voices joined in, speaking in support. 'What did this man do? Why punish him?' a serious-looking elderly man asked bitterly.

Grandmother ran towards the panchayat officials, shouting, 'What wrong did he do? You can't harm him.'

The chairman stared at Grandmother as though she had no right to speak, then he unhurriedly stood up and slapped her. 'You better shut up. Your husband is as guilty as his brother. Couldn't he keep his brother in check?'

That was not an argument others could accept. The crowd began to turn against the chairman. After all, he was known to have a mistress of his own among the servant women he kept in his home. After a few torturous minutes, the chairman decided to let both Grandfather and his brother go.

Everything that followed seemed like a movie stuck in fast-forward. I remember walking home with my grandmother, both of us in tears. Grandfather was by his brother's side, holding him by his shoulders as he limped along, wracked with pain. Shame had seized them and neither brother could look up.

I couldn't let myself become a source of shame to my family. I knew my father was proud of me. That mattered a lot, and I couldn't let him down. There was so much I had learnt from both of my different upbringings, in the village and at Shanti Bhavan. But in the end I knew no one could do it for me; the change had to come from within.

Chapter Fifteen

Playing Parent
to Parents

Not long ago, Appa accused Amma of flirting with local men after she lashed out at him for cheating on her. Hearing his shameless charge, Amma said, 'The lightning has already struck my head and now I'm being bitten by a snake.' This expression came to my mind when Mrs. Law suddenly announced in the midst of our financial struggles that she was leaving Shanti Bhavan permanently to take care of her ailing husband and infant granddaughter.

I never thought the day would come when we would not see Mrs. Law's elegant, petite figure moving briskly through the campus, checking on classes and the dorms. It was sad to think we would no longer have her life-skills sessions and literature classes to fill our Tuesday afternoons.

What happened next was even more surprising. Passing by Aunty Shalini's room one morning, I noticed that her normally neatly arranged space had been cleared entirely. Later that day, we heard DG had sent her away. Throughout all her years at Shanti Bhavan, her use of corporal punishment and her verbal abuse of children had been hidden from DG. The day he found out was her last.

The departures of Mrs. Law and Aunty Shalini were hard to fathom. For the next several days, it was the only topic of discussion among staff and children. We were afraid that no one was experienced enough to fill the void. These two women had been in my life ever since I entered the school at the age of four and, however complicated the relationships, I would miss them. *Who could be as good as they had been?* It was then that DG himself arrived, quickly taking charge of daily operations and reshuffling responsibilities of several staff members. Change swept through the school like a wild fire as we flexed and adapted. Thus began a new era in Shanti Bhavan under the guardianship of DG.

Despite the kindness and understanding I had met with in the session in Mrs. Law's office, I still had the lingering sense that

DG thought poorly of me, so his constant presence on campus was not something I looked forward to with any pleasure. I was careful not to do anything that would land me back in his office. I avoided running into him on campus, fearing he would scold me for having done something wrong. Once I was walking along the school corridor when I saw him approaching. I quickly ducked my head, turned around, and darted into the music room, worried that DG had seen me avoiding him.

I tried just as hard to avoid run-ins with my classmates. In the aftermath of my disastrous first contacts with men, and the lasting consequences of my betrayal of my best friend, I felt safer distancing myself from everyone. Sheena had graduated and gone without ever softening towards me. I was certain none of my remaining classmates really liked me. They didn't include me in their conversations and didn't invite me to join in their escapades. Once I found them sitting in a circle behind the school building, reliving their secret expedition to the fruit orchard in pursuit of mangoes. My presence was simply ignored.

I was defiant, again, determined to show that I could do without them. But this time, instead of fighting with anyone, I disappeared into books, reading with furious intensity to prepare for the coming twelfth grade national exams. I had to prove to my classmates I could rise above them in something. But on late evenings, alone, that fierce stubbornness faded into the hollowness of my isolation. I blamed Sheena for my loneliness and the absence of affection from anyone. It didn't occur to me then that no one could satisfy my constant need for attention. 'You're like a bottomless pit,' Sheena used to say. I'm surprised she wasn't even more exasperated, burdened as she was by my need to be showered with affection at all times.

Even Vijay, a boy to whom I had taken a liking, resented my demands. But for some reason he seemed prepared to put up with me for a while, and liked me well enough to display his affection in private and sometimes to acknowledge me as a friend in public. He was usually very quiet and hardly spoke to anyone, rarely taking part in school events like debates and dances. Still, everyone noticed him because of the brown leather gloves and bandages he wore to protect his arms from the bright sun.

Vijay never knew who his father was. When he was four years old, a group of men promised his mother, a young, pretty woman, that they would find her a well-paying job outside her village. Believing that God might be helping her to find a way to look after her son, she left with them in their vehicle, only to be gang raped on the borders of her village.

Shattered and disgraced, she returned home to face the insults of the villagers. Many placed the blame on her, saying she had tempted the men, and condemned her as a woman with poor morals. Unable to bear the humiliation, the tormented woman poured kerosene on her own body and lit herself on fire. Seeing his mother ablaze, little Vijay ran to embrace and protect her. His mother didn't survive, and Vijay was gruesomely burnt. The scars on his arms are grave reminders of that horrible night.

Seated next to Vijay in the dining hall, I would try not to stare at his scarred arms, though it was hard not to. In the evenings, he would often step off the football ground and come up to where I'd be watching on the side, just to say a quick hello or ask me what I thought of his dribbling skills. To feel wanted and liked by someone was what I wished for, and once I decided I had his affections, all my problems vanished and I focused on enjoying every bit of our burgeoning relationship.

When Keerthi said, 'It's just an infatuation. You will break up,' I refused to speak to her for days. I was convinced it was true love. That is, until Vijay sent me a message through one of my classmates that he didn't want to continue the relationship. He never told me why, but I suspect now that I was just too overwhelming.

I disappeared back into my studies, determined to get into a top college. Teachers constantly reminded us of the importance of these exams, urging us not to waste precious prep time. Grandmother would tell me that if I prayed hard enough, I would do well, but by now I was certain that prayer alone couldn't take care of my future. One miracle had already set me on this path, and God might not choose to grant me another.

In the midst of our rigorous class schedules, DG would ask us to take turns escorting visiting guests on tours of the Shanti Bhavan campus. The chance to do these tours meant that I got to talk to interesting people—journalists from the *New York Times*, academicians, business executives, philanthropists, and artists from Broadway plays. As we walked around the campus, they shared their life-stories and adventures, carrying me away to a vast world of possibilities outside the iron gates of Shanti Bhavan.

Most visitors were amazed by the subtle natural beauty of the landscape, framed with long stretches of lush green grass, fruit orchards, and a wide variety of birds, squirrels, and chameleons that made their homes with us. I often pointed out to visitors my favorite spot on campus—the majestic dark rocks just behind my dormitory which sat like devout sages, appearing to pray in the direction of the northern sky. I told them, 'Sometimes after sunset, I lie on top of the largest rock, gazing into the night to spot a shooting star to make a wish.' But I sighted shooting stars on only two occasions in all my fifteen years at Shanti Bhavan and both times I prayed to God to protect my mother and bring her back home safely.

Apart from seeing the school facilities, visitors were often curious to learn how we were being brought up by the school authorities who had taken over much of that responsibility from our parents. Some seemed bothered by the fact we were living for most of the year at school, away from our families from a young age.

It was always difficult when visitors asked, 'How do your siblings feel about not being able to study here?' Kavya's livid face would flash before my eyes and I would struggle to answer. Each time I responded truthfully: that my younger sister felt unhappy about my having gotten the chance to live a finer, wider life than she, but my brother seldom expressed any disappointment.

'At times I too questioned the policy of one child from each family. It causes bitter conflict amongst siblings,' I admitted. 'But in the end I feel the rule is right.' DG had told us that Shanti Bhavan had to strictly enforce this policy in order to spread the benefits to as many families as possible. One child was enough to take care of the rest in the family. Many visitors agreed that this made sense, but there were others who found it divisive.

Some visitors were concerned that we were losing touch with our cultural and indigenous heritage as they called it. I could see why they might feel that way, but I explained that we were familiar with the ways of our villages. The nearly three months we spent at home during annual vacations over the years were part of our childhoods. I had witnessed the hardships my parents and grandparents faced each day, their struggle to provide for the family, the beliefs they lived by, and the customs and traditions that chained them to old ways. My siblings were a constant reminder of how hard it was to grow up in a society that looked down upon us socially. I didn't think it was necessary to live through it every day to recognize it.

The many incidents that I had witnessed—Appa being beaten by a landlord's men, the fights among neighbors, and my own family's quarrels with our relatives—had marked me. This was a life far different from that at school. I adjust to each situation depending on where I am, and with whom. The two cultures are equally a part of me. But I did not like being told by my grandmother that girls had to marry the person their elders chose for them while it was okay for men to decide for themselves, nor could I agree that Aunt Maria's husband should be free to take away all her savings simply because he felt he was entitled to it. I chose not to follow those of my family's beliefs that I felt were dictated by caste-based practices, superstition, and ignorance of the outside world.

'The school teaches us to read widely and be prepared to think for ourselves,' I said. 'Living in the village to preserve its culture and traditions is not a responsibility I can take on or want to accept.'

Some visitors agreed with me while others thought I was too westernized or arrogant and had lost touch with my roots. One visitor even commented, 'You can't act like you are in America. Why don't you learn about the Ragas and the Vedas?'

I was taken aback, embarrassed at not knowing enough about them. 'We do. But I need to read more,' I said.

Most Indian visitors enquired whether our upbringing included spiritual and religious teachings. I replied that we did not practice any particular religion in Shanti Bhavan, but followed the universal teachings of all major religions. They were happy to see the holy books of different faiths displayed next to each other in the prayer hall, along with the bronze idol of a tree branch that was meant to symbolize open-mindedness and growth. 'Some of us pray together silently in the hall,' I said. 'And we don't question each other's beliefs.'

Upon hearing that we celebrated major festivals of different religions, one visitor replied with a chuckle, 'That's because you all want to have more holidays.'

The question about boys was always embarrassing, and I certainly didn't want any of the staff to hear my answers. My own silly romantic moments with Vijay were all the dating experience I had had. Though it was short-lived, the excitement of getting to know a boy was enough for me to like the idea. I told visitors that the school discouraged it, although we always found our way around that. Sometimes I would tell them about Kavina's relationship with her senior, Avnith, which had survived seven long years of restriction by the staff, and how, despite being away in college, Avnith still managed to send letters to her through secret channels. I said that I wanted to choose my partner in life, but only after I finished college; I had much to accomplish to start a good career.

I wanted visitors to know that all of us felt free to make our own choices and were not constrained by traditional practices of any kind. 'Shanti Bhavan takes no official position on political or religious issues. We don't follow the philosophy of any one individual or community,' I said. 'Instead, we strongly believe in living by globally shared values such as honesty, integrity, and transparency. We grew up recognizing the importance of humane qualities such as kindness, generosity, and humility. These were taught to us by example as much as by books.'

It was through telling others of these experiences that I was able to look beyond the conflicts I had faced at school and understand how my difficult past had in mysterious ways paved my present. It was the honesty with which we were being brought up that amazed me. There is a paradise in every childhood, and for me it was Shanti Bhavan, an enchanted place where life was simple and the air was fresh, where there was laughter even when there was pain, and always a chance to start all over again.

After eight years working abroad, Amma decided to return home for good. I learnt of her decision from the last letter she sent me from Singapore. It was the best news I had had in a long time; the thought of reuniting with my mother was simply ecstasy for me. But something that Amma scribbled at the end of the letter troubled me: 'Chinna, if I die here, there will be no one to cry for me. I cannot die alone in a strange land.' At first, I couldn't understand why she was talking about death, and it scared me. As I tried putting myself in her shoes, I began to understand how desperate she was to reunite with her loved ones. No amount of insistence by my father could get her to remain longer in Singapore.

Every time the girls in my class and I spoke about our mothers and all the difficulties they endured in their lives at the hands of alcoholic husbands, ruthless money-lenders, and the demands of a dowry system, I couldn't help but feel a sense of pride in Amma for courageously living through the hardships of her early years. The anger that I had harbored towards her for abandoning me had eased but not disappeared completely.

Appa called one of the school staff, and asked that I be informed of my mother's arrival. The thought of reuniting with her left me sleepless with excitement. Every time I passed by the prayer hall, I stopped to say a special thank you to God for bringing my mother safely back to me. I couldn't wait to get to our village, and when we did, I didn't let Appa walk me home from the bus stop either. I ran all the way to our house, and almost broke open the front door in my eagerness. Amma unlocked the bolt and greeted me with a wide smile and eyes gleaming. I cried out to her and dove into her arms.

'My chinna, you have grown big and beautiful,' she exclaimed, hugging me tight and covering my face with kisses.

'You look so different. You've become as chubby as me,' I said, noticing that the hollowness around her cheekbones had disappeared.

Amma laughed, and ran her hands over my hair and pulled me close. There was so much urgency in her every action. There could be no doubt that she still loved me. My fear of her resentment towards me for rejecting her brother quickly faded. I kissed her cheek and put my arms around her.

That night, there couldn't have been a happier family than ours as we sat together on the floor, sharing a delicious meal of steamed rice and chicken curry that Amma had prepared. It was almost like a small celebration. I laughed watching Francis's failed attempt to steal Kavya's share of the chicken from her plate. Kavya pinched him and he yelped. I was grateful that we were finally a family again.

I would soon find out that our life together was not to be what I had imagined. I struggled to get used to Amma's presence in our lives, just as she struggled to reclaim her role as a dutiful wife and mother. She was anxious to please us, but her attempts to discipline Francis and Kavya never seemed to work; they just wouldn't take her seriously.

At first I hardly left her side as she went about cooking, washing our clothes, going to the village market to buy vegetables, stopping by a neighbor's home to gossip, and visiting relatives who lived close-by. I noticed how everyone seemed to scrutinize her foreign ways—her outright rejection of the sari and the lack of hesitation to express her opinion. While others resented the change in Amma, I silently celebrated it as I wanted to find similarity to my own changing outlooks towards life.

My mother's return brought about sudden changes in our living conditions at home. With her savings, she arranged to have a kitchen, a living room, and a bathroom built adjacent to the poorly furnished hut we had known. Now that I was older and finding the early morning trips to the fields very embarrassing, I was relieved we were finally getting a bathroom built inside the house. It was all a lovely change, one that I hadn't even dreamt of.

Word about Amma's grand construction plans shot through the village like a bullet. Neighbors came by to praise her for being the first woman in the village to work abroad and earn money. Unemployed men seeking income from construction work eagerly turned up at our doorstep. Kavya, Francis, and I were a nuisance to them, as we kept getting in their way in our excitement to be of help.

We were not the only ones in the village whose lifestyle had taken a turn for the better. The economic boom that was taking place in urban India prompted many villagers to take up jobs in cities as factory workers, laborers, and mechanics. They brought home higher wages than they had earned working for landlords. Thatched roofs were replaced with tiles, while some people built more comfortable homes. Part of the forest had been cut down for planting crops and a few more bore-wells were drilled for supplying water. But all these developments also robbed the village of what was once its raw and sublime appearance. It was no longer the place I had grown up in, its natural beauty lost to human industry to make life better.

All the same, the usual practice of women with buckets and pots gathering every evening near common wells continued. This was their opportunity to share news about their lives, to inquire about others, and simply to gossip. No news is kept secret in the village; there are happy stories of young girls getting married, and sad stories of their broken relationships. Women seem to enjoy talking about other women and their children, especially about those who are not married by sixteen. As for men, prosperity meant more money in their hands, which in turn meant more drinking and chasing other women. The newfound wealth was like a thick moss covering the surface. But underneath, not much had really changed in Thattaguppe.

However, with passing days, the slow flow of life began to feel the pressure of discord within our family. For one thing, Joseph Thatha came to live with us in a small room built for him with Amma's money. The fact that he still had not talked to her or treated her with civility since she married his son did not stop him from moving in with us. Yet, despite her generosity, he refused to eat anything she cooked, and so Uncle Philip would supply him with food twice a day.

'That old man will realize one day how good I've been to him,' my mother often said to me with a quiver in her voice, her words barely audible.

Most nights, we could hear Joseph Thatha coughing and chattering to himself, his senses completely overtaken by the local liquor he somehow managed to get hold of. He seemed haunted, and I was often disturbed by his cries for his late wife, 'Arpuda! Where are you? Bring me dinner.' He was probably struggling to face the reality that the power he once held over his wife and his children had vanished into his sullen past and he was living on the generosity and kindness of his despised daughter-in-law.

I dreaded entering my grandfather's dark room that reeked of stale urine and worse. The walls were almost bare except for a large picture of the *Last Supper of Jesus* that rested on two rusty nails by the doorway. The few times I went to his room to give him meals, there was no sign he recognized me.

'I am Shilpa, Thatha,' I would remind him each time, placing the steel plate filled with rice on the mat and helping him to sit up.

'Which Shilpa?' he'd ask, peering into my face with a look of distrust.

'I am Kavya's elder sister,' I would say, trying to place myself in his memory. Accepting that I was no stranger to the family, he would reach for my hand and give it a squeeze. He would ask me a few questions, the same ones each time I saw him. He reminded me of a still, giant clock that had lost track of time. I often wished I could just sit down by his side and hear him tell me stories of his life, so I could understand why he'd sunken to be the man he was in his late years.

But it was hard to ignore Appa's anger towards his father who had for so long made him feel weak and useless. He always described him as a cruel man who cared little about his family. Once, hearing Appa talking about his father, Amma teased, 'If he hears you saying bad things about him, he will beat you like he did when you were a boy.'

'If he enters our room, he'll regret it,' Appa retorted. I recoiled at the resentment and bitterness in his voice.

There was little stability in my life at home. A self-indulgent father, a distressed mother, and a perennially drunken grandfather all living under the same roof made for a chaotic family that offered no tranquility. The comfort of living in a larger house made no difference in the absence of peace.

Even worse was my relationship with my mother. Until now, Amma had been the missing part of my puzzle, and now that we were all together, I still couldn't feel whole. No matter how hard I tried to open up to her, there was a perpetual distance between us. It was like we were constantly out of sync, unable to connect. Whenever she complained about one thing or the other, I found it difficult to remain patient and sympathetic towards her.

Kavya and Francis were also struggling; they would show their annoyance and brush off the restrictions Amma tried to place on them. Kavya didn't feel attached to Amma and didn't bother to hide it. She spent most of her time in Grandmother's house and talked very little with Amma. From the sad creases around her eyes, I could see Amma was hurt by us. We had drifted away from each other, and I knew it was going to take a long time for us to find our way back.

Most nights, tucked away with my siblings on the new cot that Amma had bought for us, I lay awake wrestling in my mind with the changes that were pulling our family apart at a pace I couldn't keep up with. I often overheard Appa and Amma talking to one another in whispers, usually about money matters. I pretended to be fast asleep, blocking out the sound of their arguing. It was harder when their whispers turned into angry brawls. Even with Amma back home from abroad, we couldn't live together in harmony.

And it was not just our family members who had noticed Amma's transformation. On her way to buy vegetables from the market, women passing by would stop to stare at her fancy dress and footwear—tight, colorful salwar and matching leather sandals bought abroad, replacing faded saris and worn-out rubber slippers. She had also stopped ornamenting herself with cheap, gold-plated necklaces and elaborate bangles and earrings, distinguishing herself from other village women. Her new attire helped hide her large, bulging belly scarred by ugly stretch marks, but it didn't help her make friends with local women who resented her sophistication.

I, on the other hand, loved Amma's new style. It brought out her youthful beauty and suggested her eagerness to live a full life. But I could also see that in the long years she had been abroad, certain feminine attributes she once had, attributes traditionally considered important—gentleness, humility, acquiescence—had been lost. I was surprised by her boldness in contradicting my father even when it risked turning him violent. Having seen how women interacted with men in an affluent society, she was no longer willing to accept her husband's orders implicitly. Of course, I was supportive of her expressing her wishes, but others in the family made disparaging remarks about her. Grandmother once said to me, 'Your mother has turned into a man. She's no longer the old Sarophina I knew.'

I tried to understand who my mother had become. Her time abroad had turned her into an assertive woman who refused to remain silent when challenged by others. Amma's varying roles as a daughter, wife, mother, cook, housekeeper, liquor saleswoman, servant, and farm worker had trained her to adapt to every situation. She could now handle what others threw at her with wit, vigor, cunning, and deceit.

I couldn't help but notice that Amma was frightened of candor, finding it necessary to manipulate others to get what she wanted. Every time I snapped at her for resorting to lying to escape from a difficult situation, she would firmly justify her actions by pointing out that they were only for the good of the family. According to her, the society was not sufficiently fair or truthful to be dealt with in a forthright manner. I tried to convince her it was wrong to lie or act dishonestly, as I was taught in school. But she wouldn't budge.

'You can't feed a family with truth alone. When you lie for another's good, it is not a lie,' she said. Her words troubled me, but the more I thought about it, the more I found myself wanting to agree with her, or at least not judge her. I still revered the principles of truth and honesty but how could I judge my amma harshly for dishonesty when it was for the family's survival?

There was no doubt that Amma was proud of me and longed for my company. She would show me off to her friends and anyone who came to see her. 'You remember my daughter Shilpa? I never thought she would grow up to be smarter than any of us,' she would say to others with immense pride, kissing me on my forehead. Embarrassed, I would beg her to stop, but she would simply ignore and do it again when we ran into someone else.

Amma often wanted me to escort her to the village market, or go with her on evening strolls along the lane where we lived. But I had grown increasingly argumentative, often fighting with her over family matters. I thought she was wrong to demand that Kavya do so many household chores when she had homework to complete. Whenever Appa brought home vegetables picked from the landlord's farm, I would ask her whether he bought or stole them. Amma lied every time, and once replied casually, 'What does it matter whether he paid for them or not?'

The conflict between my parents was the worst part of being home. They simply could not get along with each other, fighting over everything. On several occasions, when their quarrels turned ugly, Amma threatened to take her own life. Once she tried to hang herself from the wooden rafter of the hut, but was stopped by Grandmother who came running when I yelled for Francis to fetch her. Another time, she folded the few saris she owned into a bundle, and screamed that she was going to run away, and if Appa managed to track her down she would kill herself by jumping into a well. It was clear she had lost all hope for the kind of life she thought she might be able to lead after working abroad. I was living with the constant fear of when the next crisis would erupt.

Once I had to send Kavya to fetch our grandparents. Appa was raging about Amma's claim that there was no money left in her bank account. He didn't believe her and repeatedly accused her of hiding what she had earned in Singapore. Grandmother arrived, dragging Grandfather along with her, just in time to stop Appa from beating Amma.

Although my grandparents' intervention broke up the fight, there was no resolution. Appa looked my way with sad, red eyes, and then walked out without a word. I wanted Amma to ignore him so the fight could be over, but she confounded me by calling out, 'Anthu! Anthu!' and running after him.

In the space of a single second, all her bold declarations of wanting to be free of my father's tyranny vaporized and her emotional dependence on him was exposed. She couldn't consider living alone in a village where single women are not safe. I was furious with her for behaving as though it was all her fault, but my grandparents were glad to see her trying to make amends, for they considered it a woman's duty to be a 'good wife,' which to them meant always shouldering all the blame and appeasing her husband.

My upbringing in school taught me to question what had long been the expectations in our society. Having been brought up in a place where boys and girls were treated as equals, I found it hard to understand why women would allow themselves to be 'slaves' to men. Even when women worked in the fields and earned money to meet the needs of the family, men didn't seem to appreciate their contributions. I rarely noticed a village woman questioning her man's bad behavior or lack of concern for their family. They even accepted the excessive drinking habits of men. Clearly, the two worlds I was living in saw women differently.

Despite the way my feelings had changed towards Amma, I spent most of my time at home comforting her, assuring her she wasn't alone in the world. In turn, Amma showered special attention on me. Once, when Kavya saw that Amma had bought hair clips and face cream for me, she burst out crying, 'I want to go far away so you will get me good things when I come home. You treat one daughter like a queen and the other like a slave.' Kavya stormed out of the house, almost tripping over the wooden threshold.

Upon her return, Kavya shouted at Amma, 'What do you give us? Every day it's the same rice and ragi. Not even good clothes to wear. You don't take us to visit places.' It was the first time I had heard her express disappointment about what our parents couldn't give her.

'Is it my fault I was sent to Shanti Bhavan?' I shouted at her, but she didn't respond. For a moment, I wished I had never left home. It was hard to believe Kavya was only twelve. She was already well aware of her situation—what she longed for and what she couldn't have. Her resentment towards me for my good fortune was so fierce and implacable I didn't know how to make peace with her.

As time passed, I began to take a more active role in settling disputes between my parents. I openly disapproved of my father's heavy drinking and my mother's habits of pitying herself and gossiping with neighbors. Contrary to the widespread village notion that girls should not voice their thoughts, I put my disappointments and frustrations on full display.

Playing parent to my parents was the most difficult task I had ever undertaken. I wasn't conscious it was even happening until it hit me in the aftermath of one of my father's violent attacks against my mother. In the midst of one of their quarrels about money, Amma foolishly revealed to Appa that she had gotten involved in gambling while in Singapore and had lost considerable sums. Enraged, Appa slammed Amma in the face with his fist, catapulting her to the floor in pain.

'He wants to kill me! All he cares about is my money,' Amma wept loudly, as Appa moved towards her again, fist raised to deliver another punch.

Francis grabbed Appa from behind, shouting at him to stop. I don't know how he managed to control our father who was probably much stronger than he was. I wished my uncles were there to see my brother at that moment. They often teased him that even a boy half his size knew how to ride a bullock cart, hack wood, and catch the drifting attention of girls who passed by. Even Appa had once remarked that any thief who came into our house would initially fear my brother because of his bull-sized frame and broad shoulders, but would quickly be filled with laughter realizing that my brother 'only squeaked and didn't bark.' I resolved never to let Appa forget how Francis handled him this time. Now he knew his son was capable of more than squeaking.

The next morning, I forced my parents to sit far apart from each other on the floor, and insisted that they discuss the events from the night before. I felt awkward and nervous in my new role, but they listened and responded like two earnest children being disciplined by their teacher. They appeared completely helpless.

'Amma, you caused him to punch you,' I said bluntly to my mother, blaming her for aggravating the situation with her arguments. I must have learnt the place of women at my grandmother's feet; I was the product of the village after all. 'Appa will use your words as an excuse to hit you. You know how short-tempered he is with you!'

She raised her eyebrows sharply, disappointed at my reasoning and hurt by what she saw as my insensitivity. Despite her swollen lips and left eye, she looked ready to take on Appa again. She pointed a finger at him and let loose a fresh stream of accusations, railing at him about his infidelity.

I did my best to calm her down, relieved that Appa didn't react. He avoided eye contact with her and stared out the window, unable to hide the guilt that bled through his stony mask.

I turned to Appa. 'It is wrong of you to abuse my mother. You know this.'

He nodded, but didn't speak.

After nearly an hour of talking to my parents, I congratulated them for having stuck together all these years. They left smiling as though they had finally understood the root cause of their problems. From that day on, I became the mediator in their quarrels.

I am humbled by their trust, but lately have come to resent and dread my position. With every new fight, I awaken to the truth that they are both immutable. These days, when Amma calls me and cries about the thrashing she received from Appa the previous night, I feel helpless and even sometimes wish she would just leave me alone. Appa always has an explanation for losing his temper. As they battle like bitter enemies, I watch from afar, wondering why my father went to all the trouble to win over my mother—a woman with real guts—to be his wife.

Appa never seems to attach much importance to his bad behavior. He probably thinks it is his right as a man. On the other hand, having had a taste of independence while she was in Singapore earning her own money, Amma is no longer prepared to give up all her rights, especially her right to an opinion.

Nothing has changed for my parents. There is no possibility for altering their existence. Life is a brutal ritual for them both, a never-ending battle. They seem to live, I think, for the sake of living.

As I was about to leave home to return to school at the end of the vacation, Uncle Naresh and I made eye contact briefly. The look he gave me was that of a stranger. 'Bye, Mama,' I said. Then I walked out. That was it. I felt sad for him but knew there was no turning back.

Back at school, I heard from my cousin Devya that my grandparents were looking for yet another girl for Uncle Naresh, as the previous proposal had fallen through. Now I knew for sure the family had given up on me marrying him and I was relieved. Looking back, I can't explain why I allowed myself to get caught up in my grandparents' vision of us together. Maybe it was for the excitement of it—to have a man's affection and to be wanted. It was beginning to dawn on me that this need to be wanted was at the root of much that had gone wrong in my life.

I also heard that Kavya had become friendly with the same two louts who had confronted me. She believed them when they promised to take her away from the life she hated and buy her the things she desired. It frightened me to think that she was often with them, but sitting miles away at school, there was nothing I could do about it.

Chapter Sixteen

Passing Through Danger

Ms. Nirmala charged into our class and ordered, 'Children, none of you may leave the school building. There will be no snack break and assembly today.' I stared in confusion. Beads of perspiration dotted her face; I had never seen her so frightened before. 'The cleaning staff is on strike. They have shut down the kitchen and locked the main school gate. It is not safe for any of you to leave this building,' she said, before stopping at last to catch her breath. She didn't pause to answer the questions we threw at her, and fled the room to spread the instructions to all the other classes.

'Why are they protesting?' I asked, turning around to face those behind me. Amuda looked blank.

'Let's go see what is happening,' Avinash suggested, jumping up from his chair and rushing towards the doorway.

'Sit down. We'll get into trouble with Ms. Nirmala,' I warned.

But everyone was too excited to sit quietly, and followed him to the small balcony that provided a clear view of the campus. After hesitating for a few moments, I too ran after them, unable to resist the temptation any longer.

We watched Ms. Nirmala and the senior managers trying hard to pacify a group of furious cleaning staff. Malamma, the eldest and most aggressive, stood slightly in front of the others, her fist raised in a threatening gesture at the school staff. They were shouting in Kannada and Telugu all sorts of demands. Their foul cursing reminded me of the way women in my village became embroiled in bitter arguments with their neighbors over stolen chickens or suspected affairs.

Just then Ms. Nirmala noticed us peering from the balcony. 'Get back to your classrooms. Please listen to our instructions, children,' she shouted. We obeyed, but only because we sensed punishment would follow if we didn't.

Dread filled my stomach. This was utterly strange. I had never before seen any of these women behaving offensively. In the past, every time I ran into them, we would exchange smiles and catch up about each other's families. They showered me with affection and warmth as if I were as dear to them as a daughter. Watching them working hard around campus reminded me of my own mother during the years she was toiling away as a laborer.

Nearly two dozen laborers from the nearby villages worked at Shanti Bhavan. They cleaned the dormitories and school buildings, swept the grounds, took care of the laundry, and washed kitchen utensils. Workers who had left recently for their own reasons were not replaced as we had taken on some of the day-to-day tasks in the wake of the financial crisis. Until now, there had not been any strike or lockout.

Back in our classroom, the uncertainty of the standoff left everyone in suspense. Keerthi posted herself at the doorway, gathering news from any staff who walked past and faithfully conveying information to the rest of us. Some of the teachers stood in small groups whispering amongst themselves. They seemed as perplexed as we were. I sat anxiously waiting for someone to assure us everything would be all right.

Finally Keerthi excitedly announced that DG had summoned the entire school immediately for an emergency assembly. We hurried down the stairs anxiously.

DG stood tall in the center of the stage waiting for everyone to quiet down. I shot Kavina an irritated look as she continued to chatter.

'Children, you must have heard by now that the laborers are on strike?' DG opened his address. Heads nodded in unison. 'Well, they are unhappy with the Foundation for having let go several workers on our farm. But we had good reasons for doing that.'

DG explained that after stopping the banana cultivation a year ago due to financial pressures, the farm was now growing only vegetables for our own consumption on small parcels of land. Many of the excess farm workers had been retained until now to give them time to find employment elsewhere. Now that sufficient time had passed, their jobs were terminated. But they were angry at being let go and rose in protest, seeking to rally the support of the cleaning staff in Shanti Bhavan.

'Children, don't be afraid. If they refuse to work, we will,' DG said. A strong sense of determination welled up in me, and I was ready to do whatever was required to keep the school running. We had come close to losing it the year before and found a way. We would do it again. I could see that same feeling written on the faces of all those around me.

'By sunrise tomorrow morning, Shanti Bhavan will shine again,' DG said, clasping his hands together in a show of assurance. I didn't know where he found such optimism in challenging times.

We gathered with the school staff and put together a plan of action. There was eager enthusiasm amongst us to show that we could go on without the help of the cleaning staff who were still battering us with loud chants from outside the school building. We thought about locking them out from entering the school the next morning, but DG was insistent we not do anything that could lead to more hostility. 'Aggressive actions only invite vengeance. And that is not the way problems should be solved,' he said. Strangely, at that moment, he reminded me of Atticus from my favorite book, *To Kill a Mockingbird*, teaching me to remain strong and fight for what is right, but never at the risk of violence.

The next day we woke up early and began our new routine. Despite all the newly assigned work, no one complained. Some of the boys even preferred hard work like digging and shoveling to sitting in class. I felt very grown-up going from dorm to dorm, sweeping the floors and clearing out the laundry. The little ones who didn't understand what was going on mistook our work as punishment for some mischief. As I worked my way back to my dorm after putting the clothes out to dry, I found DG squatting on the lawn. At first I couldn't make out what he was doing, but as I moved closer, his sharp, practiced movements became clearer; he was weeding.

The cleaning staff on strike gathered to talk amongst themselves in the dining hall after watching all the work getting done without them. None of them had expected us to react so calmly to their mutiny. They were ready to call off the strike and return to work if DG would talk to them. But DG wasn't willing to negotiate or to let things return to the way they had been, as though nothing had happened.

'Tell them what they have done is wrong,' he said to the managers. 'Shanti Bhavan is a home and a school for children from poor families like theirs. It is not a factory.' There was no doubt in anyone's mind that DG would stand firm. He wouldn't address their grievances until we could return to our dorms. It was now a question of who had greater staying power.

To our surprise, the situation took a dramatic change for the better in an hour. The managers came back to inform DG that the laborers had called off the strike. They were afraid of losing their jobs when they realized the school could function without them and that they had lost DG's trust with their betrayal.

But we were wrong to assume the matter had been settled. Weeks later, we were surprised to see DG going about all day wearing a cap, something that he rarely did. I assumed he had just taken a liking to it. But when I saw Ms. Denny, who usually worked from her office in Bangalore, on campus that afternoon, I realized there was more to it.

News spread that DG had been hurt in an attack. At first, he didn't speak to anyone about it; he didn't want to frighten us. But eventually he decided everyone needed to be alerted to the possibility of a similar incident happening to the staff or children as he had encountered.

Early that morning around one or two o'clock, DG was awakened with a start by a loud bang. He touched his head and found blood running over his fingers. Turning on the light, he found a large stone, half the size of a brick, lying on the floor. Someone had flung the rock through the glass window, and it had bounced off the headboard and struck him hard on his head. His army instincts took over and he immediately found cover behind the dresser and lay still. He spent the next few hours on the floor, pressing a towel against the cut on his head to control the bleeding.

We learnt that a powerful landlord, Murga Gunna, was behind the trouble. Since the school opened, many landlords resented the fact that their own children were not getting the education that Shanti Bhavan offered to children from poor families. Furthermore, as many families found employment in projects run by our organization and earned fair wages, the subservient village community was beginning to gain a measure of independence, and landlords blamed the Foundation for their having lost control over the poor.

Murga Gunna had secretly joined with a manager at our farm to foment the strike. Seeing an opportunity to display their power, the workers were prepared to follow his directions; their loyalty was easy to purchase. I had heard Grandmother telling me of similar incidents where politicians incited poor people to create conflicts between communities for personal gain, usually to win elections.

DG learnt from local supporters in the village that Murga Gunna had hired a criminal to throw the rock. But DG didn't want to file a police complaint against the landlord without sufficient evidence, so instead he sent two strong men from the nearby town to warn Murga Gunna of serious consequences if he continued to cause trouble: charges for attempted murder would be filed in court. Everyone knew the police would take action if they were paid enough bribe.

But yet again, one evening after dinner, just when we thought our troubles with Murga Gunna were over, we spotted a fiery blaze raging through the wild vegetation outside DG's residence. School security guards responded quickly with water hoses to put out the fire. At that point, DG took further precautions. He kept pepper sprays in his room and office, and restricted information about his whereabouts to certain trusted staff members. Still, he was vulnerable while travelling at night on the lonely roads leading to Shanti Bhavan. It became clear to me that 'doing good' brought many dangers with it.

The time had come to secure the premises with additional guards and keep a school workforce that was friendly. Laborers who were known to be mischief-makers were assigned to the vegetable farm outside the main campus. It was risky to dismiss them immediately, so DG had to wait for the right opportunity. He finally got his chance a few months later when someone stole several irrigation pipes from the farm. The management immediately announced that what remained of the farm would also close, with all workers being let go.

A month later, the manager who was believed to be collaborating with Murga Gunna was found with a village woman in his room on campus. Crimes of that sort were looked upon seriously in the villages, though such escapades were not uncommon. He was asked to leave or face prostitution charges. The manager had no choice but to resign.

With all the troublemakers gone from Shanti Bhavan, DG assured the remaining laborers that their jobs were safe. After those incidents, no more labor problems troubled Shanti Bhavan. In fact, Murga Gunna then even tried to befriend the school management. Knowing that Gunna would cooperate if he could earn money from the school, DG instructed the staff to buy eggs from his poultry farm.

DG was tough in the face of danger but willing to compromise to win over his enemies, and soft when others needed him most. After all that conflict, I realized that true strength lies not in how many you defeat but in how many you win over.

Despite the restoration of calmness, the school's financial difficulties continued to remain a worry. Each day we waited for positive news, still harboring fears that our dreams of a good future could suddenly be shattered.

The unexpected finally happened. One morning DG came to the assembly with an announcement. Standing on the concrete stage before us, he said, 'Shanti Bhavan will not shut down, no matter what. I will not let anything destroy what we have built together.' He went on to say that all of us would share not just our joys but our hardships as well, no matter what the future held. I had not seen DG radiate so much self-confidence since the onset of the financial crisis. A bright rainbow had emerged from the thunderous storm that had kept us fearful of what the next day would bring.

'If necessary, we will grow our own food on our own land, older children will teach the younger ones, and at night we will study by candlelight. Aunties, teachers, and volunteers who wish to live in Shanti Bhavan will look after you and teach you.' A chorus of happy chatter broke from the crowd of children and staff members.

DG went on to explain that his efforts to get help from several rich industrialists had failed. Apparently, their interest in Shanti Bhavan was for investment, not charity. He concluded with a determined message, 'Children and staff, we will get through this together.'

DG's words held a different meaning for each of us. Sheena who was brought as an orphan, and Shoba—no longer recognizable as the frightened five-year-old who had come with me from my village on that first day—were being supported fully for their studies in college and never again had to fear being abandoned. For me, there would be a way out of my village. For all of us, the security of Shanti Bhavan in our lives meant we could continue dreaming of a good future. We had been given another chance at pursuing a good life. Karma had orchestrated a terrific piece of magic.

Although that day brought my classmates and me together, it wasn't long before our problems resurfaced. Except this time, it wasn't the result of any mischief. My feverish studying for the final national board examination, the results of which would determine which colleges might accept me, triggered their outright resentment, ostensibly for not spending enough time with them.

It came to a head during an argument with Avinash one day when he blurted out, 'You have been with us for the last fourteen years, but we have never been happy with you.'

Unable to control my tears, I pushed my chair aside and ran from the room to my hideout—the library. Sitting by myself amongst the rows of books, I wondered how the good moments we had had together over all these years could turn to dust so quickly. No doubt, my family problems had turned me into a defiant person in the past, but now I was at least trying to mend my ways. My feelings towards my classmates grew bitter.

That evening we were celebrating Thanksgiving at the Foundation House with volunteers from abroad, complete with a grand dinner and plenty of free-style dancing. In the midst of so many happy people, I felt lonely and miserable. My classmates made no effort to cheer me up and I waited impatiently for the party to end.

To make my suffering worse, after dinner DG surprised us with a request. Standing at the center of the hall, he asked us girls to join him one by one for a dance. No one knew any ballroom dances. All I wanted was to return to my dorm and hide under the bedcovers to avoid making a fool of myself.

'Come on; don't be shy,' DG said gently, nudging us to be brave. As usual, Keerthi, the most confident one amongst us, came forward first.

Soon it was my turn. Panic stricken, I extended my stubby arm, hand barely reaching DG's shoulder. He took my hand in his and slowly guided my feet in small steps to follow him. Despite his best efforts, I lost my balance and stumbled, stomping on his foot. He continued as though nothing had happened, but everyone saw and burst into laughter. When it was over I ran back to my seat, relieved that the embarrassment was over.

I ached to be part of my classmates' circle in all things— dancing, playing basketball, or just chatting late into the night. I argued that studying was no reason to isolate myself and began making concerted efforts to get closer to them. At first they were not interested in hearing anything I had to say, but as time went on, the ice gradually began to crack. I joined in their games, trying hard to laugh along with them. My overwhelming desire to be liked and accepted by those around me overtook my interest in schoolwork. I sought their company at every chance, even if it meant getting into trouble for doing things that were not allowed, like garden raids or accessing off-limits Internet sites.

Our carefree ways didn't do us any good. All of us performed poorly in the mid-term examination, so it came as no surprise when we were informed one evening that DG and Ms. Beena had scheduled a meeting with us. I knew we were in big trouble. That evening, DG walked into the room, his expression taut. He sat down, crossed his legs, and cast his gaze slowly across the room at each of us. I averted my eyes, quickly rubbing them as though they were itching. None of us dared move in our seats.

'You don't seem to care about your futures,' DG began somberly. 'Don't you know you are the ones who have to transform your families' lives?'

He was right about us: we had chosen to forget our main goal in life, though the staff frequently reminded us saying, 'Your families are depending on you. They are hoping you will save them from their difficulties.' In truth, sometimes I wished I didn't have such weighty responsibilities.

Appa often asked me, 'Shilpa, when you grow up, will you help the family, or will you be angry with us for not having spent a rupee to educate you?'

'Appa, I will never blame you,' I replied instantly, irritated at him for always doubting me. He hadn't seemed satisfied with my promise.

'You know, when you were little, you used to tell your mother and me that when you grew up you would burn all our old clothes and buy us new ones. You said you would build a big house for us.'

I had assured him then that I would do all those things. But now it was DG who had to remind me of the promises I'd made. I knew I had to earn enough money to help with Kavya's wedding and the dowry we would have to give her in-laws. I couldn't ignore the fact that I owed at least that as her elder sister and the most fortunate one in the family. I wasn't working hard enough to keep my word. Even as I realized I needed to balance my studies and my desire for companionship, I had no regrets over the time spent with friends because those were mostly happy moments. Now I needed to get serious again about my work. There was no other choice, no second chance. Until the exams concluded two months later, I kept to myself again. Some of my classmates surely resented me, but I had promises to keep and I would not need another reminder.

After the final examinations, while we waited for our scores, the staff prepared us to lead independent lives outside the gates of Shanti Bhavan. We listened to lectures on career choices, time management, personal health, and dealing with money. Drilled into us were the importance of good relationships, proper conduct, and how to avoid sexually transmitted diseases. I had led a sheltered life in the safety of Shanti Bhavan and found the idea of being on my own scary. I had never handled money, and was unsure how I would manage it. We were being prepared to go our separate ways.

Not long before we were set to graduate from twelfth grade, DG spoke to us about marriage. He told us that when we became old enough, he would be very happy if we found our life partners amongst our very own Shanti Bhavan classmates. 'No way! Yuck!' we exclaimed, followed by giggling and teasing.

'Aren't we supposed to be brothers and sisters?' Avinash asked, sending us all into a fit of laughter. I could sense DG was enjoying the madness he had instigated. Even though my classmates and I had made up in recent weeks, I was convinced none of the boys would choose me.

The following days flashed past. By this point, I had made a major decision: to remain in Shanti Bhavan for another year to write my memoir. It wasn't an easy decision to delay college, but it was what I wanted.

A few days later, we were notified of our examination results. I stood second in the class with a distinction; everyone had done well. Despite all the recent turmoil in my life, I had managed to focus on my studies at a critical juncture. I was satisfied with my performance, felt good about myself, and gained confidence in my abilities.

DG promptly called for an informal get-together of our entire class in the downstairs library. I was sure he would be happy with our performance in the examination. Sitting before us, he said, 'I want you to know we will be there with you through college and graduate studies. When the time comes, we will use all our contacts to make sure you land a good first job. All you have to do is work hard in college.' It was exciting to hear him speak about our future as though it were a real thing, something we could grasp with our two hands.

He waited for a moment. 'Many people told me children from poor homes could not succeed academically, even if they studied in good schools. They said that nature was more powerful than nurture. You have proved them wrong. I am a very proud man today because of you.' He struggled to overcome the tears welling in his eyes. 'It is not about the beautiful setting of Shanti Bhavan—its buildings and gardens; it is not about the people who work here; it is not about me; and it is not even about you. It is about all those combined and what we accomplish together— how lives are transformed, how families are taken care of, and what you will do for others in the ideals of equality, truth, generosity, compassion, and ultimately in reverence for life.'

I looked at my classmates. Everyone was struck by his words. The idea of caring for others has always been a part of our personal mission in life.

Our time in Shanti Bhavan had been one great experience. We had grown up together as a big family, treating each other as equals and respecting each other despite our differences. Boys didn't look down upon girls. It was beautiful to realize that the same boys who witnessed their fathers kick, burn, and emotionally destroy their mothers would never raise a hand to a girl, or make her feel less worthy.

In Thattaguppe, often there were fights between people of different castes. Once I heard about a young girl who had fallen in love with a boy from a lower caste. The boy she loved was brutally beaten by thugs called in by her family, and she later went missing, now presumed dead. I cannot understand why people allow caste differences to drive wedges between them.

Looking back I was glad that the school authorities had limited my time at home during these past fourteen years. It had saved me from accepting much of what my family would have taught me. I know it sounds cruel to think like that, but it's true. But none of that diminishes my love for my mother or the rest of my family.

By the time graduation was close at hand, my determination to improve my character and to conduct myself well had transformed me. The unsettling confusion that had arisen from my family's demands about my marriage, my conduct towards men, and the two worlds I had to juggle seemed finally resolved. The upbringing I had in Shanti Bhavan brought me self-confidence and self-worth. I could not even consider walking out through the gates of Shanti Bhavan without saying to myself, *I shall follow the lessons I have learnt here all through my life. I will not entertain the thought that I am intrinsically inferior to anyone else.*

And yet, it was important for me to understand the indignity my father had endured. Through his experiences, I hoped I would learn more about myself, and that that would prepare me for the way society at large might perceive me.

Appa finally took me to see the Gunna's house where he had worked for his longest period as a servant. No one but the current servant was home. I could see why Appa thought of the landlord's house as majestic. It had several rooms arranged next to each other to cater to the family's every need—a complex architecture in a land where until recently most people had nothing more than one-room mud huts. Even with all its grandeur, the house still harbored the familiar smells of the village: fresh manure collected in the adjoining cattle shed and smoke from the firewood burning in the kitchen adjacent to the living room.

'We can't enter the kitchen,' Appa whispered as I was about to cross the threshold. I knew what he meant, that lower castes were not allowed to set foot inside, but I ignored his warning. While my father waited on the doorstep, I walked through the entire house. I wanted to know everything about the landlord's lifestyle. My courage stemmed from what I had learnt at school— that everyone is created equal.

Appa's silent acceptance of the Gunna's insulting rules and the injustice he encountered troubled me. He couldn't seek redress for unfair treatment by landlords. 'Justice' was what landlords and village heads decided. And in a land where justice is often bought, poor people can only hope for mercy. Unfortunately, mercy, too, comes at a price.

I suppose Appa has always viewed his social status as his karma. He lived through indignity to win the biggest game in life—survival. Often, he had to lose to win. I have come to believe that Appa's childhood experiences, as difficult as they were, gave him insight into what would be good for me. I am sure he doesn't want me to face the indignities he has so often faced in his dealings with those above him. He is confident a good education will ensure a prosperous future for me. He told me to study hard and get a good job, even though he never bothered to encourage my siblings. I can't help but also see a selfish motive in Appa's aspirations for me—that through my education I will bring in money for the family.

For my part, I am determined to help my family, community, and anyone else who is in need. Having experienced the kindness and generosity of strangers all through my life, I firmly believe my obligations to society reach well beyond my blood family.

Where does my duty to my parents lie? After all, I was cared for by my school for all these years and, when at home, by my grandmother. Yet somehow, I still feel an unexplainable bond with my mother and father. Even if Appa's reason for sending me away to school was a selfish one, I do not blame him. I will gladly help my family when the time comes.

Chapter Seventeen

The Graduation

The sun nestled into the orange horizon as parakeets flew across the evening sky. A light breeze carried their chirping as they darted through the air, competing with hovering dragonflies. Moving in flashes of green, they dotted the blue sky before finally settling onto long cherry branches.

A few talkative parakeets fluttered over the high roof of the school building. Two perched on the beams running across the ceiling, peering inside to watch nine young, shy girls stepping onto the stage. A happy evening of jubilant dancing and singing in anticipation of the following day's graduation ceremony was just about to conclude.

Now was the evening's grand finale, the Viennese waltz. This was a special event, one I had been waiting for ever since Sheena's class performed the waltz last year. A hush settled over the audience as the girls slowly joined the boys on the other side of the stage, facing an auditorium packed with guests, staff, and friends watching us with broad smiles. My stomach knotted.

I bowed before my partner, Avinash. I wondered if he was thinking then of the chubby clown he once was, if he remembered those early bird-watching walks around the lake outside the grounds of Shanti Bhavan as a preschooler. We had not been good friends in recent years, and both of us secretly tried in vain to convince others to switch partners. But when we could not find anyone willing, we were forced to practice together. I did not make eye contact and was a little stiff in his arms as we went through the movements. This was the first time in all our school years that boys and girls were officially permitted to hold hands and dance. Grandmother would surely have fainted had she seen me dancing 'so shamelessly' with a boy.

Although I was too involved to observe the others, I could imagine what they were like on stage—joyful faces on full display with elegance flowing from every turn. Everyone except the two of us was excited to make the most of this moment.

Who could have ever imagined that the girl in the far corner of the stage once begged on the streets, that the boy in black tie smartly turning his partner was the son of a construction laborer, or that the tall, slender girl dancing off to the side had watched her murdered father's body burn on a pyre? None of those things mattered on this day. We danced with all the fervor and grace we could muster, as in the old Hollywood movies of our dreams.

I looked down and smiled to myself, realizing that every footstep signified the culmination of fourteen years growing up in a world unrecognizable to the one I had left behind. I was now to be the architect of my future with the knowledge and confidence to free my family from the bondage of poverty. I was free to follow a road my ancestors never even set foot on, redirecting our assumed fate like a large boulder in the middle of a river, diverting its flow.

As the music ended and the dancing stopped, a painful awareness of my own beginnings overwhelmed me. I wondered why some people see me as unworthy—other than that my forefathers had engaged in work traditionally associated with very poor people. It was a thought I had struggled to let go in recent years but, finally, I was determined not to carry it with me any longer. 'From this day forward,' I silently vowed, 'regardless of how anyone else might judge my existence, the word "untouchable" will have no meaning for me.'

My bond with my classmates was what really mattered to me that night. I remembered the first time we all had met at the age of four. We came from very poor homes, but through the years we had come to see one another as no different from any other children—innocent and eager to take on the world. Each one of us displayed something unique and beautiful, like the different images in the Hindu calendar. As years passed, Shanti Bhavan had led us into the creative reservoirs of our own imaginations, teaching us to express our thoughts and beliefs without fear of being silenced. And with all our schoolmates, staff, and volunteers who cared for us, we have a much bigger family now.

I see myself as a product of two disparate worlds, and each has given me a reason to love, to be kind, and to grow strong. My education has given me the ability to choose what I want for myself and the confidence to aspire to greater goodness. I have chosen to favor my new world, and hope to change the one I left behind.

I woke up early the next morning to prepare for the graduation ceremony. There was so much to do to get ready for the occasion; it felt like time was speeding out of control. The aunties hurriedly helped me finish dressing. Amma had never before seen me in a sari; I had especially chosen one with gold trimming she would surely like.

'Shilpa, hurry up,' Ms. Nirmala called from the dorm's entrance. I rushed out, lifting my sari carefully with one hand to avoid tripping.

I stopped to ask one of the older girls to look over my hair. 'Shilpa, you look beautiful,' she said cheerfully, advising me not to worry. The girls in my class were already in the school building, still asking each other how they looked. The boys stood off to one side, dressed smartly in white shirts with ties and dark grey trousers.

As the auditorium filled up, the microphones were tested one last time, and special guests were escorted to their seats. Rows of red chairs on the left remained empty—they were for us, the members of the graduating class. I searched the crowded hall for a sight of my parents; watching me graduate would surely be their proudest moment. But they were not there. I started to panic, and held back tears only by telling myself that if I started to cry tears would wash off my mascara.

'Please take your seats,' Ms. Nirmala instructed softly.

It was time for the chief guest to arrive, escorted by DG. I frantically scanned the crowd again. Would my parents really miss this? I couldn't imagine them not being present for the occasion after waiting all these years.

But just as the ceremony was about to begin, I caught sight of Appa and Amma entering from the side door. My mother looked pretty in a pink sari. Our eyes met, and she waved at me excitedly, nudging my father to look in my direction. Appa was very presentable—clean, well-shaven, dressed in an ironed white shirt. I could see that his combed-back hair had thinned to near baldness. Once, when I asked him why he had lost so much hair, he replied that years of carrying liquor sacs and baskets full of cow dung on his head had taken their toll. My heart sank when I noticed Kavya wasn't with them.

By now all the guests had taken their seats. Prasad, who was the master of ceremonies, came up to the podium and thanked everyone for coming. The vice principal followed with a speech of welcome. The ceremonial lamp was lit, the keynote speech was delivered by the chief guest, and soon it was time for us to receive our diplomas. The moment we had been waiting for had finally arrived.

When my name was called, I nervously walked up to the podium, paying close attention to my sari not to make a fool of myself by tripping on it. Once safely up on the stage, I turned to greet the audience with a Namaste. I glanced at my parents and smiled at them before bowing respectfully and receiving my certificate.

The next item on the agenda was the announcement of special awards. 'The award for the top student in the liberal arts stream goes to Shilpa Anthony Raj,' announced the vice principal. Loud applause accompanied me as I made my way to the stage once again. I couldn't have been happier, beaming joyfully in the direction of my parents.

I wondered whether my mother liked the way I carried myself in a sari. For my father, I guessed it was probably enough for him to hear my name called out twice. He was always excited when I took home prizes and certificates with my full name printed on them. As he stared at them, I would point out, 'Appa, your name, Anthony Raj, is here too.' He'd grin with pride.

Next, Amuda, the valedictorian, walked gracefully up the steps, her head held high, carried by a wave of enthusiastic applause from the audience. Many of us knew what she was going through in her personal life and the sadness she was concealing from others. We were drawn to her, our hearts filled with admiration and love. Composed and dignified, she accepted the coveted award.

The room fell silent as Amuda adjusted her notes and prepared to deliver her talk. She began in a strong voice, thanking everyone for their support and affection. 'I have learnt in the past fourteen years that a family is defined not simply by blood ties, but by what we are to each other,' she said. Her eyes scanned the children and staff. 'As many of you are aware, my mother, the only blood family I have, cannot be present today.' Tears filled my eyes as she talked about her mother, and I could see the pain on my classmates' faces as well.

Amuda had gone to see her mother just two weeks before graduation. She had been hiding from Amuda's stepfather who was terminally ill with AIDS. Not wanting his family to live after he died, he had vowed to kill both Amuda and his wife by pouring acid on them. Amuda, terrified that he might carry out his threat, had packed up and run from their home, and she and her mother were still in hiding.

Back at school, Amuda received word that her mother had also contracted AIDS. While the rest of us rehearsed for graduation, Amuda was busy looking after her sick mother in a single-room hut they had managed to rent as a temporary hideout. She fed her, helped her to the bathroom, and frequently stayed awake at night to check for fever.

Poised and calm at the podium, Amuda turned to DG. 'Dr. George, you told me I have the potential to accomplish great things in my life.' Taking a deep breath, she continued, 'You helped me write a better beginning to my story.'

Amuda turned to us and began to address each of her classmates by name. When it came to me, she said with a big smile, 'To think of Shilpa is to think of a sculpture made with her mind.' Amuda's vivid and intuitive remarks about each of her classmates spoke to the importance she attached to all of us. She ended with the words, 'My friends, wherever you go, go with all your heart.'

The entire audience was in tears. An added wave of sadness washed over me as I realized our time together as classmates had come to an end.

We grew quiet again as DG approached the podium. He was dressed in a long white formal jacket called a kurta, with matching pants and a contrasting red shawl. 'Like any proud father, I am thrilled to watch you on this special day,' he began, his face radiant with joy. 'Despite your young age, you have overcome many hurdles and accomplished a lot.'

As DG delivered his speech, it struck me how much he meant to us. We worried about letting him down, not living up to his dreams for us, though we sometimes felt he was expecting too much from all of us. I listened carefully as he came to his parting words.

'You will transform your families in many ways, bring comfort and dignity to their lives, and offer them choices they have never had,' he said. 'You will set good examples for others with your character, ideals, and moral standing. You will be thoughtful towards others, especially those who live each day at life's mercy, and come forward without being asked to help those in need.' DG paused for a moment to look at our faces. 'When you are such individuals, then you will have upheld what this institution truly stands for in your lives and in the lives of those who will follow you.' He thanked everyone and walked back to his chair as the audience broke into enthusiastic applause.

I had been in DG's care since I was four, and he had helped shape me into the confident person I have become. I have always felt his love and caring—from my first memories of him bringing lollipops from America to the important lessons of life that he imparted over the years. Though we were afraid of him when he scolded us for misbehavior, he was never indifferent. None of the children had spent much time with him, and yet we knew he was always there behind the scenes, like Erik in *The Phantom of the Opera*, pulling strings and working tirelessly. DG had taken over the helm of the school at the peak of the financial crisis. He had steered us through difficulties with an uncanny determination and optimism that made us feel secure. He had taught me what true courage is.

I heard my mother calling my name and turned to see her hurrying towards me, her face lit with pride. I ran into her open arms. 'Shilpa, I am so happy, my chinna,' she whispered as we hugged each other.

By then, my father too had found his way through the crowd. Unable to openly express my affection towards him, I joined my hands respectfully in Namaste. He said little, but his eyes revealed joy in my accomplishment—the first in our family to graduate from high school. There were no hugs; we hadn't embraced for as long as I could remember. But we both knew the love we felt.

I told my parents I had come second in my class with nearly eighty-four percent in the national examination. My mother gave me a kiss on my forehead, but I couldn't tell if my good performance meant anything to either of them. My passing alone would surely earn the respect of the entire village for our family.

'Shilpa, if it weren't for your father, the two of us would never have seen you like this today,' Amma said, clutching my hand in hers and pinning jasmine flowers in my hair. Appa kept silent, but could not hold back a smile. None of us could forget the ridicule and scorn he had endured in the years following my joining the school.

I led them up the stairs to where the rest of my classmates were waiting with their parents to have their photos taken with DG and his wife, Ms. Mariam. She looked beautiful in a white sari dotted with green flowers. She had always been genuinely concerned about our progress and showered us with love and encouragement. She hugged me tightly.

We stood in line behind my classmate Manikaran and his family, eager for our turn. Manikaran's father had spoken on behalf of all the parents. He said in Tamil, 'I was one of the laborers who built these buildings. Today, I watch my son rising from it.' His words of appreciation for Shanti Bhavan resonated with the other parents, and on this day his quiet pride in his son was apparent. And yet, not too long after, this simple man would take his own life in desperation at not being able to repay the family's debts.

For the first time in my life, I felt no hesitation in introducing my father. I had been ashamed of him, worrying that he couldn't speak English or handle a pen to sign his name on my report cards. I remembered the times he arrived at school in faded clothes and worn-out slippers. He always smelled of sweat and it wasn't easy to sit beside him. And I remembered how, when he learnt that I found his dirtiness repulsive, he started bathing twice a week whenever I was home.

After our photos were taken, I escorted my parents to the side. I had to find the courage to tell them what was on my mind. 'Appa, Amma, I am not going to college yet. I'm staying back a year to write my book.'

The joy on their faces vanished instantly and was replaced by stark disappointment.

I struggled to sound confident, wavering at their shocked looks. 'That was why I interviewed all of you. I want to write this book,' I said, trying to sound upbeat.

'So you won't go to college?' Appa asked. 'Why are you wasting a year?'

'I am not wasting a year.' I knew it was difficult for my parents to understand. 'It is your story too, Appa.'

Amma remained silent, but from the way her lips quivered, I knew she was struggling to control her distress.

I'd find out later that, back at home, Amma found it embarrassing to tell the neighbors; neither she nor they could understand what I was trying to do. 'All the other children are going to college, but not my daughter.' Leelie would be in college, and everyone in the village had heard about it and ridiculed my parents.

The path I was preparing to traverse was bound to be worrying until I began earning money to support the family. But I couldn't be dissuaded. I had to write my story.

I believe now that from the beginning I was destined to take a different path. I had entered the world in a haunted hut in a village in South India bound to centuries of tradition, one that didn't smile upon the likes of me. Yet, I was spared a spot at the edge of the woods where baby girls like me were poisoned and buried, never to be spoken of again.

So much has changed since then. Today, I can aspire to be a writer, to travel the world and learn about other cultures. I want to be in touch with people, to interact with them, and perhaps become a psychologist. I want to be a voice for the poor and the deprived, and a catalyst for change. I can't know where my future will take me, but so long as I spread my wings, I trust the winds will carry me.

The atmosphere remained festive as we neared the end of the celebrations. I saw a group of my classmates, aunties, and a few volunteers sitting outside the Foundation House not far from the entrance to school. I could tell from the overlapping voices and laughter that they were happily sharing good memories. There was no doubt about what Avnith had once said: 'The relationships we have built at Shanti Bhavan are for life.'

I walked my parents to the school gate. The three of us remained silent. Amma tried not to acknowledge the fact that it was time to say goodbye. As I put my arms around her, her eyes filled with tears. Appa stood to one side like a shy boy watching us. 'Bye, Appa,' I called out to him. He turned to face me as I walked up to him and took his hand. 'Call us once in a while,' he said, smiling sadly.

As my parents slowly walked away from me, it struck me that they wouldn't find it easy living a life foreign to their own. If I succeed professionally, I will improve their lives by making sure they always have good food to eat and comfortable clothes to wear, but they have grown too old to be interested in learning new ways. They would prefer to be with the people they have always known, whose beliefs and customs are like theirs.

There is also the fact that my mother and I think very differently, and we will likely never agree on matters like careers or marriage. I keep a certain distance because I know I disappoint her and cannot explain myself in a way she will understand. I cannot blame her; her life has been in the ragi fields of her village, as the subservient wife of an alcoholic, and as a maid to a wealthy Singaporean family. She has never had the opportunities I have, nor experienced the independence and empowerment that come with them. Despite our separate lives, she longs for my company and craves my sympathy and love. Yet, sometimes I get the feeling that she is jealous of the life I lead. I must somehow find a way to make her happy.

I must also make peace with my own decisions. There is no way I can live with my family permanently. I have come to understand the world I left behind simply cannot accept me as I am now. This I see as the price of my education.

As I watched my parents turn towards the woods, a feeling of intense sorrow gripped me. The joy I experienced during the ceremony was marred by worries about my family. My thoughts flew to every member of my family. It hurt to think I had become distant from my grandmother, the one who had showered me with so much love. She no longer advised me on any topic whatsoever. Joseph Thatha hadn't spoken to me for many years, preferring to drink each day away. As for my parents, I couldn't foresee much change in their relationship: Amma and Appa would never get along. My brother was attending school but faring poorly in his studies and nothing I might say now could make a difference. In a few years, when I planned to be earning a salary, I would be able to help him. As for Kavya, she had taken up the company of bad men, and despite Appa's efforts to protect her from them, she found ways to evade his control. She wouldn't listen to me when I tried to guide her, and my worrying constantly about her did neither of us any good. I could only hope she would someday accept me and love me. Uncle Naresh, meanwhile, was still waiting for his parents to select a bride for him. I knew I would always have to keep my distance from him.

Appa and Amma gradually disappeared from view. A track through the countryside would lead them to a main road junction where buses stopped. Having trekked through the forest all his life, this was no difficult task for my father. But Amma would find it hard to walk over the narrow track in her sari. They left carrying my other world.

I turned around and headed back up the cobbled pathway to join my friends who had gathered around DG outside the Foundation House.

'Will you occasionally come to tell me what you have accomplished?' he asked.

All around him stood young people about to head into the city for their next big adventure, struggling with how to say good-bye to the one man who had done everything in his power to shape their lives. All replied emphatically that they would.

Finally, left alone, I reflected on my future. Despite all the excitement of the day, I was still afraid of the unknown. *Could I be destined to a life of hardship and indignity for no fault of mine?* Suddenly I remembered my grandmother's words: 'What God has written on your forehead is your destiny.' It was no comfort. I was not going to leave my prospects to a pre-ordained fate.

I had many reasons to be optimistic, and couldn't let fear overtake me. The culmination of my schooling brought me hope. Standing in the middle of the pathway that day, I knew I had been given much to prepare me for the outside world and I felt confident that my future would be what I would make of it. For the first time, I felt I was in control of my life.

Chapter Eighteen

An Ending

It was barely a year after my graduation when Kavya died. Just a few months before, she had run away from home with my mother. The rest of us did not see her again until Amma returned with her lifeless body.

Grandmother and the other women in the family believed that Amma joined in Kavya's escape not because she was truly afraid that Appa would set Kavya and her gangster boyfriend on fire as he had threatened, but because she could not bear the world she had returned to after working in Singapore. Who knows what these men might have promised both mother and daughter? If Amma, in her desperation to live free of her husband's control, had succumbed to the promise of a new and exciting life, can I blame her?

I spent nearly the whole day mourning by my sister's side. By evening, arrangements were made to take the body to the graveyard for burial. Dragging myself along at the front of the procession, I frequently turned to look back at the small wooden coffin carried by four men. My mind kept shuffling through old memories, remembering what I had wanted for my sister and what she had craved. I imagined her riding in a chariot, with me by her side, to the stone church on the day of her wedding. But now instead, here I was with the rest of my heartbroken family for her last journey—one of a vastly different kind.

Aside from our close relatives, there were no more than a dozen people in attendance. Where were all the neighbors and relatives who had taken her in their arms when she was a baby, and grumbled about her being too talkative when she had grown older? Where were the little children Kavya used to bring to our house on hot afternoons for lunch with whatever was left over while their mothers were away at work? Where were the girls she played with until sunset every evening? Where were the grown-ups who would call out to her to come to their houses and sing folk songs for them?

I found the answers on our way to the graveyard. The village women simply watched us, sitting at their wooden doorsteps, cleaning rice in straw pans. They turned to look at the procession, eyes full of pity, but not one got up to join us or show respect. Grandmother would later tell me that many didn't want to be seen taking part in the funeral ceremony of a person who had died in a 'disgraceful' manner.

The receding sun was still warm, slowing the pace of the marchers as we neared the graveyard that lay at the village entrance. The men placed Kavya's coffin by the side of a small, deep pit that a few relatives had already dug for the grave at a far corner of the yard in the secluded section reserved for those who died in unholy ways. It was hard for me to understand how my sister, even in death, could be relegated to lowliness in the same house of God where she used to worship.

My fear that the church might refuse to conduct the ceremony because of Kavya's unexplained and unnatural death disappeared when I saw the priest standing at the head of the grave, reading from the Bible. My little sister, too young to be anything worse than a fun-loving, mischievous girl, was indeed going to be blessed before her dishonorable burial.

Grandmother sat like a stone before the empty grave. I put an arm around her, holding her tight through the brief prayer. Despite her broad frame, she felt frail, small, and vulnerable. All through Kavya's life Grandmother was a mother to her, and her loss was unbearable.

As the men started to hammer down the coffin's lid, I let go of Grandmother and pushed through the crowd to the coffin. 'Stop!' I cried out. 'Please, let me touch her one last time. One last time.' I felt an unconquerable need to connect with her— something I hadn't done in recent years. The men ignored me.

Devya screamed and threw herself beside me, begging them to open the lid. 'Open it! Please open it!' We were both shouting and pleading, but the men's grip on the lid was tight. My mother joined us, sobbing uncontrollably, her arms flailing about, stopping just short of attacking the men. Finally, Uncle Naresh, who was standing closest to me, firmly asked the men to stop hammering, and they proceeded to lift the lid up just a little. Just *enough*. I slipped my hand through the opening and touched something soft and cold. Was it her face? Her hand? It felt so unfamiliar.

The hammering finally ended with one last, determined blow, and the coffin was sealed shut. There was no eulogy, no words uttered in praise of my beloved sister. Instead, two young boys quickly lowered themselves into the grave to receive the coffin and set it in place. I wanted to move forward to catch sight of it down there, but people had already begun throwing mud inside. Two elderly women filled Grandmother's small, cupped palms with soil and stayed by her side as she emptied it into the pit in one slow, lifeless motion. I scooped up less than a handful in each palm and flung it forward. Aunt Rani whispered to me to throw three handfuls. I obeyed, then lay my head on her shoulder and wept.

I was burying my little sister with the soil on which we had run around as little children after Sunday church service. There was so much innocence in her then, and now there was so much none of us knew about her. She was laid to rest without honor and with no one to speak for her. My sorrow at her ending was simply unbearable. I was gripped by the feeling that I couldn't go forward with my own life. I was already at my funeral.

'Light the candles,' Grandmother whispered into my ear, wiping away her tears. Then my brother held out a plastic bag before me, filled with small, pale red roses. Seeing my blank expression, he instructed softly, 'Throw them in.'

Large-winged birds from the heavens hovered above, watching us part with my sister below. In the distance, the forest rustled—the sound of the wind through the branches offered Kavya's most eloquent requiem. As in life, she had in death wandered into an unknown land. I wanted to know how she had died and where she was now. The afterlife suddenly mattered terribly.

I looked up to see Appa leaning against a tree, half-hidden in the shadows, all by himself, weeping. His shoulders shook with every sob and he occasionally wiped his nose on the cuffs of his sleeves. He looked so pitiable that I felt sad for him, even though I was not prepared to absolve him for his absence from my sister's life—for the indifference he had shown towards her in recent years. Did he weep like this over his sister's unexplained death as well, years ago? Was our family history destined to repeat itself?

The crowd soon began to disperse. Darkness had set in all around us and Grandmother called to me to come away from the grave. Aunt Rani dragged me through the tall, wild grass, keeping a firm grip on my hand to keep me from running back to touch the soil over the grave. I just couldn't bring myself to leave Kavya.

'Aunt Rani, how will I know in the morning which grave is hers?' I cried, realizing that I couldn't even tell where we were in the graveyard. She didn't answer.

Incense burned on the fresh mound, and a small fire was lit by its side. I wanted to wait for the flames to die, but Aunt Rani wouldn't let me. Everyone was moving away.

Once outside the graveyard, I found Ms. Denny and the driver waiting to take me to Shanti Bhavan. She informed me that DG had telephoned with clear instructions not to let me stay back home after the burial, out of fear for my safety. 'Darling, don't be afraid of anything. We are with you,' DG had said when he called me earlier from America. I was too choked with tears to answer him.

'Shilpa, say goodbye to your brother,' Grandmother said, her voice breaking.

I could see Francis was terribly distressed. Before his tall, broad frame, I often felt small, but now he looked weak and broken. 'Study well,' I whispered to him. 'Be a good boy.'

He nodded, forlorn. I took his hand and said, 'Don't worry. I am there for you.'

'You also study well and don't be crying all the time,' he replied. There was a wealth of love in his words even though we knew little about each other. He looked lost and lonely and I knew well I could never give him the companionship he had known with Kavya.

I found comfort on my grandmother's shoulder. 'Don't cry now,' she said, soothing me. 'Don't cry. It was her fate. She was meant to go and she went.'

'If I had gone instead of her, wouldn't you have been less sad?' I asked, tears flowing.

Grandmother gasped, her face contorted with shock. 'What a thing to say! How can you say that? Didn't I bring you up also?'

'No. Kavya was the one you loved more. She was your daughter, your favorite,' I said, suddenly heedless and angry at everyone. I knew this to be true, though I couldn't blame her. Kavya had been living with her all those years. I had only passed through.

Appa moved forward to hug me, something he hadn't done in years. I stiffened, feeling awkward in his arms. 'I have only two children now,' he sobbed, no longer trying to control his tears, and pulling me to him in desperation. I couldn't respond. I didn't have any words to comfort him, and I wasn't prepared for it yet.

'Appa, can you take me to the place where Kavya was with those men who used her?' I needed to learn the truth about what had happened to her, but knew this was in every way dangerous.

Appa raised his brows in surprise and answered me with deliberate silence.

'Please, Appa. I need to know what happened. I can't live with this.'

Grandmother stepped close to me and listened, not saying a word.

'I already lost one daughter. I can't lose you too,' Appa replied, the sadness in his eyes belying the anger in his tone.

I had earlier asked my uncles to take me, but they too rejected my request without giving any reason. I could not bear not knowing how my sister died. How could we find closure without uncovering how and why it happened? To this day, the circumstances of Kavya's death remain a mystery. It seems no one truly wants to understand, no one explains—at least not to me—what really took place.

As I turned towards the jeep waiting to take me back to the school, an elderly relative whispered, 'Don't come back to this village. Study well and become something. There is nothing here for you.'

I nodded. I felt he was right. At least for now, I could not be a part of this village. The people my family represents—the village poor—are integral to a culture that is accustomed to what had happened. The hardships Kavya faced in her short life, and her sudden death, are not uncommon. There are millions of girls like her among the lower castes—butterflies without wings— growing up in families troubled by domestic violence and danger. In a society bound by traditions, there is no escape for them.

Women in these families have little or no control over their destinies; they suffer innumerable cruelties and lead lives regulated strictly by men. This way of life is not something I am prepared to accept as a natural order.

Kavya's short life was like the intertwining patterns of rangoli she taught me to draw upon the sand, and now she had vanished into the earth. The thought that she could have gone to college, become a teacher or a doctor, travelled the world, and fallen in love with a man who would be a caring partner to her, if only she had had the opportunity I received, added to my crushing guilt and sadness. I sought comfort in Grandmother's words: *It was her fate.*

I liked being Kavya's sister. Now that she is gone, do I stop being her sister? *No matter what, love doesn't die with death,* I consoled myself. Despite her leaving me, there is still the possibility of connecting with her in some way, I thought. Inescapably, Rabindranath Tagore's words I had read in school came to my mind: 'Death is not extinguishing the light; it is only putting out the lamp because the dawn has come.' I want to believe that life outlives death. Through me, she will live on.

After exchanging hugs and kisses with my loved ones, I stepped into the vehicle, struggling to pull the door shut. Once again, I was leaving my village just the way I had fifteen years before. I turned to look back, not wanting to lose sight of the fire devouring the camphor, flowers, and candles. As the jeep took a sharp turn, the dark tree branches and the hill shadows hid their glow from my sight.

Epilogue

Nearly a year has slipped away since we lost Kavya. For much of that time, I found myself alone, contemplating in the park and crying in the chapel, thinking about my little sister and how our lives turned out so differently. But no more. I have finally gained the inner strength to resume my studies in college. Ms. Denny and Ms. Jayanthashree take care of my needs, ensuring that I follow a steady routine and do well in college.

I seldom return to Thattaguppe. Appa feels the village is unsafe for me with the two hoodlums still around. Weekend visits to Shanti Bhavan offer great comfort. I hold special English classes for those appearing for the national board examination. When DG is there he talks to me about the importance of not letting the past cripple my future. His presence gives me a sense of security and belonging, and I find reassurance and hope in his words. He is constantly striving to improve the school and to encourage us to do well in life.

Several of my old classmates are with me in Jyoti Nivas, the girls' college in Bangalore where I am now studying. The strong emotional bonds and trust we have in each other make up for what I miss most being away from Shanti Bhavan. I am trying to make new friends, many of whom come from affluent backgrounds. I have no difficulty adjusting to their ways. Some find me too westernized, and refer to me as 'ABCD'—'American Born Confused Desi'. I don't mind being called that; I was shaped into the person I am today by my exposure to different cultures.

Sheena and I have forgotten our old quarrels, and I am happy to see the self-reliant and confident young woman she has become. She will be graduating from college this year and has already been offered a good position at a major multinational company.

There isn't much peace at home. Appa frequently comes home drunk. Every time he gets angry, he accuses Amma of causing Kavya's death. Amma works as a maid in a business executive's home. She earns more money than before, but somehow my parents are still unable to make ends meet, having borrowed large sums at high interest. I have no influence over them and things continue to disintegrate.

Francis is not motivated about anything since Kavya left us. He dropped out of school after failing tenth grade, and took up a job as a security guard. I try to be more of a sister to him than I was to Kavya. I can't imagine the pain he goes through without his younger sister and closest companion. It is hard to think how he sleeps on the same cot he and Kavya shared as children, or how he walks about in the house that was once home to the three of us. Since Kavya's funeral, I can't get myself to set foot inside our house, and Appa and Amma have given up asking me to.

Every time Appa and I fight, he reminds me sadly, 'Shilpa, I lost one daughter. I have only you and your brother.' He grieves for Kavya all the time and none of us can bring him any consolation. He frequently returns to the forest, as that is the one place he finds peace. 'Listen to the woods. There's magic in its music. It's the only comfort for a heart-broken man like me,' he once told me.

Amma and I hardly talk about Kavya anymore. I have given up trying to get answers from her because each time I ask her questions she starts crying. She says, 'Like the rest of them, are you also going to torture me?' I get the feeling she is struggling with her own guilt, whatever it might be.

Grandmother is weaker and is losing her eyesight, but she still tries to keep the family together. I have great affection towards her for all she was to me when I was a child. I worry that nobody will be there to take care of her. Her only joys are in the children of my aunts and uncles and the small troubles the little ones bring her.

Despite all the difficulties, my family manages to keep going. Sometimes I feel bad about having found my escape, but my guilt does them no good. There is nothing I can do for them right now other than to offer words of comfort, and give them hope that I will one day be able to make their lives better. I will be there for them in the ways that I can be. I love them.

I find myself more interested in studying child psychology than in pursuing a career in journalism, and hence, I am majoring in that in college. I recognize that my need to be close to people can be fulfilled only by caring for them individually and personally. I want to work with children who have undergone trauma and distress and find ways to help them overcome their pain. I know I possess sufficient empathy for this task, and now I must acquire the needed skills.

I am moving forward in my life, but still have the urge to connect with my sister in ways I cannot explain. I don't know when I will see her again. Until then, I will search for little children like her who need a loving hand, a warm hug, and someone to guide them. I will be there for them. And in them I will find Kavya.

NETFLIX DOCUMENTARY: DAUGHTERS OF DESTINY

A four-part documentary based on the lives of the author and four other children of Shanti Bhavan School is available through NETFLIX. The film is directed by Oscar Award winner Vanessa Roth, and music by the highly acclaimed composer and director, A.R. Rahman.

If you wish to learn more about Shanti Bhavan project, visit www.shantibhavanchildren.org.